RUNNING AGAINST THE

Joseph V. Hughes Jr. and Holly O. Hughes
Series on the Presidency and Leadership

James P. Pffifner, General Editor

RUNNING AGAINST THE GRAIN

How Opposition Presidents Win the White House

David A. Crockett

Texas A&M University Press • College Station

The paper used in this book meets the requirements of
ANSI/NISO Z39.48-1992
(Permanence of Paper).
Binding materials have been chosen for durability.

LIBRARY OF CONGRESS CATALOGING-IN-PUBLICATION DATA

Crockett, David A.. 1963–
    Running against the grain: how opposition presidents win the White
House / David A. Crockett.. — 1st ed.
        p. cm. — (Joseph V. Hughes Jr. and Holly O. Hughes series on the
presidency and leadership)
    Includes bibliographical references and index.
    ISBN–13: 978-1-60344-010-3 (cloth : alk. paper)
    ISBN–10: 1-60344-010-0 (cloth : alk. paper)
    1. Presidents—United States—History.   2. Presidents—United
States—Election—History.   3. Political campaigns—United
States—History.   4. Opposition (Political science)—United
States—History.   I. Title
JK511.C77   2008
324.973—dc22   2007037950
ISBN–13: 978-1-60344-131-5 (pbk.)
ISBN–10: 1-60344-131-X (pbk.)

In memory of Valerie Earle and Elspeth Rostow

—With great appreciation

CONTENTS

TABLES

PREFACE

In many ways, studies of the American presidency and presidential elections walk hand in hand in form and content. Regardless of the analytical focus, similar volumes can be found in each subfield. This is true in both academic work and popular literature. For example, the dominant focus of journalism is on the immediate and transitory, both in campaigning and governing. The strangely ahistorical methodology of this school is encouraged by the ubiquitous presence of public opinion polls that reinforce the notion that the only thing that matters is what is current. If any attention is paid to history, it is on the most recent, with anything prior to one or two presidential terms past treated as archaeology. Just as numerous books hit the stores, giving us insider information on the inner workings of the West Wing, so other books, with varying levels of skill, mine the details of presidential campaigns for interesting stories and anecdotes. The major purpose of these tomes is to explain why a president or candidate won or lost a particular conflict—what strategic move or brilliant maneuver led to victory (policy or electoral), or what tactical misstep or gaffe brought defeat. I have on my bookshelves at least ten journalistic accounts of various aspects of the Bill Clinton presidency and as many as twenty accounts of different presidential elections, beginning with Theodore H. White's first *Making of the President* book from 1961. For the ambitious politician seeking wisdom, the lesson would seem to be that one should focus on the detailed accounts in these books in an effort to repeat the success or avoid the failure of the most recent counterpart. Presumably, one is supposed to "learn the lessons" of the previous president or candidate. Thus, for example, Clinton purposed not to repeat the mistakes of Michael Dukakis or Walter Mondale, and George W. Bush purposed not to repeat those of his father or Bob Dole.

Scholarship has done a better job at exploring the deeper importance of specific events and at uncovering the interconnections often missed in instant analysis, but the logical connections between presidencies and presidential elections remain. Every president is now treated to regular *First Appraisals* and *Legacy* volumes, just as every presidential election gets the obligatory quadrennial treatment in the various *Election of xxxx* books. Such works do an admirable job of peeling back the many layers of an individual presidency or election, examining them from a variety of perspectives. This is only fitting, since the presidency is a unitary office, the character of which is very much dependent on that of the individual inhabiting the position.

A different subset of the literature examines the presidency or presidential elections in the context of a specific historical era. This methodology has an intuitive appeal, for scholars like to employ labels such as "Era of Good Feelings" and "Gilded Age" and "Progressive Era" to demarcate periods from each other and to highlight specific characteristics that typify these periods. In the area of presidential elections we find the occasional book that treats earlier eras in American history, such as Richard McCormick's *The Presidential Game*, which details the development of the presidential electoral system up to the beginning of the strong party system. Far more common are the books that analyze—usually on a quadrennial basis—the vicissitudes of the modern plebiscitary system, usually marked as beginning somewhere between 1968 and 1972. Similarly with the presidency as an institution, we find books such as Ralph Ketcham's *Presidents above Parties* and Brooks Simpson's *The Reconstruction Presidents,* which analyze the office in a specific era. More common are works that are presumably most relevant to current leaders, those dealing with various aspects of the "modern presidency." Richard Neustadt's seminal work *Presidential Power* made the case for such a distinction most powerfully, and certainly the dominant trend in presidency studies has made the modern presidency its principal unit of analysis. Indeed, Fred Greenstein argues that "the presidencies that provide the most useful lessons to a contemporary chief executive are those of the final two-thirds of the twentieth century."[1] One can only imagine that something similar should be said about the quest for the presidency.

At one level, Greenstein's assertion rings true. The very notion of a "modern presidency" assumes that we can make a clear distinction between presidents who came to office before and after 1932, and one can certainly make the case that the transformation effected in the presidency by Franklin Roosevelt was profound and durable.[2] The problem is that this perspective is historical in only one sense. By highlighting what presidents in the modern era have in common with each other as distinct from earlier presidents, the focus too often assumes that modern presidents are all created equal. This focus ignores the many ways these presidents are quite dissimilar to each other—and perhaps more similar to earlier presidents. It also tends to ignore the many ways in which the Constitution gives *all* presidents across time similar functions, powers, and responsibilities.[3] In the same way, literature on presidential elections that limits itself to the modern plebiscitary era also misses a mother lode of valuable insights and historical data from earlier periods. While we should work to understand what presidents and candidates have in common with each other in specific eras, it is not necessarily clear that this perspective tells us all that is important about these individuals. In a sense, one could argue that the political leader seeking wisdom in the modern presidency school will find it, as with the journalistic school, by seeking to "learn the lessons" of his or her nearest chronological neighbor.

One way out of this dilemma is that small subset of the literature that examines all presidencies or presidential elections in one broad historical sweep. As with the other two subsets, this one also finds the literature analyzing the presidency tracking well with the literature analyzing elections. Some works focus on specific areas of analysis as they illuminate aspects of American political development. For example, James Ceaser's *Presidential Selection* traces and evaluates the presidential selection process from the Framers' ideal to modern times, while Jeffrey Tulis's *The Rhetorical Presidency* does the same thing for presidential power. These works retain a very tight focus even as they break free from the modern presidency construct. Other works are mainly general surveys or textbooks designed to address the ahistorical tendencies of contemporary college students, but these broader overviews often sacrifice historical nuance in an effort to cover everything. In this sense, all presidencies are apparently created equal, and the contemporary political leader seeking wisdom will not really know where to turn—and will thus probably try to "learn the lessons" of those closest to him in chronology. In these latter cases, the notion that George W. Bush could learn anything significant from Benjamin Harrison, or Bill Clinton from Zachary Taylor, seems rather absurd. But is it?

Another category of analysis—one that crosses over and redefines some of the above genres—is exemplified by Stephen Skowronek's *The Politics Presidents Make.* In that work, Skowronek analyzes individual presidencies in a fair amount of detail. He also examines presidencies according to specific eras, detailing what distinguishes the eras from each other. Finally, he manages to effect an analysis of the presidency as an institution—without being encyclopedic—from Washington to Clinton. He ably illuminates some transhistorical aspects of presidential politics through his focus on "political time" as opposed to chronological time. In Skowronek's schema, different presidents face different leadership projects depending on when in a political era they take power. "Reconstructors" are presidents who repudiate the established order and redefine politics to inaugurate a new era (taking the New Deal era as an example, this would be Franklin Delano Roosevelt [FDR]). "Articulators" are orthodox innovators who follow the reconstructors in their work, attempting to further the agenda of the new dominant party while adapting it to changing times (Harry Truman, John Kennedy, Lyndon Johnson). "Disjunctors" have the misfortune of taking power when the dominant coalition is crumbling in the face of a new repudiator (Jimmy Carter to Ronald Reagan). Finally, "preemptive presidents" come to power opposed to the dominant party in a specific era and desire to preempt its agenda (Dwight Eisenhower and Richard Nixon).[4]

Skowronek's accomplishment invites deeper study and analysis along multiple avenues. In previous work I have focused in detail on the preemptive presidency category, labeling it the "opposition presidency" in an attempt to understand more fully the leadership dilemmas faced by these often odd presidents. Opposition presidents are political leaders whose ideal objectives or purposes run against what Richard Neustadt called the "grain of history." In that work I explored what made such presidents more or less successful, both from an individual perspective and a systemic perspective. It made great sense to me for a Bill Clinton to "learn the lessons" of a Zachary Taylor or Dwight Eisenhower.[5]

If other subsets of presidency scholarship see a close connection in form and content with studies of presidential selection, Skowronek's work should be no different. While he touches occasionally on campaigns and elections in his work, much more waits to be done. Just as his separate categories of presidents in political time warrant greater analysis and examination,[6] so too do the elections that brought these presidents to power, for there is a close connection between the process of presidential selection and the practice of presidential power. Certainly the Framers of the Constitution thought so, for Publius includes his discussion of presidential selection in the section of *The Federalist* that discusses the institution of the presidency more broadly.[7] How a prospective reconstructor obtains power has an effect on the reconstructive project as a whole. Similarly, how an opposition party candidate becomes an opposition president has an effect on the preemptive project as a whole. Just as we can study the presidency as an institution in political time, so we can study presidential elections in political time.

This project is an attempt to begin doing precisely that. It constitutes a type of "prequel" to my previous work on opposition presidents.[8] If such presidents as Zachary Taylor, Dwight Eisenhower, and Bill Clinton operated against the grain of history, how did they get elected to begin with, running against that grain? Yet, sixteen times since the birth of the modern party system in the 1820s an opposition party candidate has succeeded in capturing control of the executive branch. Four of those cases—Andrew Jackson, Abraham Lincoln, Franklin Roosevelt, and Ronald Reagan—resulted in redefinitions of the terms of political debate as American politics was transformed to favor the opposition party and make it the new governing party. The other twelve cases resulted in "opposition presidents." They remained opposition leaders even after obtaining the office, failing to reconstruct politics on their own terms. These twelve cases—seven men involved in twelve election victories—include the Whig presidents William Henry Harrison (1840) and Zachary Taylor (1848), post–Civil War Democrats Grover Cleveland (1884 and 1892) and Woodrow Wilson (1912 and 1916), New Deal era Republicans Dwight Eisenhower (1952 and 1956) and Richard Nixon (1968 and 1972), and Reagan era Democrat Bill Clinton (1992 and 1996). Through a comparative analysis of these victorious opposition candidates, I identify the features common to this specific scenario.

Skowronek calls these presidents "the wild cards of presidential history,"[9] but that description is not accurate when it comes to getting elected. In fact, there is a striking commonality among these individuals that indicates what it takes for opposition party victory at a time when the governing party is still robust. The reconstructors mentioned above ran campaigns that called into question the legitimacy and credibility of governing philosophies that were no longer resilient. They repudiated the core values of the governing party and used their campaigns to help claim the power to define politics for an entire era. Opposition candidates running at a time when the reigning governing philosophy is still resilient cannot afford to attempt such a dramatic change in politics. Such an effort is doomed to fail. These seven men acted, intentionally or otherwise, as though they understood that dynamic and tailored their campaigns accordingly. Their campaigns exemplify those qualities necessary for an opposition party victory. In the chapters to come I explore these features of successful opposition candidacies. These features are not equal in importance, nor are they present with the same force in each successful opposition party campaign, but there is more in common between the campaigns of William Henry Harrison and Bill Clinton, and between Zachary Taylor and Dwight Eisenhower, than generally recognized.

This book focuses on the question of how opposition parties obtain the presidency, using historical data to make generalizations and draw conclusions about these factors, describing how they have been employed over the years and evaluating their relative importance in opposition party campaigns. Chapter 1 begins with a discussion of campaigns and elections in historical context, laying out a framework for how to think about and use history in this type of study and sketching out a model of the successful opposition campaign. Chapters 2 through 4 then explore each of these features. In each of these three chapters, I begin with general analysis and conclusions, frontloading my major findings to highlight what the evidence suggests. I then use the specific successful campaigns as case studies, fleshing out the details of the story to compare these successful cases to unsuccessful ones. In chapter 5 I draw conclusions about the relative importance of these various factors to opposition party victory. Finally, because campaigns are the first step in the governing process, I conclude with some remarks about the impact this type of campaign has on the ability of opposition presidents to govern.

Authors typically claim responsibility for any shortcomings in their work, and I am no exception. It is important, however, to acknowledge those who have assisted me in the process of writing this book. Many thanks go to those scholars who read parts of this book in its earliest form and gave me advice and support: Bruce Buchanan, Jeff Tulis, Walter Dean Burnham, and Rod Hart. Thanks must also go to the anonymous reviewers who critiqued the work at various stages and to the panel members, chairmen and discussants, and audience members at several professional conferences who heard smaller parts of this argument and made suggestions. Significant portions of chapter 3 were previously published as the article "In the Shadow of Henry Clay: How to Choose a Successful Opposition Presidential Candidate," *Congress and the Presidency,* 33 (Spring 2006): 47–74. My university and department have been very supportive with funds and time to conduct my research, and my colleague John Hermann provided invaluable methodological assistance.

I must acknowledge a significant debt of gratitude to two special women: Valerie Earle, my undergraduate mentor who instilled in me a love for the study of politics, and Elspeth Rostow, who encouraged me at the graduate level. Neither lived to see the publication of this book, but I would not be where I am today without the active interest these two scholars took in my professional development, to say nothing of my development as an individual. They are my models of what it means to be a great teacher, and it is to them that this book is dedicated.

Finally, I must thank my family—my parents for their love and encouragement, my wife Stacy for her love and patience and support, and my three sons, all of whom were born at various points during this project, and who never cease to remind me what is most important in life. This book will never be as interesting to them as the Land of Oz or the town of Radiator Springs—and that's as it should be.

RUNNING AGAINST THE GRAIN

Chapter 1

CAMPAIGNS AND ELECTIONS IN HISTORICAL CONTEXT

There is a tendency when studying elections to treat them all the same. The reams of data lend themselves to this type of analysis in the same way that baseball statistics allow fans to compare players and teams across decades of time. In the popular mind we do the same thing to presidential campaigns, thinking of them as baseball teams or Olympic athletes meeting for some championship match. The assumption is that the rules are the same for both teams and that both sides will play under similar conditions on the same field, with similar equipment, training, and conditioning. The watch is calibrated the same for both sides, and victory is the same distance away. The only thing necessary to determine victory is relative skill on that given day. Thus, the winner of the election is the one with the smarter, shrewder, more skillful campaign.

This perspective is a journalistic fallacy that ignores historical context. By pretending that all campaigns are created equal, this perspective ignores the contextual and contingent aspects of American politics. In fact, some campaigns enter an election contest with no prayer of winning, through no fault of the candidate or campaign. Although the sports metaphor is common, especially that of the horse race, there are years in which one candidate is allowed to run in dry conditions with a breeze at his back while his opponent is forced to slog through mud and water against the wind. There are years when we look at the situation facing the contestants and say, "Wake us when it's over." We do not consider this to be unfair—it is simply the facts of political life, brought into play by the larger forces of history. Perhaps a war metaphor is more appropriate, with some election contests resembling equally matched foes along World War I trench lines and others the outmatched French knights facing English archers at Agincourt.

What makes certain campaigns "unfair" in the sporting sense? There are several elections in American history that appear to be more consequential than others, and the key quality of those elections is that they place one political party in an advantaged position for an extended period of time, usually a long generation or more. This makes intuitive sense to most students of history, for we think of the Democratic Party as enjoying a partisan advantage over its Whig opponents during the Jacksonian era, just as the Democrats enjoyed a partisan advantage over the Republican Party (GOP) during the New Deal era. The principal advantage enjoyed by the favored party is the power to define the terms of political debate, an advantage that has generations-long effects. That is why these eras are labeled as they are—because it was the Democratic Party that defined politics. The intellectual substance of political parties consists of competing visions of justice and the proper role of government. As E. E. Schattschneider pointed out, the supreme instrument of power is the definition of alternatives.[1] Whoever is able to define what politics is about, what issues are legitimate, and what constitutes legitimate discussion of those issues—what constitutes justice and the proper role of government—will tend to control the political agenda. Political parties define the alternatives in American politics, and newly advantaged parties set the terms of political debate for a long time. In a sense, that party's governing philosophy becomes the reigning governing philosophy, and that party the governing party. From this perspective the disadvantaged party in an era can be seen as the opposition party. It operates at a disadvantage because it is forced to play by rules and according to definitions established by the governing party.[2] For example, slavery and secession gave tremendous moral capital to the new Republican Party to establish itself as the governing party, just as the Great Depression gave Democrats the ability to define the long-term policy debate in terms decidedly unfavorable to Republicans. Of course, no governing party ever has unilateral control over the debate—one still has to convince sufficient numbers of voters to see the central issues of the day as the governing party sees them—but the parties rarely stand on equal ground. Even when exceptionally close elections indicate rough parity between the parties, the governing party tends to have an institutional advantage by virtue of its stronger position in an era.[3]

The larger historical context of presidential elections has a direct effect on the practice of presidential leadership. Redefining elections can be seen as national conversations in which the people and their political leadership re-create their political world. They tend to occur during crisis times, and these crises arm presidents with tremendous energy. Such redefiners have the greatest ability to set the national agenda by clarifying questions and establishing goals that are long lasting, and that process usually begins during the election campaign. It is at these times that presidents and candidates are most free to exercise national leadership, and it is at these times that such leadership is most demanded. As a unitary official, the president is uniquely qualified to exercise such leadership, a mandate that does not exist for the heirs of the great redefiners. Later presidents must find a way to govern within the universe they inherit.[4] The same is true for presidential candidates, for redefining periods settle certain issues for a time, and candidates who seek power during the "normal politics" phase of an era must be mindful of that dynamic if they are to be successful. As much as an opposition party candidate might want to redefine politics in his favor, the time may not be ripe for such a project.

One natural objection to this analysis might ask why, then, do opposition parties ever win presidential elections? After all, Eisenhower led the GOP to victory in the New Deal era. How could this happen if the GOP were in such a disadvantaged position? Did Eisenhower's victory make the GOP the new governing party? That is precisely the focus of this project. To anticipate the argument, however, we can safely say that Eisenhower did not redefine the terms of debate away from New Deal politics onto grounds that favored the GOP. He did not transform his victory into a new Republican era, and he did not remake the GOP into a new governing party. In fact, despite controlling the two elective branches of government for two years, the GOP under Eisenhower remained an opposition party. This analysis can be confusing because of the fragmented nature of the American constitutional system. Unlike parliamentary systems, one party does not necessarily control both elective branches of government in the United States at the same time. In his analysis of our "separated system," Charles Jones makes clear that divided government is not an unusual outcome of our constitutional system.[5] Indeed, the existence of divided government by itself does not determine the identity of the governing and opposition parties. The focus of this project is not centered on the vagaries of institutional control but on more foundational and longer-term dynamics. The principal idea lying at the foundation of redefining elections is that, at key points of vulnerability, one party overthrows the other, transforming itself into the new governing party and redefining the terms of political debate for the long term. The governing party essentially determines what Richard Neustadt calls the "grain of history."[6] This term is a rhetorical device that simply means there are aspects of politics within a specific era that constrain and limit the options of political actors. The debate tends to be oriented or defined in one direction, to the advantage of the governing party. In terms of electoral politics, it becomes the norm for the governing party to defeat the opposition party in presidential elections, and the opposition party is, as a general rule, forced into a defensive posture. Nevertheless, opposition parties do capture the White House, for predictable and systematic reasons.

Scholars have long struggled to define and understand these larger forces of history. They argue over the location of transformative moments in American history and over what large-scale forces affect this or that election. Perhaps the most interesting and intriguing subfield in this endeavor is the research that conceptualizes American politics through the lens of electoral eras and cycles. For over fifty years political scientists have attempted to describe and decode the cyclical and secular aspects of American politics.[7] Although there are variations in the details, there has emerged a rough consensus that American political history can be described as a series of political eras bounded by realigning elections.[8] The metaphors used to illustrate this concept vary widely from scholar to scholar. Walter Dean Burnham once preferred a geological metaphor, in which realigning elections are seen as earthquakes.[9] Samuel Lubell employed an astronomical metaphor, in which the majority party in an era is seen as the sun and the minority party the moon.[10] Edward Carmines and James Stimson chose a biological metaphor, in which "punctuated equilibrium" describes unpredictable cataclysmic changes in the evolution of American politics.[11] Responding to his critics, Burnham embraced his own version of the evolutionary model, calling it "punctuational change."[12] Debate continues over the details, but the rough consensus remains—some elections are more consequential than others because they produce durable and long-lasting change; that change tends to favor one party in a specific era, and it has long-term policy consequences.[13]

More recently, scholars have done battle over the place of realignment in the post-1968 world. Has there been a realignment since 1932, and if so, when? One reason there is debate about this topic is the small number of realignments in American history. As much as the lexicon of presidential elections helps simplify a complex world, there are simply too few examples of realignments to generalize with confidence about many things. There is, in fact, no single way in which realignments manifest themselves. Perhaps the last undisputed example of realignment occurred in 1932, when the Great Depression allowed the Democratic Party to supplant the GOP as the majority party in the country. The "System of 1896" looks somewhat similar, sparked as it was by economic disaster in the form of another "great depression"—but in that case the Republicans succeeded in extending their dominance for another generation rather than turn over power to their rivals. The Civil War realignment, of course, was sparked by the secession crisis, which one could argue was based on economics to the extent that slavery constituted an economic system.[14] However, it seems equally plausible to argue that the trigger event here was more a question of philosophy and political values, and the result was the destruction of one major party (the Whigs) and its replacement by a brand new one (the Republicans). If we push the examples back to the second party system, we find even more idiosyncratic elements, the trigger event in this case being the disputed "corrupt bargain" of 1824, leading to the establishment of our first modern party system. Given this diversity in terms of manifestation, it is little wonder that 1968 or 1980 look different from 1932. It seems likely that no two realignments will look exactly alike.

The debate over the location of the most recent punctuational change is exacerbated by the tendency for some realignment specialists to emphasize an excessively deterministic or predictive quality to the construct, at the expense of contingency.[15] In fact, as important as realigning elections are, they retain a significant number of contingent aspects that should give the prophet pause. For example, the "Revolution of 1800" depended both on the actions of such personalities as Alexander Hamilton in the House contingency election and on the fact that Thomas Jefferson's initial victory over John Adams was secured by the Constitution's three-fifths clause, which amplified the electoral count in Jefferson's favor through the partial count of slaves in Southern states.[16] The brief promise of united Whig government in 1841—possibly the beginning of a realignment—was destroyed by the untimely death of William Henry Harrison and the rise of John Tyler, his vice president, a man disinclined by partisan background to pursue what was thought to be the victorious Whig agenda. Lincoln was a minority president who was greatly advantaged by having a significant number of his opponents leave government in the secession crisis, giving him greatly amplified powers of the sword. Even the Republican victory in the realigning election of 1896 was made possible only because that same party had the great fortune of losing the very close election of 1892, just in time to be out of power when the Depression of 1893 hit. Had Benjamin Harrison won that election, one would have to give William Jennings Bryan the nod in 1896, and American history would look remarkably different. One can only imagine what a President John Nance Garner would have done to the New Deal in 1933 had the assassination attempt against Franklin Roosevelt been successful.

Stephen Skowronek reworks this analytical field by marrying the problem of presidential leadership to the notion of punctuational change. The presidency is both a creative and disruptive force in American politics, and given the right historical context the officeholder can reorder politics in dramatic ways. It is no accident that such reconstructors as Andrew Jackson, Abraham Lincoln, and Franklin Roosevelt helped herald partisan realignments that set the course of politics for a generation. It is no accident that such articulators as James K. Polk, Theodore Roosevelt, and Lyndon Johnson struggled to live up to the demands of their partisan patron saints or that such disjunctors as James Buchanan, Herbert Hoover, and Jimmy Carter faced such impossible circumstances. The cyclical nature of these regime sequences—from reconstructor to reconstructor or from realignment to realignment—allows us to compare presidents from seemingly quite different eras who faced the same leadership dilemmas, thus broadening the number of cases we can employ when studying leadership problems. It also adds much-needed nuance to the one-size-fits-all modern presidency model. There is a chronological aspect to Skowronek's work, for there is a sense in which this specific dynamic of American political development is changing and evolving with secular time (as opposed to political time), for the tasks facing different types of presidents are getting easier or more difficult. What interests us here, however, is the ability to perform a cross-era or cross-regime analysis of presidential candidates. There are some minor differences between Skowronek's regime schema and realignment theory, but they are easily explained.[17] The benefit of this perspective is that it gives us an opportunity to place presidential elections more clearly in historical context.

Taking Skowronek's analysis as a starting point, the notion of governing and opposition parties is easy to see. During the Jacksonian era, from 1828 until 1860, Democrats won six out of eight presidential elections. They controlled both houses of Congress in eleven of sixteen congresses, and lost control of both houses only once. Republicans took fourteen out of eighteen elections from 1860 through 1930, controlling both houses of Congress two-thirds of the time and losing control of both houses only five times, three of those during Wilson's presidency. In the New Deal era, 1932–1980,

Democrats won eight of twelve presidential elections, controlling both houses of Congress in all but two congresses.[18] This pattern is disrupted in the contemporary era, in which divided government has been the norm. From 1980 through 2004, Democrats won control of Congress four times and Republicans won control six times. The parties split control of Congress three times, and the GOP lost united control of Congress five months into the 107th Congress. Nevertheless, Republicans have won five out of seven presidential elections so far, and Ronald Reagan marked a clear change in political debate from the New Deal era.[19] In that sense, Skowronek's schema remains a solid one. From this brief account of American political history we can identify which parties are advantaged in specific eras, which ones controlled the definition of political debate, and which stood in opposition. It is the norm for the governing party to win the presidency anywhere from two-thirds to three-fourths of the time. The minority examples—the twelve cases of opposition party victory mentioned in the preface—remained opposition leaders even after obtaining the office, failing to claim the power to define the political debate for the long term. Instead, they had only limited power to define short-term events and developments in their favor. It is in this decidedly unequal context that presidential campaigns take place.

Of course, the ability to divide American history into a series of partisan regimes does not mean that the historical context within those regimes is always precisely the same. The relative strength of the governing party varies from era to era and from year to year within eras. For example, Republican Party dominance from Ulysses S. Grant through Grover Cleveland was not nearly as strong as it was from William McKinley to Herbert Hoover, and the Democratic Party enjoyed a stronger position in the New Deal era as a whole than the Republicans have enjoyed in the Reagan era. On the other hand, this observation is complicated by the fact that the Democratic Party in the New Deal era had greater difficulty keeping its fractious coalition together (due to the conservative coalition in Congress) than Republicans have had in the Reagan era—at least to date. The complexities of what James MacGregor Burns calls "four-party politics"—the notion that there are presidential and congressional wings of both major parties that operate in tension with each other—can make a strictly partisan analysis somewhat deceptive.[20] Still, one cannot be comprehensive in an analysis of this scope, and institutional control matters. The partisan focus, while masking some ambiguity, serves to identify major trends, dominant governing philosophies, and the basic direction of political forces. The historical surveys that follow are necessarily general and may overlook what at times is a more complex reality.

This book explores how presidential candidates from the opposition party can be successful in the general election running against the grain. Opposition party candidates operate at a disadvantage because they belong to a political party that is in a defensive posture. That is, the governing party has been able to fashion the long-term political debate on its own terms. What are the requirements for electoral success for a candidate from an opposition party? Are there aspects of these victorious campaigns that are common to all opposition party candidates? The fact that the opposition party does not control the terms of political debate should have an impact on campaign strategy, and the type of campaign the opposition party candidate must wage may be different from that waged by the candidate of the governing party. Since all opposition candidates face roughly the same historical context, one that makes their options quite constrained in an era in which they do not control the terms of political debate, it is possible to make inferences and to generalize about this type of candidate. For the purposes of this exploration, I accept as a given Skowronek's breakdown of political history. Since the notion of legitimate opposition did not gain credence in American politics until the Jacksonian age, I limit my examination to the modern party era that began in the late 1820s.[21] Studying campaigns in such a transhistorical fashion demonstrates that the quest to attain leadership—as much as the practice of leadership—is a contingent and context-bound phenomenon. Just as we can study the presidency as an institution in political time, so we can study presidential campaigns in political time.

Studying Opposition Party Campaigns

It should be clear from the discussion above that in the lexicon of presidential elections the most popular subject of research and analysis has been the realigning election. Realigning elections are roughly equivalent to Skowronek's reconstructions, maintaining elections to his articulations, and deviating elections to his preemptions.[22] The literature on realigning elections is legion, but little work apart from voting behavior has been done focusing specifically on the other types of elections as distinct categories. The earliest treatment of deviating elections—opposition party victories—can be found in Angus Campbell's chapter on election classifications in *Elections and the Political Order*. There Campbell and his colleagues employ survey research data to draw some conclusions about the elections of 1952 and 1956, when the Republican candidate Dwight Eisenhower won the presidency during a normally Democratic era.

In a deviating election, the basic division of partisan loyalties remains relatively unchanged, but some short-term forces allow the minority party to defeat the majority party.[23] In Campbell's analysis, Eisenhower was successful not only in capturing the vast majority of Republican votes for president, both strong and weak identifiers, but also in winning an unusual number of independent and Democratic votes. Independents voted nearly two-to-one for Eisenhower in 1952, and the general was able to carve out over one-third of weak Democrats. So, despite the fact that Democrats outnumbered Republicans in the electorate, 47 to 27 percent, according to Campbell's research, Eisenhower won the office. What distinguished this outcome from a realigning election was that the victory was temporary and largely personal. Eisenhower's 1952 victory brought a very slight gain for Republicans in Congress, just enough to win control of both chambers for two years, but they lost control in 1954 and failed to retake Congress in 1956. Voters apparently made a distinction between Eisenhower the man and the party he led. The GOP was unable during this time to effect any long-term shift in partisan strength in its direction, and it certainly failed to alter the basic direction of national policy. It remained the minority party, and the majority party regained control once Eisenhower left the scene.[24]

Perhaps the reason less work has been done studying campaigns in other categories of elections, apart from elections in general, is the persistent controversy over the place of realignment in the post-1968 world. The persistence of divided government and the lack of consensus over the location of the dividing line that marks the beginning of the contemporary electoral era make identifying deviating elections in the current era somewhat difficult. If scholars are unsure about the location of the most recent realignment, they will be equally unsure in labeling other types of elections. Part of this problem is due to the fact that it is difficult to understand fully the larger context of an era when one is situated in the middle of it. The struggle to understand how to think about electoral politics in the 1980s and 1990s, and how to classify Clinton as a president, is very similar to the struggle 1950s-era social scientists faced when trying to understand electoral shifts in that decade.[25] The prevalence of survey research as a dominant methodology also restricts the number of campaigns and elections we can study. Because so much work in this area relies on survey research data, it is impossible to analyze voter behavior prior to the 1940s with modern precision. For these reasons, the only systematic exploration of deviating elections and their campaigns is relegated to those seen in the 1950s. If regime cycles accurately describe American political history, there are many other deviating elections to be studied, and the detailed historical analyses and comparisons that mark work in American political development may help unpack some of the story.

The focus of this analysis will be on those temporary forces, such as candidates and campaign strategies, that bring victory to opposition parties, rather than long-term forces such as party identification.[26] This does not mean that long-term forces will be irrelevant to such a study. On the contrary, if there is anything to the vast scholarship on electoral eras, it is that Jackson's victory in 1828 and Lincoln's victory in 1860 heralded major changes in the political system that likely included changes in party identification. However, because we do not have the survey research tools to pin down with any sense of certainty the voting behavior of "weak Whigs" or "weak Jacksonian Democrats," we have to look elsewhere for knowledge. If it is true that realigning elections or reconstructive presidencies exist, it is possible that there are common elements shared by those victorious campaigns, and that those common elements tell us something about why such campaigns win, and how in turn those presidents exercise leadership. That is certainly the suggestion of Skowronek's work, as well as that of realignment scholarship in general. By the same token, it seems quite likely that there may be common elements shared by victorious campaigns in deviating elections. If we can generalize about this type of campaign, it may suggest what is required for any opposition party candidate to win in presidential elections. We will be able to approach an answer to the question of how a Whig candidate could win the presidency during the Jacksonian age, how a Republican candidate could win the presidency during the New Deal era, and how a Democrat could win the presidency in the Reagan era.

The leading scholars of voter behavior did not ignore this question. In their treatment of deviating elections, Campbell and his colleagues suggested possible common features of victorious opposition party campaigns. A close reading of the pertinent passage reveals at least three features these scholars thought might be common to victorious opposition campaigns. First, as the very definition of deviating elections suggests, there are likely short-term forces at work that lead to the majority party's defeat. The defeat is not so strong that the majority party loses its preeminent place in the political system, but it is enough to dislodge the party from institutional control of the presidency for a term or two. In Campbell's words, such an election is "a temporary reversal."[27] Such short-term forces can be diverse in nature. Campbell discusses Woodrow Wilson's victories, pointing to the Republican split in 1912 and incumbency and war fears in 1916, but the circumstances are quite different with Eisenhower in the 1950s. What is common to the two presidential victories is the existence of short-term forces that provoke a defection of majority party voters toward the minority party candidate.

Second, the authors indicate that such elections might be typified by opposition party candidates who are in some way popular heroes. Eisenhower is the obvious example—commanding general of Allied forces in Europe during World War II who defeated Nazi Germany and retained a type of nonpartisan popular appeal and heroic image in the years to come. Campbell cites another study that suggested a similar dynamic for other popular war hero candidates, including Washington, Harrison, Grant, Taylor, and Jackson. He argues that it appears that such candidates lack "ideological content" and that "the public image of these gentlemen has little to do with great issues of public policy." Instead, the appeal of the candidate is purely personal. The candidate is able to exploit whatever immediate circumstances have placed him in this position and ride that wave of public approval to electoral victory. Because the election is a personal victory, when the individual passes from the scene the political context reverts to its norm.[28] In this way, this second common feature of deviating elections is linked to the first. Campbell here does not mention Wilson, who was hardly a war hero figure, but his analysis is clearly not meant to be considered comprehensive—merely suggestive.

Third, the authors suggest that deviating elections tend to be void of great policy debates. They do not argue that these elections are completely void of any policy debates. Issues such as corruption and the Korean War, for example, were on voters' minds in 1952. The argument instead is that such elections tend to have "little to do with great issues of public policy"—the types of issues that tend to be present in realigning elections, especially those that put the dominant party into its privileged status. Part of the reason for this is the popular hero status of the opposition party candidate, whose background, often military, lacks ideological content. This is certainly true of Eisenhower, and may be true of other war hero presidents. The personal appeal of these figures overshadows the core issues that tend to divide political parties, making for a less ideological campaign. Just as the "popular hero" aspect of these elections is linked to the "short-term forces" element, so is this "issueless campaign" element connected to the other two features. This final feature is so important, however, that the authors state their belief that "it is this absence of great ideological issues which provides the basic quality of these deviating elections."[29]

One difficulty with this list of observations is that there is clearly an overlap among the three categories. The seven victorious opposition presidents—the seven men who won deviating elections—are William Henry Harrison,

Zachary Taylor, Grover Cleveland, Woodrow Wilson, Dwight Eisenhower, Richard Nixon, and Bill Clinton. To take Eisenhower as an example, it may be difficult to separate the extent to which his status as a popular war hero was an advantage distinct from the nonideological nature of the 1952 campaign. Was it Eisenhower's status as a war hero that contributed to a campaign void of great issues? Was his mere presence on the ballot enough of a short-term force to place the governing party at a severe disadvantage? Similar arguments could be made about Harrison and Taylor, the other two war heroes. At one point the authors suggest that it is the absence of great ideological issues that defines this type of election, but the definition of deviating elections suggests the centrality of short-term forces. Thus, it is not clear which of these elements is more important or more influential than the others.

A perhaps more troubling problem with these observations is their lack of universality. Campbell's discussion does not make it precisely clear which short-term forces led to Eisenhower's victory in 1952, unless it was simply the presence of a war hero in the election. Clearly the Republican split in 1912 aided Wilson's victory, but there was no similar party split in 1840. The authors give credence to the idea that the presence of a popular hero may be a common theme in deviating elections, but only the three war heroes obviously meet that definition. There are four other presidents on the list, and it is difficult to imagine Cleveland or Nixon as "popular heroes" in any sense of the term.[30] The same problem exists for the supposedly nonideological nature of the campaign. The election of 1840 is infamous for its issueless quality, and Campbell has reams of data to support the idea that the presidential elections in the 1950s were void of great ideological content—but can the same really be said for the epic struggle in 1912 between Woodrow Wilson, Theodore Roosevelt, William Howard Taft, and Eugene Debs? Would anyone suggest that the election of 1968 was a placid affair?

These objections are intuitive complaints about the list of opposition party victors. Campbell acknowledges them by avoidance. He mentions the Republican split in 1912 when discussing the short-term forces that helped Wilson win the office, but ignores Wilson when discussing the issue of popular heroes. The existence of such objections need not derail the quest to understand what is typical of opposition party victories, however. Just as there is a substantial degree of diversity among realigning elections, it seems likely that there will be an equal amount among deviating elections. Our task is to think more systematically about what Campbell and his associates suggest in their brief treatment.

At this point, scholars of elections and campaigns may object that I am reaching too far. Most contemporary election models tend to focus on such things as the economy and public opinion polls when predicting results, not such features as placement in the regime cycle. In fact, Campbell's observations concerning short-term forces connect very well to contemporary scholarship on the effects of campaigns on election results. For example, James E. Campbell has written that all campaigns are inherently limited in their effects due to the presence of partisanship in the electorate, and that all campaigns are heavily influenced by features that actually predate the start of the general election season, such as incumbency, the state of the economy, and the natural narrowing effect of the campaign. Thus, the fundamentals of most elections are firmly in place before the campaigns even begin.[31] It seems quite possible that all or some of these elements could factor into the short-term forces mentioned by Angus Campbell. Is there, then, any reason to move beyond the predictive models?

I think that there is. Take James Campbell's incumbency variable as an example. Campbell argues convincingly that presidential incumbency is an advantage for presidents seeking a second term, or for in-party candidates seeking a second presidential term for their party. This advantage is lost when the in-party seeks a third term.[32] As an empirical observation about elections in general this makes sense, but if there is something to the notion that opposition parties operate at a systemic disadvantage when seeking the presidency, as opposed to governing parties, then we should see some evidence of that disadvantage. This can be seen by examining the relative long-term success of governing parties and opposition parties in electoral eras. It may be difficult for successful presidents to pass on the office to their in-party successors, but it is not unheard of. In the modern partisan era, successful three-term sequences include Jackson to Martin Van Buren, Warren Harding to Herbert Hoover, and Reagan to Bush. The McKinley-Roosevelt-Taft succession is the only example of a successful four-term sequence. The Roosevelt-Truman years represent the only successful five-term sequence, while the Lincoln-Chester Arthur reign is the only six-term sequence, aided as it was by extra-electoral factors in 1876. What is intriguing about this list is that, without exception, the presidents listed are members of the governing party. In fact, there is no example of an opposition president successfully transferring power to an heir apparent through an election. There have been some close calls—Nixon in 1960, Gerald Ford in 1976, and Al Gore in 2000 come immediately to mind—but they have always come up short. If there is no wider contextual distinction between governing parties and opposition parties in presidential elections, why would these differences exist? Surely random chance would give the opposition party a three-term sequence somewhere! If Angus Campbell and his colleagues are correct, however, opposition presidents win at least in part due to purely personal factors—their status as a popular hero, or as a nonideological figure. Such an idiosyncratic element would be very difficult to pass on to an heir apparent. Governing parties do not depend as much on such personal elements, enjoying as they do a built-in advantage during the regime they control. This distinction alone is enough warrant to study what is peculiar about successful opposition party campaigns.

The task ahead, then, is clear. If there are differences between successful governing party and opposition party victories, they should be apparent in the conduct of the campaigns. If there are systematic commonalities among regimes throughout American history, it is possible that what is common to opposition party victories is fairly constant through time, even as nomination processes change. If so, we should be able to examine those campaigns and draw some conclusions about what is required for opposition parties to win. This will allow us to draw from a larger pool of elections to gain understanding about the requirements of success. Such a contextual view of presidential campaigns may suggest that the differences in leadership style witnessed between opposition and governing party presidents have their roots in the campaigns that brought them to power.[33]

A Model for Getting Elected

In pursuing this investigation, it seems reasonable to begin where Campbell and his colleagues left off. In their brief analysis of deviating elections, they identified three features they believed might be common to this type of victory. So, in examining what contributes to opposition party victories, we can begin with those same features. As suggested before, the boundaries separating these three features may not always be clear, but it is worthwhile to define them as clearly as possible, and then see where the evidence takes us. If these three features hold up under analysis, then presumably the evidence will allow for sharper distinctions to be made.

Before beginning, however, it is important to recall the basic task facing the opposition party candidate. The primary objective for any opposition party candidate is to attain the office of the presidency, but potential opposition presidents already operate at a disadvantage by campaigning in a political party that is in a defensive posture. That is, the governing party has been able to fashion the national political debate on its own terms. Nevertheless, even a party of opposition is not helpless, especially when favored by events beyond its control. All victorious presidential candidates are able to define politics to their benefit in an election, but there is a difference between a long-term redefinition, such as happens in realignment or other punctuated change, and a short-term redefinition, such as happens in most elections. The opposition president is unable to redefine politics in any fundamental way, so he may seek victory along lines that do not strike at the foundations of the governing party.

I. TAKE ADVANTAGE OF A GOVERNING PARTY IN TROUBLE. Before addressing what an opposition party candidate can do to win an election, it seems clear that the larger historical context has to be favorable to victory. Certain fundamental features need to be in place for the normally disadvantaged party to beat the advantaged party. Campbell refers to these as short-term forces that lead to a temporary reversal for the majority party, and he mentions the Republican split in 1912 as an example. The implication is that even robust governing parties face difficult times, and those times may have the great misfortune of coinciding with election years. In a political era that normally favors one party, there are elections that simply are not "Republican" or "Democratic" years. If the opposition party understands the nature of the trouble afflicting the governing party at such times, it will take advantage of it.

What factors lead to a temporary reversal for the governing party? Perhaps the most obvious one is the status of the governing party incumbent. If the governing party has no incumbent running for reelection (Democrats in 1952), the race is an open one, and open races always give hope to the challenger. By the same token, if the opposition party has succeeded in wresting control of the presidency from the governing party, and runs an incumbent of its own for reelection, the advantage of incumbency now works in its favor (Eisenhower in 1956). Alternatively, a governing party incumbent might be weakened by any number of negative short-term forces, including scandal, economic trouble, or foreign policy crisis (Bush in 1992). None of these problems need lead to a long-term reversal of control, but they can be sufficient to call into question the credibility of the governing party in any specific election year and place it in danger. Worse, such conditions could lead to an undesirable and divisive nomination battle, placing the eventual nominee in a defensive posture in the general election. All parties face difficulties keeping their diverse coalitions in line, and governing parties are not immune to factional defection, but this problem can range from simple internal party tension to a strong intrapartisan challenge to a full-scale factional bolt—a defection of normally reliable partisans to the opposition (Republican Mugwumps in 1884). It is also possible that the presence of third parties in elections tends to work more to the disadvantage of governing parties than opposition parties (Ross Perot in 1992). All of these factors are fairly easy to measure. The key is that, by placing the governing party in trouble, they set up an electoral context that provides an opening for the opposition party.

2. RUN A "BLANK SLATE" CANDIDATE. Once the opposition party sees a weakness, it must exploit it. Its first decision is to determine what kind of candidate to run. Campbell suggests that a common feature of victorious opposition parties is the use of popular heroes. He calls special attention to popular war heroes such as Harrison, Taylor, and Eisenhower. As noted above, however, it is immediately clear that not all victorious opposition candidates are war heroes. Cleveland and Wilson hardly qualify, and neither do Nixon and Clinton in the modern era. Is there any way to broaden the scope of this concept in a more useful way?

The problem an opposition party faces is that it represents a governing philosophy that runs counter to the reigning one. Unless the party's goal is to overthrow the reigning governing philosophy and replace it with its own, it is not well served by highlighting the central differences between its ideology and that of the governing party. It would seem wiser for the opposition party to find its advantage in temperance or subterfuge. Campbell hints at this dynamic, for when he talks about popular heroes as candidates, he describes why they are effective at winning office from the opposition party. He argues that such candidates are appealing on a personal level, not due to any partisan or ideological views they may possess. Their public image is not associated with the philosophical differences that divide the parties, and they are not thought of in ideological ways. It is possible that this nonideological dimension is not limited to popular war heroes. Perhaps a candidate need not have a heroic résumé to be perceived as someone who has more personal than partisan appeal.

What is required, then, are not popular war heroes but candidates who hide or mask the central differences between the two parties rather than highlight them. Instead of boldly championing the core philosophy of the opposition party, the successful opposition candidates are politically ambiguous enough to be whatever voters want them to be. In other words, instead of presenting a clear and staunchly ideological portrait to voters, the successful opposition candidate allows voters to write their own vision of the candidate in their minds. These candidates are, in a sense, blank slates, not because they lack a national reputation or a clear set of core beliefs, but because their political views are ambiguous enough to make them attractive to a wide variety of people. Such a candidate may be truly nonpartisan in background, like a war hero, but he may simply have a nonpartisan personal style. He may be a political unknown whose low profile or lack of lengthy service has not given national opinion shapers the opportunity to sketch out a clear portrait of him to the public (Grover Cleveland). Alternatively, he may be someone whose own governing philosophy tends toward the center of the ideological spectrum, thus muting some of the criticism the governing party might throw at him (Bill Clinton). This is hardly heroic—but it is sound politics. He may even, as we shall see, be a renegade member of the governing party. The central point here is to determine the degree of ideological purity in a candidate relative to the governing party's ideology. We should find some similarity among these candidates in terms of their ability to put forward a nonideological image.

3. RUN AN INDIRECT CAMPAIGN. Once an opposition party has its standard-bearer, it is time to run the campaign. Campbell and his colleagues are least equivocal on this final point. In their view, the absence of great ideological issues is the basic quality of victorious opposition party campaigns. Some of this has to do with the previous point—the nonideological character of the blank slate candidate. However, it seems clear that Campbell sees the typical deviating election as not simply about image but also about the absence of great issues. Again these elections are not completely void of any policy debate—they simply seem to avoid "great" policy debates. To use a military metaphor, successful opposition campaigns avoid direct frontal assaults on the core issues that divide the parties, pursuing instead a more indirect approach.

Avoidance of great issues is not the natural tendency of core partisans. For the purist faction of a party that serves as its ideological anchor, it is the nature of political competition to emphasize and magnify the differences between one's party and the opposition. It is the purists who keep parties of the left and right anchored on the left and right. They do not always command the decision-making power in the parties, but they strive to keep them honest to their central convictions. While parties are more coalitions of coalitions than pure monolithic entities, even among these coalitions there are groups that tend to seek ideological purity at the expense of electoral victory. However, ideological purity is precisely the wrong thing to seek if one is a member of the opposition party. The implication in Campbell's observation is that successful opposition parties and candidates stifle or pacify purist dissent in an effort to present a moderate image. This in turn masks the differences between the two parties that the purists prefer to highlight.

The natural culmination of the first two elements, then, is an indirect campaign. It should be remembered that the typical American brand of electoral politics makes very likely the avoidance of some issues. Ceaser describes quite clearly the kind of partisan conflict that normally takes place in American elections. Partisan conflict in the United States rarely ever centers on wars between "great parties," conflicts that involve foundational regime-level issues. In that sense, virtually all American elections are issueless. Similarly, partisan conflict in the United States only occasionally involves ideological frontal assaults between fiercely principled "Burkean parties." These middle-level conflicts do occur in American politics, but they result either in the realignments or redefinitions of politics that mark the beginning and ending of governing party control in a political era, or the shellacking experienced by parties that attempt to elevate a political contest to this level when the time is not ripe, as occurred in 1964 with the GOP. Most elections involve "small parties" that fight over run-of-the-mill matters of principle on some ground of consensus established the last time a middle-level conflict presented the electorate with dramatically different alternatives.[34] Successful opposition campaigns do not wage war over the cleavage issues that define the basic partisan division that put the current governing party in power. Instead, they pursue a more indirect and moderate course.

Although Campbell argues that this final feature constitutes the basic quality of opposition party victory, it seems at first glance to be the most difficult to measure. Political parties embody ideas, and even the most im-age-centered campaign involves issues at some level. Indeed, there is no such thing as a purely issueless campaign. Many of the traditional historical accounts of the 1840 and 1884 elections emphasize their issueless quality, but more recent scholarship encourages readers to remember the legitimate issues that always lie behind seemingly contentless campaigns. Although the campaign spectacle may seem to overshadow policy substance, that substance never completely disappears. This third factor is much more relative to the specific context of the campaign. In a situation when one party's issues do not command great electoral power, however, the opposition candidate may try to downplay thóse core issue differences to place emphasis on other things. The goal is to attempt a short-term redefinition of politics by focusing on some issue or controversy that does not represent a fundamental attack on the reigning governing philosophy. Thus, "indirect" refers not to a campaign devoid of issues, but to a strategy of avoiding the core issues that divide the opposition candidate from the governing party—avoiding what Campbell calls "great questions of policy."[35] What issues do arise in the campaign may be short-term issues on which the governing party is temporarily weak. These would not be "core issues" but more peripheral issues, such as some scandal or foreign policy trouble. Undoubtedly the opposition party focuses campaign attention on whatever short-term forces have placed the governing party in trouble. Here we see the marrying of this third feature with the first. In such a case, it would be foolish for the opposition party to play up deeper divisions that do not resonate that year. Of course, the opposition party could choose to focus its attention on emotional appeals, personal attacks, and other diversions. Such "image over substance" campaigns would also divert attention from the core issues dividing the two parties.

No doubt these three strategies occur occasionally in campaigns other than those run by opposition candidates. Any party seeks to take advantage of a weak opponent, and both parties consciously work to moderate their image to the general electorate. Appealing to the center is a time-honored Downsian tactic.[36] Nevertheless, the larger political context of an era suggests that the tenor of these strategies will be quite different when governing parties employ them. When a governing party seeks to present a moderate image in a campaign, it is simply trying to reassure the electorate that the party's principles are safe. The party still persists in referencing and paying homage to its fundamental principles and founding heroes. When an opposition party seeks to present a moderate front, however, it is masking its purist anchor and trying to convince the public that the party is not as extreme as the public may think it is. It will actually play down its fundamental principles, even as it recalls its founding heroes. It may even adopt some of the rhetoric of the governing party. In a sense, the opposition party plays by the rules established by the governing party. That is why it makes a difference who holds the power of definition. Table 1-1 represents an attempt to illustrate the various features of successful opposition party campaigns under examination in this book. The table lists the successful opposition party candidates and the years they were elected. To the right are three columns that summarize in bullet form the model for campaigning as an opposition party candidate sketched above. The basic ingredients of each feature do not correspond to

TABLE I-I:

Template of Successful Opposition Campaign Features

Year	Winning Candidate	Governing Party in Trouble	Blank Slate Candidate	Indirect Campaign
1840	Harrison			
1848	Taylor	open race	military hero	core issue avoidance
1884	Cleveland	opposition incumbent	unknown	short-term focus
1892	Cleveland	scandal	centrist	image over substance
1912	Wilson	economic crisis	cross-partisan	
1916	Wilson	foreign policy trouble		
1952	Eisenhower	internal party tension		
1956	Eisenhower	factional bolt		
1968	Nixon	third party presence		
1972	Nixon			
1992	Clinton			
1996	Clinton			

specific candidates in the table—that will await the more detailed treatment in each of the next three chapters—but they ably summarize the preliminary "recipe" thus far.

Ultimately, what is at play here is a twist of that conservative Republican plea during the later New Deal era for "a choice, not an echo." The GOP suffered a devastating defeat at the polls in 1964 when it followed that advice. Instead, if this model is valid, what successful opposition parties seek is something approaching "an echo, not a choice." Oddly enough, when running against the grain of history, as opposition parties do, the candidate must run with the grain of history to be successful.

The following three chapters will dissect these three features in turn to determine several things. First, are these features common to all successful opposition party campaigns? Will we be able to generalize about candidates in similar circumstances? Second, is one feature more important to a successful campaign than the others? Or do they tend to shift in importance depending on other factors? Third, will we be able to draw some general conclusions about what is required for electoral success for opposition party candidates in such a way that distinguishes that success from governing party victories? Ultimately, what are the requirements of success for the opposition party candidate? Each chapter begins with a brief recapitulation of the specific feature and continues with analyses of the historical data, drawing inferences and conclusions about opposition victories. I then provide historical surveys of the twelve presidential elections that meet the criteria of opposition party victories, concluding with a statement of what links the particular feature to the other criteria for success.

Chapter 2

THE GOVERNING
PARTY IN TROUBLE

Perhaps the most important element in an opposition party victory, the one unquestionably present in every single example of the same, is not even under the opposition party's control. There are times when even robust governing parties face great difficulties, and sometimes those difficulties coincide with election years. Barring some catastrophic governing party mistake, some years are simply lost causes for the opposition party. Elections that follow soon after a realignment or long-term redefinition of politics are the obvious examples, such as the Roosevelt elections of 1936, 1940, and 1944, or Reagan's reelection in 1984. Elections that take place during times when the governing party and its philosophy are particularly robust also work to the great misfortune of opposition parties. Examples of these include the elections of Ulysses Grant, William McKinley, Theodore Roosevelt, and the Republicans of the 1920s. It is difficult in these cases to see what the opposition party could have done to alter history from its course. The historical data point to several factors that may indicate governing party weakness, however, and all of these cases have one thing in common: they represent or are the result of a short-term problem that adversely affects the governing party.

First, the governing party may field no incumbent in a given election. The Twenty-second Amendment now makes this situation mandatory, but it was even more common in the nineteenth century. An open race always gives hope to the opposition party. With the withdrawal of James K. Polk from the 1848 race and no incumbent Republican in 1884 after six straight victories, Taylor and Cleveland were free to play to their respective strengths in their own campaigns.[1] A similar dynamic faced Eisenhower in 1952 and Nixon in 1968. In both cases—as with Polk—the incumbent president re-

TABLE 2-I:
Opposition Party Victories in Open Races, 1828–2004

Year	Governing Party Candidate	Opposition Party Candidate	Winner
1836	Van Buren	Harrison, White, Webster	Van Buren
1844	Polk	Clay	Polk
1848	*Cass*	*Taylor*	*Taylor*
1852	Pierce	Scott	Pierce
1856	Buchanan	Fremont	Buchanan
1868	Grant	Seymour	Grant
1876	Hayes	Tilden	Hayes
1880	Garfield	Hancock	Garfield
1884	*Blaine*	*Cleveland*	*Cleveland*
1896	McKinley	Bryan	McKinley
1908	Taft	Bryan	Taft
1920	Harding	Cox	Harding
1928	Hoover	Smith	Hoover
1952	*Stevenson*	*Eisenhower*	*Eisenhower*
1960	Kennedy	Nixon	Kennedy
1968	*Humphrey*	*Nixon*	*Nixon*
1988	Bush	Dukakis	Bush
2000	Bush	Gore	Bush

Summary: Number of open races: 18 of 41 (44% of total)
Governing party victories: 14 (78%)
Opposition party victories: 4 (22%)

moved himself from the coming battle. This advantage obviously holds for opposition presidents who stand for reelection. Wilson, Eisenhower, Nixon, and Clinton all stood for reelection and won, and their elections were made easier by already occupying the White House.

On further examination, however, the existence of an open race does not appear to be as clear a discriminator as one might think. Table 2-1 lists all the presidential elections from 1828 to 2004 that were open races—no incumbent president in the race. Focusing on contests that did not lead to reconstructions of presidential politics, I exempt from the analysis Lincoln's victory in 1860. The table lists the opposing candidates in each year by governing and opposition party, and the winner. Victorious opposition party elections are in italics. Of the forty-one elections examined, eighteen were open races. Presumably, these would be races that provided the normally disadvantaged opposition party with its greatest opportunity for victory, yet fourteen of them resulted in governing party victories, and only four led to opposition party victories. That is a winning percentage of only 22 percent. Since the opposition party has won twelve of the forty-one total nonrealigning elections—a rate of 29 percent—it would appear that facing an open race does not provide a disproportionate advantage to the opposition party.[2]

Table 2-2 presents a similar analysis for presidential elections that involve incumbent candidates.[3] Again, focusing on contests that did not lead to reconstructions of presidential politics, I exempt from the analysis the elections of 1828 (Jackson), 1932 (Roosevelt), and 1980 (Reagan). The table lists the opposing candidates in each year by governing and opposing party, and the winner. I identify the actual incumbent candidate and highlight victorious opposition party elections in italics. Of the forty-one elections examined, twenty-three were races involving incumbents, seventeen of them from the governing party and six of them from the opposition party. Presumably, these would be races that presented a more significant barrier to opposition party victory. In fact, the opposition party performs only slightly better in these races, winning four of the seventeen races that involved governing party incumbents, for a winning percentage of 24 percent, slightly better than with open races but still under the overall average.[4] What is clear from this chart is the positive effect incumbency has on both governing and opposition party presidents. The governing party has won thirteen of seventeen races in which its candidate was the incumbent president, a winning rate of over 76 percent. The opposition party has won four of six races in which its candidate was the incumbent president, a winning rate of 67 percent. Thus, in terms of incumbency status, we can say that it helps tremendously if the opposition party already holds the presidency and is running for reelection, but there does not appear to be a significant advantage for the opposition party when it faces either an open race or a governing party incumbent.

A second factor indicating governing party vulnerability in a given election is the presence of a weak incumbent. I am not referring here to presidents such as Herbert Hoover or Jimmy Carter, whose circumstances were so dire that they heralded the great redefiners of politics. Rather, these are presidents such as Martin Van Buren and George H. W. Bush, who were blamed for economic strife but whose electoral losses did not result in long-term repudiations of their parties. It was the panic of 1837 and the Jacksonian philosophy of negative government that damaged the credibility of the governing party and led to the election of Harrison. It was the economic recession of the

TABLE 2-2:

Opposition Party Victories in Incumbent Races, 1828–2004

Year	Governing Party Candidate	Opposition Party Candidate	Winner
1832	Jackson (i)	Clay	Jackson
1840	Van Buren (i)	Harrison	Harrison
1864	Lincoln (i)	McClellan	Lincoln
1872	Grant (i)	Greeley	Grant
1888	Harrison	Cleveland (i)	Harrison
1892	Harrison (i)	Cleveland	Cleveland
1900	McKinley (i)	Bryan	McKinley
1904	Roosevelt (i)	Parker	Roosevelt
1912	Taft (i)	Wilson	Wilson
1916	Hughes	Wilson (i)	Wilson
1924	Coolidge (i)	Davis	Coolidge
1936	Roosevelt (i)	Landon	Roosevelt
1940	Roosevelt (i)	Willkie	Roosevelt
1944	Roosevelt (i)	Dewey	Roosevelt
1948	Truman (i)	Dewey	Truman
1956	Stevenson	Eisenhower (i)	Eisenhower
1964	Johnson (i)	Goldwater	Johnson
1972	McGovern	Nixon (i)	Nixon
1976	Carter	Ford (i)	Carter
1984	Reagan (i)	Mondale	Reagan
1992	Bush (i)	Clinton	Clinton
1996	Dole	Clinton (i)	Clinton
2004	Bush (i)	Kerry	Bush

Summary: Number incumbent races: 23 of 41 (56% of total)

      Governing party incumbents: 17 (74%)

          Winning governing party incumbents: 13 (76%)

          Losing governing party incumbents: 4 (24%)

      Opposition party incumbents: 6 (26%)

          Winning opposition party incumbents: 4 (67%)

          Losing opposition party incumbents: 2 (33%)

Note: (i) = incumbent

early 1990s, the perception of inaction on the part of the president, and the presence of intraparty strife that damaged the credibility of the governing party and led to the election of Clinton. Benjamin Harrison and William Howard Taft demonstrated similar inability to deal with short-term difficulties in 1892 and 1912.

This analysis begs the question, however. It is too easy to stipulate that economic difficulties such as those experienced in 1840 and 1992, or problems associated with war, such as those experienced in 1848, 1952, and 1968, cause problems for the party controlling the executive branch. Economic strife in the 1870s, mid-1930s, and early 1980s did not prevent governing party victories, nor did war in the 1860s, 1890s, and 1940s, to say nothing of 2004. Context is all-important. Simply stated, there is no example of a governing party losing an election without some significant problem discrediting its leadership. That is not true for opposition parties, which sometimes lose simply because they are the disadvantaged party. The real dynamic that aids the cause of the opposition party is the internal strife experienced by the governing party caused by these external factors or by other endogenous forces. Depression, war, and other negative forces have their greatest impact when they divide governing parties through the mechanism of a partisan bolt or third-party split. In fact, after eliminating from consideration the reelection of incumbent opposition presidents—for we have already seen that their status as incumbents places the governing party at a temporary disadvantage—the election of 1840 is the only example of an opposition party victory that does not involve some sort of intraparty bolt or third-party presence detrimental to the governing party. It should not be surprising that the governing party in a two-party system would have trouble keeping its diverse coalition together. In fact, it may be more difficult for the governing party to manage factional relations than for an opposition party. Nevertheless, it is the internal strife caused by war, economic bad times, and personal ambition that makes the governing party vulnerable more than those elements in and of themselves.

Sometimes this dynamic manifests itself only in internal party tension. The feuding between Republicans Benjamin Harrison and James G. Blaine in 1892, for example, or the great tensions experienced at the 1968 Democratic national convention, or the insurgency of Patrick Buchanan in the 1992 GOP primaries all helped degrade the unity necessary for a trouble-plagued governing party to stave off a vigorous opposition party effort. At other times, this dynamic manifests itself more seriously in a temporary bolt of a governing party faction to the opposition party. The earliest example of this that worked to the harm of the governing party was the Mugwump revolt of 1884, when that small but important faction rejected Blaine, the candidate of old-time Republican values and the embodiment of all the Mugwumps hated, and supported Grover Cleveland, the good-government candidate of the Democratic Party. Many contemporary observers blamed the GOP defeat that year on the loss of New York, an exceptionally close contest that may have been lost to the GOP due to Mugwump activity. Similarly, Democrats in 1952 suffered the lingering effects of the Dixiecrat split four years earlier. With a war hero as the Republican candidate, it was an easy matter for Southern Democrats to revolt against their own party under such banners as the "Shivercrats." Eisenhower would have won without such Democratic help, but such bolts do nothing to aid the cause of the governing party.

The most devastating example of partisan strife that adversely affects the governing party is the rise of a third party, often from within the very ranks of the governing party. The rise of a third party can be seen as a rebuke of both major parties, since supporters of the third party believe neither major party addresses their policy concerns.[5] With few exceptions, however, the presence of a third party in a race does not impact the two major parties in equal degrees. In fact, more often than not third parties work to the detriment of the governing party. From the perspective of contextual politics, this should not be surprising. It is governing parties that define the terms of political debate and establish how the nation talks about issues. If the governing party fails to address some issue of concern, resort to a third party is a rational step. In this sense, the rise of a third party is not just an indictment of the two-party system but also a condemnation of "the government"—that is, the governing party. Thus, the rise of a third party usually works more against the governing party than the opposition. Table 2-3 illustrates the importance of strong third-party candidates in races that result in opposition party victories. The table lists, in chronological order, all of the examples of third-party movements since the dawn of the Jacksonian era in which the third party received at least 5 percent of the popular vote. Elections that resulted in opposition-party—but not redefining—victories are in italics.[6]

As table 2-3 indicates, twelve third-party candidates, involved in ten races, received over 5 percent of the popular vote. Seven of those candidates, in six of those races, were associated with opposition party victories. Three other races—those in 1856, 1860, and 1980—were part of longer-term realignment sequences, two of those (1860 and 1980) leading to opposition party victories in which the opposition party became the governing party. Thus, the 1924 election is the sole clear example of a presidential election in which

TABLE 2-3:
Significant Third-Party Candidates, 1828–2004

Year	Candidate	Party	Percentage of Popular Vote
1848	Martin Van Buren	Free Soil	10.1
1856	Millard Fillmore	Whig-American	21.5
1860	John C. Breckinridge	Southern Democrat	18.1
	John Bell	Constitutional Union	12.6
1892	James B. Weaver	Populist	8.5
1912	Theodore Roosevelt	Progressive	27.4
	Eugene V. Debs	Socialist	6.0
1924	Robert M. La Follette	Progressive	16.6
1968	George C. Wallace	American Independent	13.5
1980	John B. Anderson	Independent	6.6
1992	H. Ross Perot	Independent	18.9
1996	H. Ross Perot	Reform	8.5

Source: Gary King and Lyn Ragsdale, *The Elusive Executive: Discovering Statistical Patterns in the Presidency,* pp. 447–53; updated by the author.

a major third-party presence did not lead to a governing party defeat.[7] The reason for that may be the desperate state of affairs the opposition Democrats found themselves in that year, taking 103 ballots to settle on a nominee at their party convention. Partisan splits do no good if the opposition party is not positioned to take advantage of them. A similar observation could be made about the 1872 Liberal Republican split, which found the Democrats so desperate that they adopted the Liberal Republican candidate as their own.[8] As a general rule, however, it would seem that governing parties have more to fear from major third-party efforts.

Not all of these third-party efforts had the same impact on the governing party. Some analysts, for example, believe Clinton would have won the 1992 election even without the presence of Ross Perot in the campaign, and Nixon might have won in 1968 without any help from George Wallace. Other cases are clearer. The Barnburner bolt in 1848 that led some Democrats to the new Free Soil Party harmed the governing party Democrats more than a similar bolt from the Whigs, and the Barnburner bolt was exacerbated by the fact that the Free Soil Party was led by life-long Democrat and former president Martin Van Buren. Similarly, the Bull Moose bolt in 1912 destroyed any chance the GOP had of defeating Wilson, and the situation was exacerbated by the fact that the new Progressive Party was led by lifelong Republican and former president Theodore Roosevelt. The combination of a weak incumbent and a bitter major party split was deadly, and the situation remained bad enough to adversely impact GOP opportunities in 1916, an election Republicans should have won but for the lingering GOP-Progressive rift. These elections constitute a solid anchor for this factor.

The story is the same in the other elections. The Populist threat did more to harm the Republican cause in 1892 than it did to hamper Cleveland's election bid, and the Wallace effort in 1968 represented a defection of a lifelong Democrat and former governor in a region that had for one hundred years been solidly in the Democratic camp. Opposition parties are not immune to third-party efforts, but the two great examples explain more about redefining transition periods than they do about normal elections. In 1856, for example, former Whig President Millard Fillmore found himself leading the last charge of a dying party that had already given way to the new Republicans. In 1980, Republican John Anderson attempted to fight the increasingly conservative tone of his own party by offering an independent alternative to Reagan. Both efforts failed, and in the latter case, Democrat Jimmy Carter accurately believed Anderson's presence in the race would come more at his expense than Reagan's.[9]

A partisan split is no guarantee of opposition victory. The one election glaringly absent from table 2-3 is Harry Truman's victory in 1948. In that year the Democrats experienced two different partisan splits, one by Southern segregationist Strom Thurmond and the other by the left-wing Henry Wallace. The situation appeared to be a classic case of partisan self-destruction, and many observers believed the Dixiecrat and Progressive bolts signaled certain death for Truman's effort. Ultimately, of course, the internal Democratic problems proved not to be as bad as expected. Wallace's support was thin and Thurmond enjoyed support only in the Deep South. Neither candidate broke 3 percent of the popular vote, and the two third-party efforts together did not reach the 5 percent threshold of table 2-3.[10] It is fairly easy to examine the match-ups in tables 2-1 and 2-2 and construct a list of contests in which the opposition party candidate was a stronger establishment figure than the governing party candidate—Clay versus Polk, Cox versus Harding, Nixon versus Kennedy, Gore versus Bush, and others. The general rule remains solid, however—no opposition party has ever won the presidency in the absence of the types of problems described in this chapter.

Having now surveyed the general terrain, it is time to examine in greater detail how these short-term forces have manifested themselves in opposition victories. Following are brief summaries of the general context of each victorious opposition effort, focusing specifically on what led the governing party to be open to attack.

1840: Harrison takes advantage of the first great depression

By 1836, the Jacksonian era was eight years old. The new Whig Party, competing in its first presidential election, forsook the idea of running one candidate. Instead, the party ran three regional candidates in an effort to throw the election into the House of Representatives. The strategy failed, and Martin Van Buren, Andrew Jackson's vice president, took the reins of the executive branch. By 1840, however, prospects looked much better for the Whig Party. The Whigs benefited from the fact that the party in power was being blamed for a severe depression. Thus, its candidate, the incumbent Van Buren, was considerably weaker after four years in office.

The problem for the Democrats began in 1837 when the consequences of Jackson's fiscal policies hit the national economy. Jackson's famous war against the Second Bank of the United States led to the transfer of government deposits from the national bank to state-chartered banks. Those banks in turn increased the money supply, leading to inflation and massive speculation. Jackson responded by issuing, by executive order, his Specie Circular, essentially ending land speculation by requiring that purchases be made only in gold or silver. Land prices fell, banks were squeezed by numerous defaults, and the result was an end to the economic boom, the first great crash on Wall Street, and the beginning of the first great depression. In the panic of 1837, bank failures led to the suspension of payments in specie. Businesses folded and factories shut down, resulting in unemployment. States that had gone into debt to finance large canal and road programs had to curtail their work, which further exacerbated the unemployment problem. There followed a cutback in credit and depreciation of state bank notes. In 1839, another panic hit, leading to an even more severe depression. The prolonged contraction lasted nearly seven years.[11]

Blame for the depression fell on the party that had been in power since 1829. Although it was Jackson's policies that paved the way for economic disaster, it was Van Buren who suffered the consequences. Jackson left office just before the depression struck, leaving Van Buren to manage the mess.

The situation for Van Buren was not helped by his party's ideology or its response to the depression. Democrats adhered to a governing philosophy that stressed strict construction of the Constitution and negative government. They believed that the government intervention advocated by Whigs produced inequalities and privilege and favored some at the expense of others. Democrats sought to preserve equality of opportunity by having government do nothing, including relief for people suffering in the depression. It was not the government's job to make people rich or poor, or to infringe on the liberties of some to satisfy the demands of others. Van Buren remained faithful to this doctrine, choosing not to seek relief energetically. In his message to the special session of Congress that convened in 1837, Van Buren argued that the Founding Fathers "wisely judged that the less government interferes with private pursuits the better for the general prosperity." He faced a Whig Party that believed in positive government intervention in the economy to promote growth and recovery. Whigs saw government action as helping everyone and thought government should either provide capital for economic growth or help people accumulate it. They were merciless and relentless in blaming the economic situation on Jackson's policies.[12]

By 1840, the Democrats had experienced three years of bitter partisan debate over the Independent Treasury bill, which would free government funds from any connection to state banks, before finally passing it. The party also faced foreign policy troubles in boundary disputes with Great Britain and Canada, tensions with Mexico over Texas, and the Second Seminole War. By this time, the Whig program of positive and active federal relief looked very appealing. Opposing the inactivity of the Democratic regime, the Whigs promised "two dollars a day and roast beef."[13] The Whigs approached the 1840 election facing a party blamed for a severe depression and a weakened incumbent representing that economic turmoil. Although, unlike many of the other examples of successful opposition elections, the Democrats in 1840 did not suffer a partisan split or third-party threat, the presence of economic disaster (as with the GOP in 1932) was sufficient to place them in serious trouble. The Whigs called into question the very credibility of the governing party.

1848: Taylor enjoys a Free Soil split

Eight years later, the Democratic Party again faced difficulties. This time, the problems were not of an external economic nature. They were internal. The party had controlled the White House under James K. Polk for four years following Tyler's presidency, but Polk's policies had not led to a Democratic paradise, and his party lost control of the House in the midterm elections of 1846. The Mexican War divided the nation along sectional lines, splitting the Democratic Party, many of whose members joined the Whigs in seeing the war as immoral and unjust, fought only for the extension of slavery. Northern Democrats were alienated by Polk's patronage policies, while Northwesterners were incensed at Polk's compromise with Great Britain over the Oregon boundary issue. That compromise caused expansion to tend toward the Southwest, which prompted Northern Democrats to accuse Polk of favoring Southern interests. Matters degenerated to the point that non-Southerners saw the "slavocracy" as responsible for the problems facing the country, and soon nearly every political issue involved the question of whether slavery would be permitted in new territories.[14]

On August 8, 1846, the last day of the congressional session, David Wilmot of Pennsylvania and Jacob Brinkerhoff of Ohio, both Northern Democrats, introduced an amendment to an appropriations bill that provided funds to purchase Mexican lands. The amendment said that slavery should be prohibited in any territory acquired by that appropriation. Thus, there would be no slavery in any territory acquired from the Republic of Mexico. The Wilmot Proviso, as it became known, favored manifest destiny but opposed the expansion of slavery. The amendment passed the House but was halted in the Senate. The Proviso quickly split the nation and the party. In the North there was some antislavery sentiment, but there was a much greater consensus that the slave society should not expand, due in part to resentment of the greater political power of the South. Southerners, on the other hand, argued that not only did they need to expand, but they had a right to expand, and a constitutional right to carry their property, including slaves, into all territories of the United States. Embedded in this attitude were a resentment of the Northern notion that the South was inferior, a perception that the issue was a potential symbol for Southern equality, and an understanding that Wilmot represented the first step toward abolition. The issue came to a head late in Polk's term when the captured territories of California and New Mexico sought territorial governments. There was no national majority to extend slavery automatically, and there was no majority in the North to protect slavery south of the Missouri Compromise line in the conquered areas. Compounded with this was the fact that Texas claimed most of the settled portion of New Mexico, which would have made that whole area a slave territory.[15] The issue was not resolved by the time of the election.

When Polk declared that he would serve for only one term, the race in 1848 became an open one. Both parties faced internal stresses. Conscience Whigs like Joshua Giddings opposed slavery and argued that foundational Whig issues like the tariff, internal improvements, banks and public lands were no longer important. On the other hand, Northern Democrat antislavery extension "Barnburners" opposed Democratic conservative "Hunkers." With no incumbent in the race, the party that best held together its various pieces would have the advantage. On that matter, the Democrats suffered the greater damage. The party nominated Northerner Lewis Cass for the presidency, a former territorial governor and United States senator. Cass denounced the Wilmot Proviso in favor of popular sovereignty, the doctrine that the inhabitants of a territory could decide the slavery question for themselves. Southern Democrats were not satisfied with that position, though they focused more on Cass's pledge to veto the Proviso should it ever pass. Northern Barnburners were even less satisfied, for they would not accept any candidate who did not explicitly pledge support for the Proviso. The split in New York was so bad that the state party essentially disintegrated. Two different delegations from New York fought for recognition at the party's national convention, and neither in the end participated. Barnburners bolted and formed the Free Soil Party with Conscience Whigs and members of the abolitionist Liberty Party.[16]

The importance of this third-party split can be seen in the identity of the man the new party chose to represent it in the presidential race. Martin Van Buren—a major leader in the Democratic Party for twenty years, there at its founding, a key player in engineering its long success, as well as its former vice president and president—left his party, throwing his home state of New York into question for the election. Joined by Charles Francis Adams as his running mate, Van Buren was seen as the only one who could detach enough Democratic votes to prevent the election of Lewis Cass.[17] In this case, the Whigs did not have to work hard at calling into question the credibility of the governing party. Factions of the governing party were doing that well enough on their own. The partisan factional rifts experienced by the Democrats in 1848 would become the norm for later examples of governing party trouble.

1884: Cleveland attracts good-government Republicans

The Republican Party sprang to life out of the ashes of the second-party system. First achieving victory at the presidential level in 1860 with Abraham Lincoln, by 1884 the party had won six straight presidential elections, a record still unmatched since the formation of modern political parties in the United States. The party was greatly weakened, however. Its last two national victories had been exceptionally close, and its elected president in 1880, James Garfield, had been assassinated in his first few months of office, leaving Chester Arthur as president. Arthur was not an inspiring leader, and the Republicans experienced a loss of unity and a general defensiveness that gave the Democrats their opportunity. Arthur himself did not win his party's nomination for another term, so the Democrats would face no incumbent in an open race.[18]

As so often happens with a governing party that has held the reins of power for a long period of time, the Republican Party began to suffer stress fractures in its partisan base. One source of Republican pain was the Mugwumps. New York Sun editor Charles A. Dana supposedly coined the name from the Algonquin word meaning "great men," the implication being that the Mugwumps were too proud of themselves. Another interpretation pictured them as fence-straddlers who sat with their mugs on one side and their wumps on the other. Mugwumps grew out of the conscientious Republicans who after the Civil War replaced slavery as the great moral evil with spoils politics. In the mid-1870s, Independent Republicans attempted to purge the party of spoilsmanship. They defined themselves as the "party of the center" and threatened to shift their support to another party if Republicans did not satisfy their demands. They were not so much a well-organized faction of the GOP as a small group of dissidents who were unhappy with the corruption they saw in politics. The 1883 Pendleton Act instituting a national civil service was due in part to Mugwump pressure. Mugwump ideals included nonpartisanship, civil service reform, and independent voting. At the local level, Mugwumps sought nonpartisan municipal government and the business administration of city affairs. Their core idea was that there was no partisan way "to pave streets, build sewers, or educate children."[19]

Mugwumps were primarily urban Northeasterners from the New York and New England area. They were white-collar professionals and entrepreneurs who usually had attained a high educational status. Many were young men who rejected Civil War issues as "old politics" and adhered to a pre-Progressive ideology that valued scientific objectivity and specialization, which led naturally to a preference for nonpartisanship and expert administration of government. They saw themselves as guardians of public morality. Mugwumps supported political activism, but eschewed partisan politics. They saw the spoils system as irrational and unprofessional. Mugwumps also tended to be antitariff, arguing that the tariff interfered with free competition, favoring large industries at the expense of other businesses, granting special privileges to a few, and leading to large concentrations of wealth. Mugwumps also tended to view negative government as best, arguing that poverty was due to immorality.[20] Although this description appears to make the Mugwumps more Democratic than Republican, the Mugwumps remained loyal Republicans during their early years, in part because of the party's image as the party of morality and in part because of the Mugwump base in the North. In 1884, however, Mugwumps saw the primary issue in the presidential campaign as moral, not political. Because they saw the platforms of both parties as not essentially different on issues such as the tariff and civil service reform, Mugwumps chose to focus on character, and it was here that the GOP ran into trouble.

The Republican nominee for president in 1884 was James G. Blaine, a Whig-turned-Republican admirer of Henry Clay. Blaine had served as congressman from Maine from 1863 to 1876, rising to Speaker of the House before moving to the Senate. Blaine had had a close relationship with President Garfield, and had served as his secretary of state. After Garfield's assassination, Blaine did not enjoy a similar relationship with Arthur, and he soon left the administration. Blaine's problem was his public reputation. A spoilsman associated with machine politics, Blaine offended Mugwump sensibilities. Worse, he had been implicated in a shady bond deal while serving as Speaker of the House, apparently using his position to promote railroad bonds. Worst of all, Blaine wrote letters implicating himself in these activities, then telling his recipients to destroy his letters—which they invariably failed to do. The most notorious example of this was a letter he sent to a business associate in 1876 while under threat of House investigation for his railroad transactions. In that letter, Blaine asked his associate to send Blaine a letter exonerating him. Wanting his correspondence to remain confidential, he endorsed his missive with the comment "Burn this letter." The letter was held by a Boston clerk named Mulligan, thus becoming known as the "Mulligan letter." Blaine was also accused of expensive living without an adequate explanation for his lifestyle, which only fostered charges of corruption. Thus, whether he was simply indiscreet or truly used inside information to his advantage, Blaine was unacceptable to the Mugwumps.

When Blaine received the GOP nomination, the Mugwumps bolted the party. One of them said, "We have not left the party; it is fairer to say that the party has left us." Added to this recipe for dissension, Blaine was engaged in a long-running feud with party rival Roscoe Conkling, an important force in the very critical state of New York.[21]

Although the Republican situation in 1884 was not as dire as the Democratic split in 1848—Rutherford B. Hayes did not come charging back Van Buren-style to lead a third party revolt—the factional bolt was still very serious in an age of close elections. The Mugwump defection set up a perfect scenario for the Democrats to take advantage of the governing party split.

1892: Cleveland returns after the "Billion Dollar Congress"

Grover Cleveland lost his bid for reelection in 1888, coming out ahead in the popular vote but losing the electoral vote. The victorious Republicans, under Benjamin Harrison, seemed not to understand the context of their victory, however. In this late phase of the third-party system, the Democrats had become much more competitive in national politics, challenging Republicans in Congress and winning the presidency. Although the 1888 presidential election centered on the tariff issue, the close nature of the result eliminated the possibility that the nation had spoken with united force on the issue in favor of the Republican position. Prudence dictated a cautious approach for the party, taking care not to press too far too fast with its agenda. Instead, the GOP laid the foundation for Cleveland's return to power. The 51st Congress became known as the "Billion Dollar Congress" because of the activism of GOP forces. Republican appropriations and subsidies expanded the federal budget, and the party provided generous pensions to veterans. Congress passed the McKinley Act, which raised tariff rates as well as fears of higher prices. The Federal Elections bill, called the "force bill" in the South, called for the supervision of elections by federal troops in an attempt to safeguard the ballot in the South.[22]

At the local level, GOP activism also caused problems for the party. At this time, the religious differences between the two major parties began to come to a head. The pietistic energy of various groups caused problems for the GOP as religiously motivated Republicans sought to redeem their party and nation. Prohibition and sabbatarian legislation became major issues while efforts to restrict parochial schools alienated GOP ethnic support. German and Scandinavian Americans in several Midwest states fought local laws mandating instruction in English in both public and private schools. The result was Republican losses at the local level in 1889–1891 as people began to see the party as going too far, threatening the church, family, and native languages.[23]

Voters reacted against vigorous government at all levels in the 1890 midterm elections. Democrats attacked Republican activism and excessive expenditures and made racist assaults on the Federal Elections bill in the South. The GOP was hammered across the board, portrayed as legislating too much in both economic and moral areas. It was a wide-scale repudiation of activism. While the GOP retained the Senate, Democrats swept the GOP from power in the House, dumping many incumbents and taking control with a 231-88 majority.[24]

Also elected in 1890 were fourteen Populists, who represented a threat to both major parties. To understand that threat, it is necessary to review the changing nature of American society in the second half of the nineteenth century. The Northeast remained the manufacturing center of the nation. Though comprising only one-seventh of the nation's area, the section contained 75 percent of its manufacturing wage earners. These manufacturing concerns were responsible for the dramatic growth in railroads after the Civil War. The railroad boom provided many opportunities for speculation, produced an intensification of competition, and led to the growth in monopolies. At the same time, the nation saw a tremendous growth in its cities, which became marked by heterogeneous populations with varied economic interests. Farm mechanization led to a decline in the agricultural population, and the farmers who remained were more dependent on policies generated from the cities. Thus, farmers experienced a loss of control and a diminished competitive position.[25]

Agrarian discontent centered on the problem of high debt and low prices. Railroads, high mortgage rates, and the harsh climate all led to a view of the integrated economy as a conspiracy of the affluent East. Farmers saw cities as sinful places that corrupted the youth and generated a loss of individualism. They saw rural counties bearing the costs of city government and enjoying few of the benefits. They saw banks favoring urban investment instead of farm credit. The potential arose for a West-South alliance of farmers and workers, perhaps uniting poor whites and blacks. The People's Party was formed in 1890, and in 1892 it went national. Populists wrote a platform that called for free coinage of silver, a graduated income tax, an enlarged banking system, government ownership of communication and transportation, regulation of land monopoly, a free ballot with no federal regulation, liberal veterans' benefits, immigration restrictions, a six-year presidential term, and direct election of senators. In a shrewd attempt to bridge North-South sectionalism, the party nominated former Greenback candidate and brevetted Union general James B. Weaver of Iowa for the presidency, and listed former Confederate major James G. Fields as his running mate.[26]

The People's Party was a threat to both major parties because of its sectional nature. In the South, it threatened to steal Democratic votes and break up that party's lock on the section by combining poor black Republicans with poor white Democrats. In the Midwest, it threatened the GOP, which had used Civil War loyalties for nearly thirty years to keep those states in its column. Given the ability of Southern Democrats to play the race card to keep its white farmers in line, and given the Democrats' inherent electoral advantage by retaining the loyalty of the "Solid South," the Populists were more of a threat to Republican chances.

In addition to these problems, the GOP faced difficult intraparty tensions in 1892. Harrison quickly became unpopular with many of his party leaders. He remained somewhat independent of political machines and thus demonstrated little concern for their welfare, so elements in the party began to explore options for replacing him in 1892. Among the options was Harrison's secretary of state—James G. Blaine. Speculation concerning Blaine did not help matters between the two men, and Blaine made no definitive statement regarding his plans. Things became bad enough that Harrison asked Blaine either to announce his candidacy or resign. Blaine resigned on June 4, three days before the opening of the Republican national convention. Blaine's resignation was seen by many as a move to throw his hat into the presidential ring. Even Blaine's friends and allies regarded it as an open declaration of his candidacy, despite Blaine's protests to the contrary. It was too late, however, for Harrison's party organization was strong enough to lock up the nomination on the first ballot.[27]

The important point to remember in all of this is that the GOP was in general disarray in 1892. After winning the presidency and Congress in 1888 in an apparent validation of its leadership, the party overreached with its activism and suffered a severe backlash in 1890. It now faced a potential third-party threat in the Midwest, and its leading politicians spent more time feuding with each other than rallying the troops for combat. It was the perfect time for Democrats to strike with the candidate who had won the previous two national popular votes.

1912: Wilson watches partisan self-destruction

The election of 1912 must go down as the quintessential partisan disaster. Republicans did not face the problem of dire economic conditions or war. They did not have an unknown running for election. There was no great scandal to discredit the party. Instead, the GOP literally self-destructed. It was the Progressive movement that provided the spark for that immolation.

The seeds of conflict were planted during Theodore Roosevelt's presidency. During his two terms, Roosevelt tended to defer action on the tariff, thus increasing the tension that existed between GOP conservatives and progressive insurgents. Roosevelt also supported railway and antitrust regulation, measures resisted by conservatives as government interference in private decisions. Nevertheless, Roosevelt used his political skill and force of personality to keep Republicans from splitting. He then left a rather delicate intrapartisan mess for his hand-picked successor, William Howard Taft, to deal with. In the area of antitrust action, Taft was actually a more vigorous progressive than Roosevelt, prosecuting ninety cases of antitrust violations in only four years, as compared to Roosevelt's total of fifty-seven. Still, Taft was not seen as a progressive by progressives themselves. In seeking to consolidate and administer Roosevelt's gains, he succeeded only in painting himself as a conservative.[28]

Taft's troubles began almost immediately. He alienated Roosevelt supporters by picking others for his cabinet, and he very early became aligned with party conservatives by working closely with Speaker Joseph Cannon in the House and Nelson Aldrich in the Senate, both party regulars. When insurgent House Republicans moved against Cannon, Taft supported the Speaker. When the tariff issue finally broke into the open in the form of the Payne-Aldrich bill, dividing Senate Republicans, Taft sided with conservatives against the progressives. Taft then became embroiled in a dispute over conservation with his chief forester, Gifford Pinchot, a close associate of Roosevelt. Taft fired Pinchot, who retaliated by painting Taft as unfaithful to Roosevelt and progressives everywhere. Taft compounded his problems by insisting on party loyalty—resisted by progressives—and then working in a failed effort to defeat progressive Republicans in the Midwest primaries in 1910.[29]

By the time Roosevelt returned from his African safari, he had already heard consistently negative reports about Taft. He began meeting with insurgents, and on August 31, 1910, Roosevelt gave a speech in Kansas called "The New Nationalism." In it he praised such progressive reforms as the regulation of industry, workman's compensation, child labor laws, graduated income and inheritance taxes, and primaries. During the midterm elections, Roosevelt campaigned for insurgents while Taft supported conservatives. The result was a catastrophe for the party. The GOP lost fifty-seven seats and control of the House for the first time since 1894, and the Senate came under the control of a coalition of insurgents and Democrats. Many states that were normally Republican, such as Massachusetts, Connecticut, New Jersey, Ohio, Indiana, and others, voted in Democratic governors. The final blow to party unity came in October 1911, when the administration indicted U.S. Steel for creating a monopoly, partly due to its absorption in 1907 of the Tennessee Coal and Iron Company. Roosevelt had approved that merger, making Taft's action look like a betrayal. Meanwhile, Taft and his fellow Old Guard members became energized by Roosevelt's constant criticisms of the courts.[30]

GOP progressives, represented by the new Progressive Republican League, opposed Taft's nomination for another term and began looking for an alternative. They first looked to Robert LaFollette, but Roosevelt changed the political equation in February 1912 when he told reporters "My hat is in the ring." Three days later he formally announced his candidacy for the Republican nomination. A variety of reasons have been posited for Roosevelt's action, from legitimate policy differences to a desire for greatness by recreating a party along reform conservative lines to simple boredom with private life.[31] Whatever the reasons, Roosevelt's action split the GOP, threatening Taft and the Old Guard and promising to remake the party in his image.

Knowing he could not win the nomination through traditional means, Roosevelt chose to build support by proving his popular appeal in the primary system. Roosevelt fought in thirteen primary states, finishing the season with 278 delegates to Taft's 48 and LaFollette's 36. Roosevelt even beat Taft in the president's home state of Ohio. The two candidates were exceptionally vicious toward each other. Roosevelt called Taft a "puzzlewit" and "fathead," while Taft referred to Roosevelt as an "egotist" and "demagogue"—hardly dialogue that would foster party unity in the general election. Taft forces controlled the national convention in Chicago, and despite Roosevelt's popular victories in the primaries, convention authorities awarded most of the disputed seats to Taft. When Roosevelt led his supporters out to form a rump convention, Taft got the nomination on the first ballot. Roosevelt's rump convention led to the formation of the Bull Moose Party, splitting the GOP down the middle and presenting the Democratic Party with a prime opportunity. As with the Van Buren-led Free Soil split in 1848, a former

Republican president led a factional bolt into a full-fledged third-party split. Taft knew he would never win, but he remained in the race as an inactive contestant to defeat Roosevelt.[32]

1916: Wilson runs as an incumbent

One of the important factors that may be in place prior to the beginning of a campaign is presidential incumbency. Scholarly research indicates that incumbents seeking a second presidential term for their party have an advantage. That advantage seems to disappear when incumbents seek to extend their party's reign further. Van Buren sought a fourth consecutive term for his party in 1840, and Taft sought a fifth consecutive term in 1912. Both men lost to opposition party challengers. There was no incumbent running in 1848 or 1884. To anticipate the story, readers will recall that George H. W. Bush sought a fourth consecutive term for his party in 1992 when he lost to Bill Clinton. Harrison lost in 1892 after only one term, of course, but incumbency is an opportunity, not a sure thing.[33] No opposition presidential incumbent defended the office in 1844 and 1852, and Cleveland lost a close race in 1888 that saw a popular vote-electoral vote disjunction. Woodrow Wilson is the first example of an opposition president who successfully defended his seat in a bid for a second term, and certainly one factor that placed the governing party in trouble was Wilson's status as an incumbent. It is always helpful to actually hold the office one is trying to retain four years after a partisan change has taken place.

Aside from Wilson's incumbency status, the reigning Republican Party still had factional issues in 1916. The ruling faction in the GOP made a conscious decision to throw the election in 1912. The party essentially chose not to fight, trusting that things would turn in their favor by 1916 and that Roosevelt would no longer plague them. Through much of Woodrow Wilson's first term, especially through the 1914 midterm elections, the governing party was confident of victory. Then war became an issue. Still needing to heal the rifts of 1912, the party now faced internal divisions over neutrality and preparedness. Eastern Republicans such as Roosevelt, Henry Cabot Lodge, and Elihu Root tended to be interventionist, but the majority of the party opposed such a stand. Taft and progressive Republicans opposed risking war, and traditionally Republican ethnic groups such as German-Americans opposed anyone supporting a pro-allied stance. The party that sought to retake the White House had to balance all of these forces.[34]

Republicans also faced the ghosts of their recent past. Having lost in 1912 because of a progressive split, the GOP saw that it needed to keep those forces in the family this time, so party leaders chose as their candidate Supreme Court Justice Charles Evans Hughes. Hughes had built his reputation investigating the life insurance business. He had been a progressive governor of New York, someone seen as working against political bosses and therefore not a pure party man. He was a moderate on economics and had no clear record on most of the divisive issues of the day. He was now a Supreme Court justice who had been out of politics for several years and someone who never openly sought the nomination. When the Republican and Progressive parties met in Chicago, there was an immediate effort to heal old wounds. A "harmony committee" formed to try to forge agreement on issues and candidates. The platforms of the two parties were very similar, agreeing on preparedness, Americanism, the tariff, regulation, and criticism of Wilson's administration, but most Progressives wanted to nominate Roosevelt again and force the GOP to accept him. Roosevelt urged a delay of the nomination to cooperate with the GOP convention. There, three ballots were sufficient to nominate Hughes. Progressives promptly nominated Roosevelt again, but this time Roosevelt declined. He had wanted the GOP nomination, but he wanted a united front to defeat the Democrats even more, and he saw Hughes as an acceptable candidate. Most of the Progressives disbanded.[35]

With the endorsement of Hughes by Roosevelt, one would think that the party would unite and march forward together in its mission to oust the Democratic usurpers. Such was not the case. The party knew it had to bring Progressives on board, but not all Progressives and Republicans were eager to work together again. The Progressive National Committee endorsed Hughes, but many state and local GOP organizations did not welcome Progressives back with open arms. Much residual tension remained. The problem was most evident in California, where Progressives were still powerful. There, Roosevelt's 1912 running mate, Hiram Johnson, reelected governor in 1914, was running against another GOP candidate for the party's Senate nomination. GOP and Progressive forces were at war with each other during the fall campaign when Hughes arrived to tour the state. To bring insurgents back into the party, Hughes had to deal with Johnson. Johnson himself wanted to support Hughes, but GOP forces stifled any Progressive alliance and ignored Progressive forces in the tour planning. Hughes was ignorant of the situation, saying things that antagonized Progressives and even failing to meet with Johnson when the two men were by chance in the same hotel.

Hughes left the state never having met with Johnson, and the Republican-Progressive split, supposedly healed in Chicago, was a major factor in GOP troubles—troubles that would redound to Wilson's benefit.[36]

1952: Eisenhower campaigns against "Korea, Communism, and Corruption"

After twenty uninterrupted years of Democratic control of the presidency, the GOP could be forgiven if it thought it would never again sit in the seat of executive power. Only the 1861–1885 Republican reign was more dominating, and even there the Democratic accomplishment can be considered greater, for Lincoln's untimely death placed a Democrat in office, and Republicans had to bargain their way into office in 1876. By 1952, however, Democrats were exhibiting severe weaknesses. Inflation plagued President Harry Truman throughout his administration, exacerbated by his disbanding of the Office of Price Administration in 1946, and by the advent of the Korean War in 1950. Added to his economic difficulties were a series of scandals that discredited Truman's leadership. Investigations began in 1949 of Truman appointees who received money for obtaining government contracts for friends, and the Kefauver Committee—led by Democratic senator Estes Kefauver—established links between organized crime and urban Democratic party leaders.[37]

Truman also faced a new cross-cutting issue in communism, a concern that affected both parties but which the GOP could use more effectively against the governing party Democrats. On the domestic side, various espionage cases and a general fear of nuclear war allowed Senator Joseph McCarthy to exploit the issue to attack the administration, becoming a celebrity with his detailed charges of enemy infiltration at the highest levels. On the international side, Truman failed to extend his successful bipartisan foreign policy of containment in Europe to the Asian continent. The defeat of the Nationalists in China in 1949 looked like a setback for the United States, leading to the charge that Truman had "lost China." Then, after General Douglas MacArthur's initial success in the Korean War, Truman changed the objective of the conflict and made the decision to unify the peninsula by invading North Korea, bringing China into the war and resulting in stalemate and all of the problems associated with limited war. Truman's subsequent firing of MacArthur aided the Republican cause by focusing attention on the conduct of the war. The experience joined the foreign policy issues of

Korea and containment to the domestic issue of anticommunism. McCarthy leveled a broader array of attacks, and Republican candidates like Richard Nixon exploited the issue to win office.[38]

Democrats also faced severe internal problems stemming from tensions that had been building in the party since Roosevelt's first victory. Truman's position as president was weak. He was the only Democratic president from 1921 to 1995 to face a Congress controlled by the Republican Party. Despite his dramatic victory in 1948, the close election was no mandate for more reform. Truman ran on protecting New Deal accomplishments, and there was little public enthusiasm for his Fair Deal proposals, evidenced by his low approval ratings. His uncompromising stand on civil rights led to the Dixiecrat split in 1948, and that Southern revolt had not healed by 1952. There remained the threat of another Dixiecrat-style bolt, and Southern states like Texas and Mississippi were severely divided on the question of party loyalty before the national convention. Southern states were further angered when Truman vetoed a measure giving them title to offshore oil in the tidelands oil dispute. Eventually, several Southern governors, headed by Texas governor Allan Shivers, led the so-called Shivercrat revolt against their own party's candidate in 1952, working for the election of Eisenhower.[39]

Finally, Democrats had no incumbent in the race in 1952. Truman planned early on not to run and entered the race for the nomination only because he could find no suitable successor. He exited when he was humbled by Kefauver in the New Hampshire primary. There was still no clear leader in the race by the time of the Democratic national convention. Kefauver personally campaigned and won most of the primaries, but he did not enjoy the support of his party leadership. Truman supported Illinois governor Adlai Stevenson, a one-term governor who at the time of the convention had consistently maintained that his only desire was to seek reelection in his state. Before the nominations began, Stevenson had a change of heart and asked Truman for his support. With Truman's help, Stevenson won the nomination on the third ballot, giving the Democrats a candidate who was a relative unknown on the national stage.[40]

With the lingering potential of another Dixiecrat-style split, a whole host of issues gave the GOP an opportunity to call into question the credibility of the governing party. "Korea, Communism, and Corruption" became the eventual battle cry. All the Republican Party had to do was suppress its own in-house troubles and find a candidate who had what the Framers once called a "continental character."

1956: Eisenhower runs as an incumbent

As with Wilson in 1916, Dwight Eisenhower entered the 1956 election season as an incumbent attempting to extend his party's control of the executive branch for a second term. That fact alone placed the reigning Democratic Party at a disadvantage. Unlike Wilson, however, who went to bed on election night not knowing if he had won, there was never any real doubt about Eisenhower. The governing party remained in trouble in the one sense that really mattered: a popular war hero-president was running as an incumbent during good economic times, facing the same candidate he had trounced just four years before. Eisenhower's moderate leadership had given the majority party identifiers no reason to fear him, and his position only became stronger as the campaign progressed. Stevenson reversed the traditional Democratic focus on defense and foreign policy, coming out in opposition to the draft and in support of an all-volunteer force and a nuclear test ban. Open support of these positions by Soviet leaders embarrassed the Democratic candidate. Foreign policy crises in Europe and the Middle East dominated the end of the campaign and served to solidify Eisenhower's status as a steady and experienced hand in troubled times. The governing party never had a chance.[41]

1968: Nixon watches partisan fratricide in Chicago

Everything about the election of 1968 presents a picture of a governing party in severe crisis. Myriad problems faced the Democrats, and the problems were so intertwined that it is difficult to separate them. Lyndon Johnson wanted to be the greatest president in history, ending poverty and communist aggression, but he found himself repudiated by his party and country, unable to wage war on poverty and communism at the same time. Violence and social unrest prompted by race and a youth counterculture seemed to portend the breakdown of the social order, and television magnified the problem by enabling people to watch it all from their living rooms.[42] There was little warning for this situation. After the Democratic landslide of 1964 and the early successes of Johnson's Great Society, observers could be forgiven if they thought the Democrats had achieved an almost insurmountable advantage in national politics. Instead, everything worked to undermine the credibility of the governing party, to the point that a more visionary Republican could possibly have effected a long-term redefinition of politics. To understand how much the governing party was in trouble, it is necessary to separate the various problems while also remembering that they were not, in fact, separate issues, but interwoven elements seemingly beyond anyone's ability to control.

The war in Vietnam was the first culprit. By 1968, Johnson had raised the number of troops in country to over half a million, relying on a draft to man the military effort. The rise in troop strength coincided with a rise in casualties, from over one thousand in 1965 to twelve thousand in 1968. The war itself was difficult to understand, an unconventional and limited war employing unfamiliar strategies such as counterinsurgency, quite different from the massive maneuvering armies of World War II. There was little public understanding of the war's objectives, even though it was the first televised war in history. Eventually, armed conflict lost popular support. Sixty thousand citizens marched on the Pentagon in November 1967, and the draft sparked the youth movement and the beginning of campus unrest. The youth movement brought to light social developments in the area of music, drugs, sex, dress, and hair, which gave many people the impression that the social order was breaking down. Then, despite the fact that American forces won decisively in the Tet offensive in January 1968, people saw the nation's embassy in Saigon threatened on television and heard reporters speak of the war as unwinnable. Johnson drew dissent from within his own party establishment. People who had served in the Kennedy and Johnson administrations, who had been involved in developing and supporting policy in Vietnam, came out in opposition to the war, tagging a Democratic president with the blame. Many Democratic leaders in Congress opposed their own president, and soon Vietnam was known as "Johnson's war."[43]

Crime was another area of trouble for the Democrats. In August 1965, the Los Angeles ghetto Watts exploded in violence, with rioters killing thirty-four and injuring over one thousand. A thousand buildings were destroyed, and over fifteen thousand National Guardsmen and law enforcement troops were deployed. An annual ritual of summer urban violence followed in such cities as Chicago, Cleveland, San Francisco, Newark, and Detroit, sparked by racial tension, police arrests, and youthful violence, climaxing in 1968 with the assassination of Martin Luther King Jr. A week of violence in over one hundred cities, including Washington, resulted in thirty-nine deaths, twenty thousand arrests, and the calling up of more than fifty thousand troops. Added to this urban violence was the unrest of the student protest movement. Organizations such as the Students for a Democratic Society and the Youth International Party began their lives involved in the civil rights movement but moved on to Vietnam through such mechanisms as teach-ins, street protests, campus violence, and Pentagon demonstrations. With the public burning of cities, flags, and draft cards, it is little wonder that "law and order" became a campaign issue in 1968.[44]

The result of this unrest was great stress in the governing party. The issues of race and crime provoked George Wallace, former Democratic governor of Alabama, to reject his historic ties to his party and run for president as head of the American Independent Party. Wallace had been remarkably successful in his limited challenge to Johnson in 1964, actually winning over one-third of the primary vote in Wisconsin, Indiana, and Maryland. Johnson's Great Society, the Civil Rights Act of 1964, and the Voting Rights Act of 1965 gave Wallace a foundation to run again in 1968, this time making appeals on issues such as law and order, an arrogant federal bureaucracy, and a political system that eliminated real choice. Indeed, it was Wallace who said "there's not a dime's worth of difference in any of 'em, national Democrats or national Republicans." Wallace appealed to a people alienated from and fearful of the federal system as it had evolved, and in doing so he became a national candidate.[45] Wallace threatened both parties, but his threat to the Democratic Party was greater, for his third-party defection was from the reigning party, and his attack was against the system created by that party.

Party fratricide continued when Minnesota senator Eugene McCarthy challenged Johnson for the nomination. Dissatisfied with the conduct of the war, McCarthy chose the New Hampshire primary as his battleground, aided by thousands of young campaign workers dubbed the "children's crusade" and the timely occurrence of the Tet offensive. Johnson forces ran an organized write-in campaign, but he succeeded in beating McCarthy only 49-42 percent. The unexpectedly close race was a moral victory for McCarthy, but the party nightmare was only beginning. Robert Kennedy, who had previously said he would not run, got into the race on March 16. Johnson exited the race on March 31, stating in a surprise announcement on national television that he did not want to involve his office in partisan divisions at such a critical time. On April 27, Vice President Hubert Humphrey entered the race, eschewing the primaries. When in early June Kennedy was assassinated, Kennedy forces shifted their support to George McGovern, not McCarthy, making for even more division.[46]

The final spectacle took place at the Democratic national convention in Chicago, where antiadministration forces (McCarthy), pro-administration forces (Humphrey), and Kennedy holdouts (McGovern) collided. The party witnessed platform divisions on Vietnam, with the majority plank supporting Johnson's policies and the minority plank demanding an end to the bombing, withdrawal, and reconciliation. Along with the possibility that Edward Kennedy might enter the race, there was lingering uncertainty about Johnson's intentions. In the end, Humphrey received the nomination despite not having won any primaries, though only a small percentage of delegates were selected by primaries in 1968. His victory was tainted by violence, for student protesters seeking to provoke violence clashed several times with police. The worst incident took place the evening of Humphrey's nomination, as rioters clashed with the police and National Guard outside the Conrad Hilton Hotel. Television coverage interrupted Humphrey's nomination, giving credence to the mob's chant that "the whole world is watching." The violence did not conclude until the end of the convention.[47]

Massive social unrest had undermined the credibility of Democratic Party policies. A Southern Democratic governor had provoked a third-party split that threatened the party's ability to hold onto the South. The incumbent president had removed himself from the election, throwing open the nomination fight to all comers. The party had faced severe internal dissension in a fight over the nomination, lost one of its more dynamic leaders to an assassin's bullet, and given the prize to a man associated with the very administration that had lost credibility. With tear gas wafting into the very room where Humphrey tallied his nomination votes, it seemed as though the whole New Deal system was falling apart.

1972: Nixon runs as an incumbent

Richard Nixon became the third twentieth-century opposition president in a row to stand for reelection and win. His status as an incumbent seeking to extend his party's control of the presidency for a second term placed him in an advantageous position. Although he remained a divisive figure, his position was strengthened by the persistent disarray within the Democratic Party. The governing party did some soul-searching in 1968, in the process rewriting the nomination rules in such a way that power was pulled away from party leaders and traditional Democratic voting blocs and given to more extreme elements. Practitioners of "New Politics" focused on racial and gender quotas, ousting from the 1972 national convention the Illinois delegation led by Mayor Richard Daley because it failed to meet the appropriate quotas, in favor of one led by civil rights activist Jesse Jackson. Senator George McGovern, architect of the new rules, won the nomination, but he was an antiwar partisan, so much so that many Democrats could not support him. Former Johnson secretary of state Dean Rusk termed McGovern's defense policies "insane," while AFL-CIO head George Meany called him "the candidate of amnesty, acid, and appeasement," a phrase turned around by Republicans to become "acid, amnesty, and abortion." Historian Stephen Ambrose describes the national convention as appearing "anti-religion and pro-drugs, anti-profit and pro-welfare, anti-family and pro-abortion, anti-farmer and pro-migrant worker, anti-Saigon and pro-Hanoi, anti-armed forces and pro-draft dodgers." Some Democrats said, "We did not leave the Democratic Party, it left us." Nixon received tacit or open support from John Connally and George Wallace, and "non-opposition" from Lyndon Johnson and Meany. McGovern's inept handling of his own party organization and campaign provided Nixon with a healthy boost before the fall campaign had even begun.[48]

1992: Clinton reads Bush's lips

As the 1992 election season approached, all early indications were that the GOP would win in a walk. The unexpected collapse of the Soviet bloc led to the fall of the Berlin Wall, the end of communist rule throughout Eastern Europe, the destruction of the Soviet empire, the end of the Cold War, and the rise of democracy. Many interpreted events as a vindication of Reagan's policies, presided over by his heir, George H. W. Bush. The swift victory of American-led forces over Iraq in the Gulf War further vindicated Reagan's military buildup, and reinforced Bush's image as a master player on the world stage. Less than a year before the presidential campaign began, Bush enjoyed an approval rating of 91 percent. Democrats were in disarray, with strong challengers like New York governor Mario Cuomo, Congressman Richard Gephardt, and Senators Al Gore, Jay Rockefeller, Bill Bradley, Lloyd Bentsen, George Mitchell, and Sam Nunn all declaring themselves out of the running. The party was left with six late and relatively unknown participants.[49]

Yet these very foreign policy triumphs posed a problem for Bush. The end of the Cold War removed a key element of the GOP's ideological appeal. For two decades Republicans had painted Democrats as too soft and liberal on national security issues, but the removal of the principal international threat required Bush to construct a coherent post–Cold War vision for foreign policy, and "the new world order" remained ill-defined. Bush might have compensated for this difficulty had the economy remained strong, but his foreign policy victories coincided with economic recession. Unemployment hit 7 percent by June 1991, and the situation was exacerbated by corporate "downsizing." White-collar workers lost their jobs as companies restructured, many of them moving away from permanent jobs, with good wages and benefits, to temporary and part-time jobs. While economic matters in 1992 were not desperate, the recession had a larger impact on the middle class than had earlier downturns, and rising health care costs and worries about unemployment fostered uncertainty, anxiety, and apprehension in the middle class about the future. Bush's energy in foreign policy did not compare well with the public's perception that he was inattentive and indifferent to domestic troubles. He seemed unwilling to acknowledge the problem, giving the impression that he cared more about foreign policy than domestic ills. The locus of concern in the public was the reverse. The end of the Cold War reduced the concern about peace and placed even greater focus on prosperity. In that area, the public had a decidedly negative view of Bush's stewardship.[50]

Bush also faced dissent within his own party. He had based his 1988 campaign on the singularly memorable line "Read my lips: No new taxes." He had pledged to uphold Reagan's vision, calling it a matter of trust. So, when in 1990 he compromised with the Democratic Congress to raise taxes to reduce the deficit, conservatives charged him with betrayal of core principles. A majority of his own party voted against the budget deal, and conservatives blamed their midterm losses on Bush's flip-flop. Then, when Bush signed the 1991 civil rights bill—one he had vetoed a year earlier as a "quota bill"—conservative commentator and former Nixon and Reagan speechwriter Patrick Buchanan charged Bush with heresy and entered the race for the GOP nomination. Buchanan was never a serious threat, but Bush was exceptionally late starting his campaign, seemingly unaware of the dissatisfaction in the nation with his handling of the recession and of the discontent within his own party. Even though Bush never lost a primary, Buchanan focused attention on "King George" and the "Bush Recession." Instead of defending himself, Bush acknowledged his guilt and promised to do better. He stated that if he had it all to do over again, he would choose another course because of "all the flak it's taking." The GOP platform even included a plank criticizing Bush for supporting the 1990 tax increases. Then, Bush essentially repudiated himself when in the fall debates he promised to get rid of his current economic advisers and turn over domestic policy to Secretary of State James Baker, presumably putting someone in charge in whom the people had more faith.[51]

Finally, two days before the New Hampshire primary, Texas billionaire Ross Perot launched a quixotic independent campaign of his own on CNN's *Larry King Live*, pledging to spend his own money if volunteers put his name on the ballots in all fifty states. Perot was a type of folk hero, famous for his attempts to aid American prisoners of war in Vietnam and for rescuing his own employees from Iran. His unconventional campaign made use of alternative media such as talk radio, morning news shows, and lengthy "infomercials," eschewing press conferences and "spin doctors." By mid-June he was first in the polls. Although Perot ran against both major parties, his anti-incumbency message hurt Bush more. He attacked the government for the domestic mess, and since Republicans had occupied the White House for twelve years, such an attack targeted Bush. In fact, Perot largely ignored the Democrats and aimed most of his ammunition at Bush, constantly harping about "politics as usual" and budget deficits, and on the need to roll up sleeves and "get under the hood" to fix things. Even his temporary exit from the campaign was a slap against Bush, for his reference to a "revitalized" Democratic Party implied that it would best achieve Perot's objectives. Bush had hoped to run as a successful world leader, and Perot's third-party threat focused attention on Bush's failures and helped create the political climate that defeated him.[52]

As with earlier examples, Republicans in 1992 faced the triple threat of an unpopular incumbent, internal partisan dissension, and a self-financed third-party threat. Bush's unpopularity due to economic troubles was akin to that faced by Van Buren. The internal tension was similar to that faced by several earlier governing party incumbents challenged from within for the nomination. The third-party threat would prove to be the most serious one since Theodore Roosevelt's Bull Moose effort in 1912.

1996: Clinton runs as an incumbent

Bill Clinton became the fourth twentieth-century opposition president to win reelection—a perfect record for all elected opposition presidents in the century. Perhaps as divisive a character as Nixon, Clinton's first term got off to a rocky start, culminating in the 1994 midterm election that saw the GOP take control of both houses of Congress for the first time in forty years. That Republican victory, however, may have saved Clinton's political future. The 1995 budget battle between Clinton and Republican Speaker of the House Newt Gingrich laid the foundation for Clinton's reelection.

Very early on Clinton was able to portray the GOP as extremist, and that fact worked to the disadvantage of Senator Bob Dole, the eventual Republican candidate. Clinton took every opportunity to associate Dole with the unpopular Gingrich, running television ads that criticized "Dolegingrich" and the "Dole-Gingrich Congress" for trying to cut Medicare. He strove to paint Dole as just another Washington politician, a leader of Congress, while Clinton himself was presidential—the nonpartisan head of the nation. Clinton took full advantage of his incumbency status.[53]

That advantage might not have occurred had the most attractive Republican entered the race, but retired General Colin Powell bowed out early. Dole endured a difficult primary season before locking up the nomination; and by that time he was broke, giving Clinton free run of the airwaves. Ross Perot returned to run as the first candidate of the Reform Party, but Dole's bigger problems lay within the GOP, for key party leaders believed that retaining control of Congress was more important than winning the presidency. A variety of conservative interest groups recognized that fact and made decisions accordingly. Dole's party made a calculated decision to cast him aside. House Republicans rejected Dole's wishes that they challenge Clinton, deciding instead to work with the White House to build a record of accomplishments. In the final insult, Republicans campaigned against united Democratic government by running ads admitting Dole's probable defeat and warning against giving Clinton "a blank check." Governing party division and opposition party incumbency proved a devastating combination for the Republican hopeful.[54]

Conclusions

There are times when political elites simply sense that a certain election is "not a Democratic year" or "not a Republican year." When an opposition party understands that and understands the nature of the problems facing the governing party, it can take advantage of the situation and achieve victory. In a sense, much of what really matters in an opposition party victory occurs before the general election campaign even begins. This is to be expected, as a wealth of research on presidential campaigns indicates that they have at best limited effects on the outcome, with the most important influences on the results being in place prior to the actual campaign. Factors such as partisanship and economic conditions place constraints around what campaigns can achieve.[55] In this case, if the opposition party has done its job, it takes advantage of whatever short-term forces exist that have placed the governing party in trouble prior to the campaign ever beginning. The campaign becomes the opposition party's to lose. The result is a temporary reversal for the governing party. Thus, taking advantage of a governing party in trouble is perhaps the single most important factor in opposition party victory.

Recent research on the divisive primary thesis—which asserts that the party with a more divisive nomination battle tends to lose the general election—argues that general election outcomes are more a factor of how incumbent presidents are evaluated in the first place than they are of a divisive primary process. In other words, the critical issue for incumbent presidents is not whether they draw a primary challenge but whether they demonstrate critical weaknesses and failures that provoke a primary challenge. A unified party is important for victory, but it is preexisting weakness that disrupts that unity.[56] The challenge of one minor partisan against an incumbent prompted by the incumbent's supposed betrayal of party principles, as happened in 1992 with the battle between George Bush and Pat Buchanan, is far more damaging to the governing party than a multicandidate primary contest in an open race, as occurred between George Bush and several other Republicans in 1988.

Something similar can be said about governing parties more broadly throughout the modern party era. Preexisting weaknesses and failures by the governing party create problems with managing the party coalition. Whether the division manifests itself as a personality feud or a full-fledged factional revolt, the danger is the same, and it creates the opportunity for opposition party victory. In most cases, the third-party threat rises at least in part from a governing party split (e.g., Van Buren, Roosevelt, Wallace) or from a movement that represents some element that is dissatisfied with the governing party (e.g., Weaver, Perot). The impetus may be war or the economy; it may be cross-partisan issues such as slavery or civil rights; it may be simply the inability of a party to manage the ambitions of its leaders. In any case, when considered with the previous examples of temporary factional bolts to the opposition party, the evidence indicates that the greatest danger to the governing party is not the opposition party itself but the ability of the governing party to manage its own affairs. Trouble on those grounds is a necessary condition for opposition party victory. Once the opposition party understands its opportunity, it must wrestle with the question of whom to choose as its standard-bearer.

Chapter 3

THE BLANK SLATE CANDIDATE

The historical data in chapter 2 indicate that preexisting trouble in the governing party is a necessary condition for opposition party victory. These short-term forces lay the foundation for governing party defeat. The opposition party has its own part to play, however, and the most important area in which the opposition party has control over its election strategy is in the choice of its presidential candidate. Even given the existence of a governing party in trouble, the opposition party is not well served by launching a full frontal assault against the reigning governing philosophy. Instead, the successful opposition party seeks to downplay the central differences between its ideology and that of the governing party. At first glance, this concern would seem to be a question of issue focus, and chapter 4 addresses that aspect of presidential campaigns in detail. Before the party addresses issue differences, however, it needs to have a standard-bearer. Individual political leaders serve as symbols of political parties and their associated philosophies. They are emblematic of what the parties stand for and can be just as much a flash point for controversy and divisiveness as the issues themselves. So, in its effort to take advantage of a governing party in trouble, while also avoiding a direct attack against the still-resilient fundamental principles of that party, the successful opposition party picks a candidate who helps mask the core differences between the two major parties, giving rise to enough ideological ambiguity on the part of the electorate to allow voters to write their own vision of the candidate in their minds. Rather than convey in digital quality what differentiates the two parties from each other, the "blank slate" candidate has a background and biography sufficiently blurry to allow voters to construct the candidate in their minds as they see fit.

Some of these opposition party candidates eventually run as incumbents, and no incumbent can be a blank slate candidate, having spent four years in the public eye and acquiring something of a record. Presumably the incumbent has had an opportunity to do things that the reigning party can attack, thus placing him on the defensive in an age that does not naturally favor his party. On the other hand, as demonstrated in the previous chapter, an incumbent with a good record must be considered a favorite for reelection, and presidents running for reelection can govern in such a way as to preserve their ideological ambiguity—to continue to encourage voters to write their own vision of the candidates in their minds. This scenario would be another example of the short-term forces that put the governing party at a disadvantage. The reelection experiences of the twentieth-century opposition presidents—Wilson, Eisenhower, Nixon, and Clinton—are a testimony of that dynamic. The question for the moment, though, is in what way these four presidents, as well as the other three elected opposition presidents, may be considered "blank slate candidates" in their first election victories.

Perhaps the easiest way to understand the need for a blank slate candidate is to look at the negative examples of purists nominated by the opposition party. Henry Clay, for example, received a presidential nomination three times and lost each of those times. He attempted to acquire the Whig nomination on three other occasions, but Clay was too much of an ideologue, too closely associated with core Whig beliefs, to be successful running against the governing party, and usually his party understood that. William Jennings Bryan is another good example of a staunch ideologue who acquired the opposition party nomination three times, only to lose all three times. Republican Barry Goldwater is the best modern example of a spectacular electoral catastrophe. He was the very embodiment of contemporary American conservatism, even writing books labeling himself as such and repudiating the reigning governing philosophy. His 1964 campaign suffered one of the worst popular vote defeats in American history. Other examples of purist opposition party candidates include Al Smith, Walter Mondale, and Michael Dukakis. In each case, the opposition candidate failed to diminish the distance between his party and the governing party.

Perhaps the most important aspect of blank slate candidates is that they are not like the above individuals. They are not Clay, symbol of Whig principles, or Robert Taft, who was known as "Mr. Republican." Instead of playing the part of the purist warrior, the blank slate candidate is generally some type of ambiguous centrist. The candidate may be genuinely nonpartisan, and thus not strongly associated with the core issues and battles the opposition party has been fighting with the governing party. The candidate may be a political unknown, with little of political substance for the governing party to attack. He may simply be from the centrist branch of his party, holding to a personal governing philosophy that tends toward the center of the ideological spectrum, again muting some of the possible criticism the governing party can throw at him. The extent of ambiguity retained by blank slate candidates varies, making precision about this variable impossible, but whatever the case, the successful blank slate candidate gives rise to enough ambiguity in the population to allow voters greater freedom to interpret their candidacies as they see fit. Table 3-1 lists, in chronological order, opposition party candidates since Jackson's election whom I classify as blank slate candidates, individuals who meet the above criteria, along with the year in which they ran, the party that nominated them, and a label describing in what way they were blank slate candidates. Winning opposition party candidates are in italics.

By this count, opposition parties have run blank slate candidates in twenty-seven of the forty-five elections since the beginning of the modern party system, winning twelve of those races. The candidates can be classified into fairly clear categories. Early in the modern party system, the military hero was the most popular form of blank slate candidate. Seven of the first eight blank slate candidates were military heroes, picked more for their popularity and name recognition than because they were active leaders of a political party. The popular appeal of the military hero goes back at least as far as Cincinnatus and Julius Caesar, but the "caesarism" inherent in this appeal is understandable for opposition parties. Often the recognized political leaders of the parties are closely associated with controversial issue positions and bitter political battles, and that can work against the election of candidates from the party not favored in a certain political era. They become unelectable. Military leaders, especially if they are career officers, usually generals, are associated with courage and valor, duty and nonpartisan service to their country, and battles and wars that cross partisan lines. Much of Jackson's appeal, in fact, came from his reputation as a military hero. His electoral success established the model for Whigs to emulate (given their lack of success with Clay), thereby establishing the template for future blank slate efforts.[1] Thus, Harrison was marketed as another Jackson; Taylor, Scott, and Fremont were heroes of the Mexican War; McClellan and Hancock were Union generals during the Civil War; and, Eisenhower was a hero of World War II. The three victorious opposition party generals, Harrison, Taylor, and Eisenhower, enjoyed the favor of partisans who preferred electoral

TABLE 3-1:

Blank Slate Candidates by Type, 1828–2004

Year	Candidate	Party	Type
1836	William Henry Harrison	Whig	Military hero
1840	William Henry Harrison	Whig	Military hero
1848	Zachary Taylor	Whig	Unknown/Military hero
1852	Winfield Scott	Whig	Military hero
1856	John C. Fremont	Republican	Military hero
1864	George B. McClellan	Democrat	Military hero
1872	Horace Greeley	Democrat	Cross-partisan
1880	Winfield Scott Hancock	Democrat	Military hero
1884	Grover Cleveland	Democrat	Unknown/Centrist
1888	Grover Cleveland	Democrat	Incumbent
1892	Grover Cleveland	Democrat	Centrist
1904	Alton B. Parker	Democrat	Centrist
1912	Woodrow Wilson	Democrat	Unknown/Centrist
1916	Woodrow Wilson	Democrat	Incumbent
1924	John W. Davis	Democrat	Centrist
1936	Alfred M. Landon	Republican	Centrist
1940	Wendell L. Willkie	Republican	Cross-partisan
1944	Thomas E. Dewey	Republican	Centrist
1948	Thomas E. Dewey	Republican	Centrist
1952	Dwight Eisenhower	Republican	Military hero
1956	Dwight Eisenhower	Republican	Incumbent
1960	Richard M. Nixon	Republican	Centrist
1968	Richard M. Nixon	Republican	Centrist
1972	Richard M. Nixon	Republican	Incumbent
1976	Gerald R. Ford	Republican	Centrist
1992	Bill Clinton	Democrat	Centrist
1996	Bill Clinton	Democrat	Incumbent

Source: Biographical information from Paul F. Boller Jr., *Presidential Campaigns,* and Irving Stone, *They Also Ran.*

victory over the nomination of their recognized party leaders, Henry Clay and Robert Taft. In the case of Taylor and Eisenhower, their military careers were so nonpartisan that forces from both major political parties sought them as candidates.

The governing party is not immune to the lure of the military hero. War veterans were so popular after the Civil War that the governing party Republicans could not seem to get enough of them. Indeed, every Republican presidential candidate from Grant through McKinley, with the exception of Blaine, was a veteran of the Union Army, and Roosevelt laid claim to military hero status with his exploits in the Spanish-American War. Of course, it makes a difference that your party is the party of Lincoln and Union victory. When Democrats chose Union Army generals, they were encroaching upon natural Republican territory. For a variety of reasons the military hero has become less prevalent since the nineteenth century. Republicans flirted with Leonard Wood in 1920 and Douglas MacArthur in 1952 but did not move in their direction, opting for the more politically ambiguous Eisenhower in the latter case. The GOP toyed with this tactic again in 1996 when former chairman of the Joint Chiefs of Staff Colin Powell explored the idea of running for president. Powell's ambiguity on key issues, however, made him anathema to the anchor wing of the GOP, resulting in great ambivalence about his possible candidacy, despite the need to find someone who could defeat Bill Clinton. Contextually, Powell better fit the model of the opposition party candidate described in this chapter. In terms of personal biography, he would have been an ideal Democratic Party candidate in the Reagan era. As the opposition party, Democrats explored this option in 2004 when former NATO commander Wesley Clark sought the nomination. The eventual candidate, Massachusetts senator John Kerry, embraced the model when he chose to focus more on his record in Vietnam than his service in the Senate.

Another type of blank slate candidate is the cross-partisan candidate. This is an opposition party candidate whose political background actually lies with the governing party. It is not intuitively obvious why a party would choose a candidate from among its enemies. There are, however, two examples of this rather extreme form of blank slate candidacy, and neither was successful. Horace Greeley, one of the founders of the Republican Party and the nominee of the renegade Liberal Republican Party in 1872, was also endorsed by the hapless Democrats as their nominee that year, despite his opposition to Democratic principles. Wendell Willkie, a Democrat who supported Roosevelt in 1932, broke with his party because of the Tennessee Valley Authority and was nominated by the hapless Republicans in 1940.

Both cases represent extreme attempts by opposition parties to break the strength of the governing party by nominating their own rivals. A more recent example of a similar attempt was the campaign of former Texas governor John Connally for the Republican nomination in 1980. Connally was, for most of his life, a Democratic Party ally of Lyndon Johnson—hardly a candidate for Republican standard-bearer. After serving in Nixon's cabinet Connally switched parties and made his move for the presidency. One powerful piece of evidence in favor of a "Reagan era" is Connally's failure to secure the GOP nomination. Had the Republican Party seen itself as disadvantaged in the face of a still-robust governing party, Connally would have been a classic blank slate candidate. Instead, the party chose a frontal assault in the person of Ronald Reagan, a conservative purist who masked nothing.

Sometimes an opposition party candidate is a blank slate simply because he is a political unknown. Taylor, who had at best a vague political philosophy, falls into this category. Although personally famous because of his service in the Mexican War, he was on no one's political radar scope in 1844, and no one was very sure of his political beliefs. Cleveland and Wilson fall into this category as well, not because they did not have strong political convictions but because, like Taylor, their rise to power was so rapid. Cleveland would have made no one's list in 1880 of potential Democratic presidential candidates for 1884. Indeed, he was not yet even mayor of Buffalo. In 1908 Wilson was simply a university president, yet within four years he became president of the entire nation. The rapid rise to power of both men meant that they had little national record to speak of, little invested in continuing political battles, and therefore little political baggage to harm them in their coming fights. They were not part of their party's long-standing political machine. The lack of a strong national political history put them in a situation similar to that of the nonpartisan war heroes.[2]

The most popular type of blank slate candidate has been the centrist candidate, the individual who does not hail from the purist wing of his party. These are, in a sense, the polar opposites of purists like Clay, Bryan, and Goldwater. In a political system that rewards appeals to the ideological middle, it is not uncommon to see this strategy employed by both major parties. Even Franklin Roosevelt and Ronald Reagan had their moderate moments. However, where the governing party can afford to run Jackson's heir apparent (Van Buren) and apprentice (Polk), or Franklin Roosevelt's ideological descendants (Truman and Lyndon Johnson), such a move does not seem to be possible for the opposition party.[3] Cleveland, Parker, and Davis were not associated with the core Bryan wing of the Democratic Party;

neither was Wilson until he moved toward progressivism. Alf Landon was a supporter of Theodore Roosevelt and Robert LaFollette, hardly conservative icons, and he was at best (for conservatives) ambivalent about the New Deal. Dewey, Nixon, and Ford are also generally not considered to be part of the conservative anchor faction of the GOP. Instead, as time has passed, they have been viewed as part of the more liberal Eastern Establishment wing of the party, more resistant to the goals of Taft, Goldwater, and eventually Reagan. Labels within parties are important, and the fact that purist Republicans speak derisively of "Rockefeller Republicans" speaks volumes about the locus of centrism in the GOP. Cleveland had the support of the business-gold wing of his party and won the nomination three times. Nixon served for eight years as vice president to the blank slate Eisenhower and also won the nomination three times. He and Ford both faced opposition from the purist wing of their party in the person of Ronald Reagan. Clinton marketed himself in 1992 as a moderate "New Democrat," somewhat akin to Eisenhower's self-proclaimed "New Republicanism," who was more in tune with middle-class values, tough on crime, strong on national defense, fiscally responsible, and, as demonstrated by his handling of Jesse Jackson and rap singer Sister Souljah, independent of one of his party's core constituencies. It was no accident that he had somewhat tense relations with such party liberals as Jackson and Mario Cuomo. Finally, Wilson enjoyed the unique opportunity of watching progressivism, a cross-partisan political movement, go to work in both major parties, further blurring the lines of distinction between himself and his opponents.

Victory further aids the opposition party, for in five cases the opposition party candidates had previously served as president. Four of those cases involved incumbent presidents seeking reelection while Cleveland reclaimed the office from the GOP after a one-term gap. Although in these five cases these men could hardly be called blank slate candidates in the sense of being political unknowns, they were successful in their first terms in maintaining, or reclaiming, their status as ambiguous centrists, and they ran reelection campaigns based on that status. Whatever the precise mechanism, the blurring of distinctions remains the key task of the blank slate candidate.

Of the three major criteria for successful opposition campaigns analyzed in this book, the status of the blank slate candidate seems most susceptible to changes in secular time. In a discussion about candidate selection, changes in the rules and norms of the nomination process make a difference. The nation has moved from a partisan nomination process controlled by party elites at conventions to a plebiscitary nomination process presumably controlled by the mass electorate. The path to power for Bill Clinton was quite different from that pursued by Harrison and Taylor, and even someone as recent as Nixon. It is possible that party elites operating in "smoke filled rooms" are better able to judge what is required for victory in terms of candidate selection than the modern primary electorate. Certainly the plebiscitary nomination system allows political unknowns to capture the big prize even in the governing party, as Jimmy Carter's remarkable 1976 campaign demonstrates. It is also true, however, that as the modern plebiscitary system has evolved and matured, it benefits outsiders and insurgents less than top-tier party candidates.[4] In fact, despite the transition to a plebiscitary nomination system, a concern with electability seems as important as ever. If party elites no longer control the process as obviously as they once did, it seems as though a type of invisible hand is at work steering partisan concerns in the same general direction they have always moved.

Running a blank slate candidate is no guarantee of victory. Table 3-2 lists all the opposition party candidates from 1828 through 2004, including the redefiners, identifying them as blank slate candidates and purists, and specifying whether they won the presidency.[5] It is interesting to note that more often than not, the opposition party has gone the blank slate route when it comes to candidate choice. However, as the table demonstrates, slightly more blank slate candidates have lost elections than won them, a number roughly equivalent to the number of purist candidates who have lost. The governing party needs to be in trouble for a blank slate candidate to succeed. On the other hand, the only purist candidates from the opposition party who have won election are those who succeeded in realigning the shape of the political universe. Absent that unusual and rare context, the odds of victory for the opposition party are decisively greater with the blank slate candidate.[6]

At the same time, compared to the shellackings experienced by purists such as Goldwater and Mondale, blank slate candidates also have a strong record of making election victories narrow for both parties. Table 3-3 lists all of the elections in which the winning candidate received less than 50 percent of the popular vote. The table lists the races chronologically, with the winning candidate and party followed by his percentage of the popular vote, followed by the losing candidate and party. Blank slate candidates are listed in italics.

Seventeen elections since 1828 have resulted in a president who did not enjoy the support of a majority of the voting public. The lowest vote getter was Abraham Lincoln, who came to power as an opposition candidate (but hardly a blank slate candidate) in a four-way race in the midst of a severe

TABLE 3-2:
Opposition Party Election Results by Type

	Blank Slate Candidate	Purist Candidate
Won Presidential Election	Jackson (1828)	Lincoln (1860)
	Harrison (1840)	F. Roosevelt (1932)
	Taylor (1848)	Reagan (1980)
	Cleveland (1884)	
	Cleveland (1892)	
	Wilson (1912)	
	Wilson (1916)	
	Eisenhower (1952)	
	Eisenhower (1956)	
	Nixon (1968)	
	Nixon (1972)	
	Clinton (1992)	
	Clinton (1996)	
	13 of 28 contests—46%	3 of 17 contests—18%
Lost Presidential Election	Harrison (1836)	Clay (1832)
	Scott (1852)	Clay (1844)
	Fremont (1856)	Seymour (1868)
	McClellan (1864)	Tilden (1876)
	Greeley (1872)	Bryan (1896)
	Hancock (1880)	Bryan (1900)
	Cleveland (1888)	Bryan (1908)
	Parker (1904)	Cox (1920)
	Davis (1924)	Smith (1928)
	Landon (1936)	Goldwater (1964)
	Willkie (1940)	Mondale (1984)
	Dewey (1944)	Dukakis (1988)
	Dewey (1948)	Gore (2000)
	Nixon (1960)	Kerry (2004)
	Ford (1976)	
	15 of 28 contests—54%	14 of 17 contests—82%

constitutional crisis and at the beginning of a long-term redefinition of politics. Leaving the extreme case of 1860 out of consideration, thirteen of the remaining sixteen races involved blank slate opposition candidates, the only exceptions being the 1844 race between Polk and Clay and the disputed elections of 1876 between Hayes and Tilden and 2000 between Bush and Gore. All the rest involved military heroes and other ambiguous centrists. Thus, nearly half of the twenty-seven races listed in table 3-1, which saw blank slate candidates run by the opposition party, resulted in minority-vote victories. Such close elections as 1948 and 1960 were nearly opposition party victories, in part because the opposition party chose blank slate candidates as its standard-bearer.[7]

Eight of these sixteen narrow victories were opposition party victories. In fact, only four of the twelve total opposition party victories are absent from this list: 1840, 1952, and 1956 all involved popular military heroes,

TABLE 3-3:
Minority Vote Presidents, 1828–2004

Year	Winning Candidate	Percentage of Popular Vote	Major Party Losing Candidate
1844	Polk (D)	49.5	Clay (W)
1848	*Taylor* (W)	47.3	Cass (D)
1856	Buchanan (D)	45.3	*Fremont* (R)
1860	Lincoln (R)	39.8	Douglas (D)
1876	Hayes (R)	47.9	Tilden (D)
1880	Garfield (R)	48.3	*Hancock* (R)
1884	*Cleveland* (D)	48.5	Blaine (R)
1888	Harrison (R)	47.8	*Cleveland* (D)
1892	*Cleveland* (D)	46.1	Harrison (R)
1912	*Wilson* (D)	41.8	Taft (R)
1916	*Wilson* (D)	49.2	Hughes (R)
1948	Truman (D)	49.5	*Dewey* (R)
1960	Kennedy (D)	49.7	*Nixon* (R)
1968	*Nixon* (R)	43.4	Humphrey (D)
1992	*Clinton* (D)	43.0	Bush (R)
1996	*Clinton* (D)	49.2	Dole (R)
2000	Bush (R)	47.9	Gore (D)

Source: Harold W. Stanley and Richard G. Niemi, *Vital Statistics on American Politics,* 2003–2004, pp. 25–29.

and 1956 and 1972 saw the reelection of incumbents. These four elections stand as the only strong popular vote victories by blank slate opposition party candidates. From another perspective, eight of the twelve opposition party victories—67 percent—were elections in which the winner received less than a majority of the popular vote. By contrast, once the four redefining elections of 1828, 1860, 1932, and 1980 are exempted, only eight of twenty-nine governing party victories—28 percent—were elections in which the winner received less than a majority of the popular vote. The governing party clearly has the advantage in both frequency of election and margin of victory. Blank slate candidates help give opposition parties a fighting chance, and make more likely a close race that will go their way.

Just as all campaigns are not created equal, neither are all blank slate candidates created equal. There is clearly a range of "blankness" present in table 3-1. The original insight of Campbell and his colleagues was that the successful opposition candidate would be some type of popular war hero, and here the truly heroic figures are Harrison, Taylor, and Eisenhower, three winners in eight attempts at running a military hero. They establish a firm anchor of this notion. Their appeal was more personal than ideological, and their public image was not associated with the core differences that divided the parties. Equally firm as an anchor for this model, however, are the truly unknown candidates. The heroic Taylor overlaps with this category, joined by Cleveland and Wilson. Certainly a lack of partisan history also made their appeal more personal than ideological, and they have a perfect three-for-three electoral record. Military heroes and true unknowns may not always be available, however, and the most common resort of the strategically minded opposition party is to seek the centrist. Cleveland and Wilson overlap with this category (as do, to be sure, the war heroes), joined by Nixon and Clinton. Nixon and Clinton are admittedly less clear examples of blank slate candidates, and there is greater room for argument about the interpretation of the centrists. Nixon could even lay claim to the position of party leader. That may be why centrists have the lowest success rate, three out of ten, with two of those successes belonging to the second-chance efforts of Cleveland and Nixon. Nevertheless, when thinking about the continuum of possible choices, these centrists lie closer to the pure blank slates than they do to the pure ideologues who often serve as the leaders of their parties. As much as is possible for people with substantial partisan backgrounds, these individuals cultivate a public image that is not anchored as much in ideological content. To that extent, people can still write their own image of the candidate in their minds.

Having now surveyed the general terrain, it is time to examine in greater detail what made these individuals successful blank slate candidates. Following are brief profiles of each winning candidate, focusing specifically on what allowed voters to sketch their own picture of these individuals.

1840: William Henry Harrison

On the surface, the logical Whig choice for an opponent to Martin Van Buren in 1840 was Kentucky senator Henry Clay. Clay was the acknowledged leader of the party, he had twice before run for the presidency, and he clearly wanted the job. One of the problems with Clay, however, was that he *had* run twice for the presidency—thus he was already a two-time loser, including a shellacking at the hands of Andrew Jackson in 1832. Clay represented the hard-line anchor wing of the party. Despite his reputation as a compromiser, he was the architect of the American System so hated by the Jacksonians. He had participated in the so-called corrupt bargain that made John Quincy Adams president instead of Jackson in 1824, serving as his secretary of state. As a senator, he had led the Senate to censure Jackson for misuse of the presidential office.[8]

Clay also faced trouble within his own party as antislavery sentiment began to build. New York Whig leader Thurlow Weed believed it was essential for the Whigs to carry New York and Pennsylvania in the coming election. Rising abolition feeling worked against Clay's candidacy, however, for he owned slaves and tended to make antiabolition speeches at inopportune times. It was Clay who first said, in reference to a speech that angered abolitionists, "I had rather be right than be president."[9] Clay was seen by some party leaders as an aristocrat who lacked democratic character and talents. These leaders wanted someone who would be able to do what the Democrats had done—appeal to the people. They believed that the best strategy for a Whig victory was to become more like the Jacksonian model.[10] Understanding both the opportunity of the party and the risk of running a purist candidate, Weed said there were two reasons Clay should not run in 1840: "first that Mr. Clay should not be subjected to the mortification of defeat; and second, that the Whig Party should not lose its opportunity."[11] A Whig circular made clear the sentiment of some in the party against their own leader. It stated that Clay could not be elected because

The old Jackson men will oppose him.

The abolitionists generally, will oppose him.

The violent anti-masons will oppose him.

The Irishmen, who have already denounced him for the attack on O'Connell, will oppose him.

The enemies of the United States Bank will oppose him.

The western squatters will oppose him.

The Southern State Rights men will oppose him.

Now, in the name of Heaven, shall we run the risk of this opposition, or even the show of it?[12]

Clay was a party leader too closely identified with too many Whig issues. In spite of the depression, the Whigs were fighting the legacy of three straight Democratic victories. They did not want to waste their opportunity by nominating a man who could motivate any self-respecting Democrat to vote with his party and who would not even be able to retain the loyalty of every faction in his own party. So Whig elites plotted against their own leader at the Whig national convention in December 1839. There, Clay had more delegates than anyone else as well as the support of the South and a plurality on the first ballot. But voting was done by delegation and the unit rule, and that prevented an early victory. Thurlow Weed's New York delegation swung the convention in favor of sixty-seven-year-old William Henry Harrison.[13] Harrison came from an old Virginia family; his father was a signer of the Declaration of Independence. His career as a military man and government official was hardly exemplary. He entered the army as a young man and then served in various government offices in the western territories, including a stint as governor of the Indiana Territory. While serving in that capacity, he fought the Shawnees at Tippecanoe Creek in 1811. The battle was first reported as a defeat, but it became the source of Harrison's future success in presidential politics. Clay helped Harrison get a commission in the War of 1812, during which he rose to the rank of brigadier general and commander of the Army of the Northwest. Financial difficulties prompted Harrison to seek a variety of government jobs, and he spent time in the Ohio legislature, the House of Representatives, the Senate, and as Minister to Colombia. He then retreated into obscurity.[14]

Harrison was hardly a nonentity, but neither was he considered presidential material until the *Pennsylvania Intelligencer* mentioned him in December 1834, and he was nominated by Dauphin County in January 1835. At that time, Harrison was serving as clerk of the court of common pleas in Hamilton

County, Ohio. Absent from politics for seven years, Harrison had not been involved in the controversies of the Jackson years, and his opinions were little known. He was one of three Whig regional candidates in 1836. His campaign focused on his military reputation, and he confined his speeches to reminiscences of a war decades past. He was only purely anti-Jackson on the issue of executive power and its abuse. The Whigs lost their fight in 1836, but Harrison had the best showing of the losers, doing well enough to be reconsidered in 1840. That campaign actually began in 1837 when the Whig convention in Ohio made its preference for Harrison. With Clay unacceptable, Harrison was seen by many as the only man who could unite the Whigs. Thurlow Weed's New York delegation supported General Winfield Scott in order to defeat Clay at the national convention. Meanwhile, William Seward, governor of New York, stated that Harrison should be the "candidate by continuation." When Clay failed to achieve victory on the first ballot, New York shifted its support from Scott to Harrison.[15]

The Whigs had nominated a man who was not the leader of their party. He was billed as a military hero, similar in stature to Andrew Jackson but also a plain man of the people. To most voters, his attitude on public questions was unknown. With his rather inconspicuous public career, he was not associated with any policy that would create controversy. Harrison masked the differences between the two parties by his very obscurity. He was essentially a nonpartisan war hero whose personal beliefs were ambiguous enough to allow the people to write their own vision of him in their minds.

1848: Zachary Taylor

In 1848, the Whigs once again faced the prospect of dealing with their party leader and perennial presidential candidate, Henry Clay. Once again Clay wanted the job and sought the nomination, but he suffered the same weaknesses in 1848 that he had demonstrated in earlier campaigns. This time, however, at age seventy-one and thrice defeated (he had been nominated for a third time in 1844), he was seen as too old. Party leaders saw his election as "uncertain." Even worse, no one seemed to care anymore about such Whig issues as the bank or the tariff.[16] Slavery had become far more important. The Whigs would have to look somewhere else.

As much as William Henry Harrison was a blank slate candidate, Zachary Taylor must be considered the true prototype. Taylor seems to have come to prominence literally from nowhere. One of his biographers pairs him with

Grover Cleveland as the two men who rose most rapidly from obscurity to the White House. No one at the Whig convention in 1844 would have believed that Taylor would be their nominee four years later. Taylor is the true template for the blank slate candidate. He was far more obscure than Harrison, who had at least held public office. Taylor had no experience in civil office whatsoever. In fact, he had never before voted in an election.[17] Taylor was a career soldier. He had been born into an old Virginia aristocratic family in 1784 but was raised on a Kentucky plantation. He and his family owned slaves, and Taylor himself became a shrewd businessman, acquiring a fortune before his death. He joined the military in 1807, serving with distinction in the War of 1812. During his Florida campaign to pacify the Seminoles he had been given the nickname "Old Rough and Ready" by his troops because of his willingness to share their hardships. He became prominent during the Mexican War when he was put in command of the American Army. However, Taylor soon came into conflict with the Polk administration, which rejected Taylor's premature armistice at Monterrey. Polk lost confidence in Taylor as the leader of the war effort and sent Winfield Scott to take over. Taylor thought the administration was playing politics by shifting the war effort to Scott. He believed the administration made a calculated and politically motivated effort to drive him from active duty, even as he became more popular after his victory at Buena Vista.[18]

Aside from his intense dislike for Polk, Taylor's political views were at best unfocused. He called himself a Jeffersonian but never defined what that meant. According to his son-in-law, Democrat Jefferson Davis, Taylor believed in strict construction of the Constitution and state sovereignty, but Davis also thought Taylor might be the *Democratic* nominee for president. Taylor himself believed the Whigs were closer to Jeffersonian ideals than the Democrats, and he looked to Clay as the likely nominee, but he believed the tariff and national bank were dead issues. Taylor also thought the Wilmot Proviso was an irrelevant issue since the North would not allow slavery in former Mexican territory and Mexican law itself prohibited it. In all of this there was a great sense of political ambiguity surrounding Taylor. Some Democrats mentioned him as a possible candidate, seeing him as a political independent akin to George Washington. In his correspondence he made naive comments about issues such as the bank, tariff, and land distribution that made him appear more Democrat than Whig. Citizen groups representing both parties made mention of his availability, and when Taylor himself began to ponder the notion of a candidacy he desired a nonpartisan nomination of the people, not one from the established parties.[19]

While one of Taylor's biographers asserts that the movement for his nomination arose more from voters than from politicians, due to his battlefield fame,[20] other scholars see the movement as carefully directed by national politicians and members of Congress, demonstrating a conscious awareness by Whig Party leaders of what was required to achieve electoral victory.[21] Taylor's views and political affiliation were unknown, and he did not even declare himself to be a Whig until April 1848. A "man above party," he even had "People's" and "Independent" and "No Party" rallies thrown on his behalf. When Thurlow Weed, himself anti-Clay, learned that Taylor was pro-Clay and anti-Jackson, he saw potential for a candidacy.[22] Taylor may have been of uncertain party affiliation, but being anti-Jackson was good enough to be considered a Whig, and being pro-Clay was good enough to draw in Clay supporters and prevent a Clay candidacy. Kentucky senator John J. Crittenden, himself a long-time ally of Clay, had told Taylor as far back as 1846 to make sure he did not return home from the war until "peace shall crown all your dangers." He had concluded that Clay had too many enemies, and that Taylor was the best hope for Whig victory in 1848. Other Whig congressmen, including Abraham Lincoln, preferred Clay but saw him as unelectable. Viewing the Whigs as a minority party, they also supported a Taylor candidacy, especially after Taylor's victory at Buena Vista established him as a hero.[23] Whig leaders believed Taylor would appeal to the South, who saw him as a fellow Southerner and slave owner who would never allow Wilmot to pass. Then, Taylor could be sold to the North as someone who would stand by Whig principles to accept the will of Congress. That is, he would use the veto only on bills involving clearly unconstitutional measures or congressional haste.[24]

Taylor's independence nearly cost him the nomination. At times he appeared too independent of the party. Once Taylor accepted the idea that he could run for president, he insisted that he be nominated by an independent convention, not a party convention. He said he would accept any nomination by citizens "provided it had been made entirely independent of party considerations," and he refused requests to state his Whig principles more explicitly. In essence, Taylor pushed the concept of the blank slate as far as it could go. Whig Party leaders went into an uproar, causing Taylor supporters to generate a letter that Taylor would sign and make public, thus reassuring the party that he was one of them. In the so-called First Allison letter, sent to Taylor's brother-in-law, Taylor finally declared that he was "a Whig, but not an ultra Whig." While still declaring that he would be a president independent of a party, Taylor also laid out his Whig political principles. He stated that he would limit vetoes to "cases of clear violation of the Constitution" or hasty action. He believed the executive should not control the actions of Congress on domestic policy but that the president should carry out the will of the people as expressed through their representatives. Presumably, in a Whig Congress, this would include such issues as the tariff, currency, and internal improvements. This effort by Taylor's allies was complicated when another letter he had written appeared simultaneously in which he stated that he would refuse the nomination by the Whig convention unless he could remain independent and "free of all pledges."[25]

Taylor remained a thorn in the purist Whig side after the convention nominated him, even accepting the nomination of a meeting of Charleston Democrats and Independents. Taylor's slate was so blank that he had to sign a second Allison letter in the middle of the presidential campaign to reiterate that he was a Whig in principle. In an attempt to reconcile his no-party statements with his Whig candidacy, Taylor again said that he would not be a party candidate "in that straightened and sectarian sense," neither would he be a partisan president, but a president of all the people.[26] Holman Hamilton sees Taylor's equivocation on issues as not representing naivete but rather a strategy to broaden his base of popular support to bring back lukewarm Whigs and draw in borderline Democrats, independents, and Southerners.[27] Whether plotted or unintentional, rarely has there been a presidential candidate with so loose a party affiliation. Taylor was the epitome of the nonideological candidate.

1884: Grover Cleveland

The Democratic Party experienced a leadership vacuum in 1884. Samuel Tilden, who had lost the bitter contest of 1876, was the only recognized national figure, but he declined to run. However, he delayed uttering a preference long enough to stall a variety of favorite son candidacies. When he finally made a definitive move, he supported Grover Cleveland. Cleveland stands with Taylor as the prototypical blank slate candidate. Few have risen so fast from obscurity to the presidency. Cleveland came from an undistinguished background, and he readily admitted that his biography was dull. Raised in New York in a minister's family, he stopped in Buffalo to see his uncle on his way west, and there he stayed. Cleveland turned to law, becoming a corporate lawyer who enjoyed partying with his friends. He avoided service in the Civil War by hiring a substitute, and he served as sheriff of Erie County. In 1881 Cleveland was elected mayor of Buffalo, earning a reputation as the "Veto Mayor." He developed his political style during these early years, and his defining characteristic was his ability to be a politician without seeming to be one. He was only vaguely identified with any organized group, and he saw himself as above the level of active, conspicuous political activity. In 1882 Cleveland was elected governor of New York. His focus on good government and anticorruption gave him a reputation for honesty and independence. Tammany Hall hated him, distrusting his governing without reference to his party. Enemies called him "Veto Governor" and "His Obstinacy." He remained reluctant to involve himself in the legislative function of government or to accept government interference as a remedy for problems.[28]

Cleveland's strength as a blank slate candidate rested on two qualities. First, he was a virtual unknown outside the state of New York. He enjoyed a lack of publicity through much of his political career and as such enjoyed a relatively clean record. In only three years he had moved from being elected mayor of Buffalo to receiving the Democratic nomination for president. There was no time to establish a long partisan history for Republicans to assault, and there was little for his own party rivals to attack. Mentioned more often as a potential vice presidential candidate, this genuine dark horse was able to snare the nomination after Tilden's withdrawal and the party's subsequent leadership vacuum. One Democrat even attacked the Cleveland nomination as one of "supposed availability, recordlessness, and mediocrity," evidence of the completeness of his blank slate quality.[29] Second, Cleveland's own principles and political style strengthened his blank slate quality. Cleveland's character and temperament were such that he hated the more partisan aspects of politics, especially patronage and spoils. His quest for good government made him a type of nonpartisan hero, not exactly like a military leader but nonpartisan nevertheless. In his fight against corruption Cleveland positioned himself against Tammany Hall, one of the core factions of the Democratic Party, thus appealing to reformers from both parties. His motto was "A public office is a public trust." When confronted on the issue of spoils, he said, "I do not think partisan zeal should lead to the 'arbitrary dismissal for party or political reasons.'" Mugwumps might not be able to vote for the Democratic Party, but they could certainly vote for a man who just happened to be a Democrat, especially one who seemed aligned with Mugwump good government values.[30]

Cleveland was aligned with the Bourbon wing of the Democratic Party, but he was independent enough to appeal to Mugwump bolters. His lack of political history, rapid rise, and personal principles gave his opponents little to attack and enabled men from both parties to write their own picture of what Cleveland was about. For the Democrats, he was the right man at the right time.

1912: Woodrow Wilson

With the Republican Party in disarray in 1912, all the ambitions of the Democratic Party regulars came to the fore. House Speaker Champ Clark and Majority Leader Oscar Underwood both entered the race for the nomination. Also running was the new governor of New Jersey, Woodrow Wilson. Wilson was born in the South and grew up there during the Civil War and Reconstruction. He went to school at Princeton and Johns Hopkins and decided on an academic career after a stint with the law proved less than satisfying. He went to Princeton again to teach in 1890, becoming president of the school in 1902. During these years, the Democratic Party was the party of William Jennings Bryan. Despite his status as a three-time loser in presidential politics, Bryan remained the party's motivating force, and any new candidate had to deal with him. Wilson had begun his adult life as a Cleveland Democrat who supported legislative government and opposed Bryan, government regulation, labor union practices, and fruitless "experiments of paternalism" in favor of "that most precious of all the possessions of a few people, the right of freedom of contract." Wilson eventually moved away from the idea of congressional government and supported the notion of an active executive who was "the leader both of his party and of the nation," who was "the only national voice in affairs," and who was the only representative "of the whole people." As he gradually absorbed progressivism, less and less separated him from the dominant political figure of his day, Theodore Roosevelt. Both men rejected the status quo, both men opposed radicals, both men sought reform within the system, both men sought greater democratization, and both men had similar views of the role of the president and the government as activist and interventionist.[31]

This history is where Wilson's status as a blank slate candidate in 1912 becomes clear. He was not a blank slate candidate by virtue of having a nonpartisan background, nor was he a blank slate in terms of his scholarly pursuits. In fact, Wilson had strong beliefs about politics, which he articulated in his writings, but these academic works were not as relevant to his partisan identity as they were to broader constitutional issues. Instead, Wilson's history as a conservative Democrat aligned against Bryan, combined with his gradual acceptance of progressivism, lent a certain ambiguity to his beliefs and positions. Conscious or not, ambiguity about personal political beliefs makes it possible for diverse groups to accept an individual as their own. That is precisely what happened to Wilson to launch his political career.

While president of Princeton, Wilson was identified with the conservative eastern wing of the party. Colonel George B. M. Harvey, editor of the *North American Review* and *Harper's Weekly*, pegged Wilson as a potential presidential candidate as early as 1906. In 1910, Harvey and New Jersey Democratic boss James Smith Jr. effected Wilson's election as the state's governor. These men were conservative Democrats who believed Wilson was an organization man whose victory would enable them to avoid a more reformist candidate. The new job would also position Wilson to run for president two years later. Wilson soon made the switch to a progressive program. The first sign of danger for Harvey and his allies was when Wilson told him after the convention that it was "no Democratic victory. It was a victory of the progressives of both parties." During his campaign, Wilson appealed to both independents and insurgent Republicans, and he praised Roosevelt's "New Nationalism." Before even taking office, Wilson turned against his conservative sponsors. Smith wanted the state's open Senate seat. He had lost the nonbinding preferential primary, but he counted on his control of the party machinery, as well as on Wilson's noninterference. Wilson, however, supported the winner of the primary against his party's established favorite. Wilson said his own election had made him "the political spokesman and adviser of the people." The people had preferred Smith's opponent, so it was "clearly the duty of every Democratic legislator, who would keep faith with the law of the State and with the avowed principles of his party, to vote for Mr. Martine." Martine won.[32]

Wilson governed as a progressive, enacting such measures as the direct primary, corrupt practices legislation, utility regulation, and workmen's compensation laws, making New Jersey a model reform state. His supporters set up shop in New York to lay the foundation for a presidential run. They wanted to make Wilson a national figure, so they took advantage of a network of Princeton contacts and had Wilson travel to other states to share his views. Wilson went on an extensive tour of the West and the South in the spring of 1911, during which he brushed off questions about his presidential aspirations and walked a line between the progressives and conservatives in his speeches. He also met with Bryan. When he finally declared himself a contender in 1912, he made the traditional Democratic issue of tariff reform his primary focus.[33]

Wilson's real threat was Speaker Champ Clark, who was a contrast to Wilson in several important ways. Unlike Wilson, Clark was a national officeholder, a long-time organization man, and a Bryan supporter. He was better organized than Wilson at the local level, having most Democratic politicians and state organizations on his side, and he entered the national convention leading Wilson by more than one hundred delegates. It is important to recognize the maneuvering that Wilson engaged in at this time. Wilson could not afford to alienate Bryan and his many followers if he expected to steal the nomination from Clark. On the other hand, because of the internal war in the GOP, 1912 appeared to be the best chance for Democratic progressives to win, but they believed they needed to attract Republican insurgents while also nailing down the Democratic base. In his own preconvention campaign, Wilson walked a very fine line in his attempt to appeal both to traditional Democrats and potential Republican defectors, sounding very much like Roosevelt in his speeches while also saying positive things about Thomas Jefferson, the party's patron saint.[34]

Thus, Wilson was a blank slate candidate on several grounds. First, he was a newcomer to politics. Like Cleveland, Wilson attained national stature as a politician only two years before the presidential election. Others had served longer and at higher levels and were more supported by the party organization as a whole. Second, Wilson's positions as a Democrat were ambiguous. Historically a conservative opposed to Bryan, the anchor of the party, Wilson began adopting reform measures as governor that appealed to Bryan voters. Third, Wilson's positions as a politician in general were also ambiguous. Identified as a Democrat campaigning on such a traditional Democratic issue as tariff reform, Wilson also made a conscious effort to appeal to progressives, blurring the distinction with Roosevelt and pointing to his record of progressive accomplishments while governor. The upshot was that Wilson could not readily be identified with any one faction of his party. He had maneuvered himself into a position such that he could appeal to a wide range of Democratic constituencies as well as to a significant faction of the Republican Party should he win the Democratic nomination.

Clark entered the Baltimore convention with the advantage over Wilson, commanding the loyalty and support of Bryanites and the regular party organization. At that time, however, prospective nominees needed two-thirds of the delegates to claim victory. By the tenth ballot, Clark had the support of a majority of the delegates, but he needed 728 to win, and many other votes were scattered among other candidates, including Underwood, who commanded the South. Tradition had it that once a candidate acquired the support of a majority, the rest would fall in line and make him the nominee. In 1912, Wilson and Underwood stood fast. By the fourteenth ballot, Bryan moved to support Wilson. On the thirtieth, Wilson passed Clark, after promising the governor of Indiana the vice presidential slot if the state supported him. On the forty-third, Wilson claimed a majority. Finally, after four days of voting, Underwood forces switched and Wilson won the nomination on the forty-sixth ballot.[35]

1952: Dwight Eisenhower

The logical choice to oppose the Democrats in 1952 was Robert Taft. "Mr. Republican" was the acknowledged leader of the party in Congress, a life-long conservative, son of a president, Ohio state legislator and senator, and three-term United States senator. He hated deficit spending and economic experimentation, adhered to a traditional individualism, and saw the New Dealers as meddlers. He also distrusted the aggrandizement of federal power that came with Democratic foreign policy. He was well known and had tried twice before to be his party's candidate for the presidency. Known as a staunch conservative, however, he was too closely identified with traditional pre–New Deal Republican issues. The faction of the GOP that had determined the presidential candidate for the previous three elections saw little hope that Taft could win by repudiating the very foundations of the Roosevelt revolution. Like the Whig elites who plotted against Henry Clay in 1840, moderate Republican elites looked for a more suitable alternative. In General Dwight Eisenhower they found what Clinton Rossiter calls "the absolutely perfect candidate of the Republican party."[36] Eisenhower was not a blank slate candidate in the sense of being an unknown on the national stage. In fact, his service during World War II made him one of the most famous men in the world. Eisenhower was from a poor Pennsylvania Dutch farming family in Kansas. He obtained an appointment to West Point in 1911, joining "the class the stars fell on," a reference to the large number of graduates who rose to the rank of brigadier general or higher. Eisenhower did not see combat in World War I, but he served diligently during the long years between the wars, eventually playing a part in preparing the military to fight the new kind of warfare it would face in the 1940s. His move to Europe in 1942 to head the American war effort began his rise to fame. Eisenhower's leadership helped bring an end to the Nazi threat. He then served as head of the American Occupation Zone, Army Chief of Staff, president of Columbia University, and Supreme Commander of NATO.[37]

Eisenhower's military service did not make him a political amateur. Although he did not vote for the first time until 1948, he rose through the ranks by relying on his bureaucratic and political skills. Eisenhower had the good fortune of serving under both Douglas MacArthur and George Marshall. He detested MacArthur's partisanship and political games and was more attracted to Marshall's managerial style. He continued to gain political experience during the war in his dealings with Allied leaders, serving as mediator, manager, and organizer. The attitude he developed during this experience can be summed up in a quote from a 1962 interview he gave in which he explained why he was a better politician than most politicians: "Because I don't get emotionally involved. I can accept a fact for what it is, and I can also accept the fact that when you're hopelessly outgunned and outmanned, you don't go out and pick a fight."[38]

The source of Eisenhower's blank slate status was the consistent bipartisan pleas that he run for office. As early as 1943 Republicans were looking for someone to oppose Roosevelt, and Democrats talked about making him Roosevelt's running mate if the GOP ran MacArthur. Eisenhower began making public his reluctance to enter political life, saying, "I can scarcely imagine anyone in the United States less qualified than I for any type of political work."[39] Both parties again courted him in 1948. Truman said he would support Eisenhower and even volunteered to run as vice president if Eisenhower accepted the Democratic nomination. Other Democratic leaders, including Roosevelt's sons, Harold Ickes, Senator Claude Pepper, and Minneapolis mayor Hubert Humphrey, tried to draft him, prompting him to declare, "No matter under what terms, conditions, or premises a proposal might be couched, I would refuse to accept the nomination." In the meantime, some New Hampshire Republicans entered a slate of delegates pledged to Eisenhower in the primary, prompting Eisenhower to reject his candidacy.[40]

Eisenhower's connection to the administration only amplified the ambiguity of his partisan status. He continued to serve at the highest levels of the military under a Democratic president. He supported Truman's Marshall Plan and was in line with administration policy toward the Soviet Union as the Cold War began. Truman made him Supreme Allied Commander Europe, and Eisenhower worked hard to put the North Atlantic Treaty Organization (NATO) on a firm foundation. Eisenhower's family was Republican, however, and he was more in tune with the GOP on domestic issues. He was a fiscal conservative, and he outlined his disagreements with Democratic policies in letters to wealthy friends, writing privately, "I could never imagine feeling any compelling duty in connection with a Democratic movement of any kind," and making clear both in public talks and private writings his hostility to "the paternalistic state" and "the New Deal-Fair Deal bureaucracy."[41]

Still, the bipartisan pleas continued. Truman tried to persuade Eisenhower to run for the New York senate seat as a Democrat, and as late as November 1951 he guaranteed Eisenhower the Democratic nomination. In the meantime, Thomas Dewey wanted Eisenhower to run for governor of New York as a Republican, in preparation for a White House run in 1952. Wealthy businessmen who had supported Wendell Willkie in 1940 against the GOP establishment joined forces with Dewey, and it was Dewey who began the successful strategy of courting Eisenhower through appeals to duty. Politics remained distasteful to Eisenhower, and he preferred to avoid campaigning altogether and receive the nomination by acclamation. The thought of a political life was distasteful enough that Eisenhower was prepared to renounce formally once and for all any presidential aspirations if Taft, the presumptive GOP heir who was already campaigning for the nomination, would only support NATO. Taft had voted against the NATO treaty, and Eisenhower was concerned about his isolationism. He saw a lack of leadership in the Democratic party, but he was prepared to avoid politics if the GOP leadership proved solidly internationalist. Eisenhower met with Taft to seek such support, but Taft disappointed him, and Eisenhower destroyed his prepared statement.[42]

Eisenhower remained reluctant as GOP elites fought to draw him in. His wealthy friends organized and financed Citizens for Eisenhower (CFE) in the summer of 1951, casting it as a nonpartisan grassroots volunteer organization. Party leaders understood that Eisenhower's popularity was much greater than the party itself, so CFE was an organization separate from the Republican National Committee, allowing the nascent campaign to be run institutionally separate from and independent of the party. GOP leaders such as Dewey and Henry Cabot Lodge, the latter named Eisenhower's campaign manager by Dewey and others, pressed Eisenhower for a commitment. Lodge told him that he was "the only one who can be elected by Republicans to the Presidency. You *must* permit the use of your name in the upcoming primaries." Eisenhower resisted, citing his NATO duties and maintaining a nonpartisan image that did not appear personally ambitious. Lodge's announcement that he would place Eisenhower's name on the New Hampshire primary ballot infuriated the general, but his public statement implied that he would accept a draft by the convention if there were present "a duty that would transcend my present responsibility."[43]

With Taft acquiring delegates, Eisenhower had to make a decision. In January, Truman submitted a budget with a $14 billion deficit. In February, Herbert Hoover, Taft, and sixteen other Republicans issued an isolationist statement to bring home American troops. Then, Eisenhower was shown a two-hour film of a carefully stage-managed pro-Eisenhower rally of fifteen thousand people at Madison Square Garden, causing him to say, "I'm going to run." Eisenhower won 50 percent of the New Hampshire primary vote without ever campaigning there in person. He received 107,000 write-in votes against Harold Stassen in Minnesota without any support from the Eisenhower Committee. With such evidence of his personal popularity, Eisenhower returned from Europe in June.[44] Allied to the Democratic administration's foreign policy, supported by Republican elites through mechanisms separated from the party institution, Eisenhower remained publicly reluctant, using the distinctly nonpartisan quality of duty as justification for his run.

The Republican platform in 1952 was an Old Guard document that repudiated the Yalta accords and containment and accused Democrats of shielding "traitors to the Nation in high places." It endorsed NATO only at Eisenhower's insistence. The convention itself also leaned right, for conservative Republicans led by Taft controlled the convention machinery, and the senator was favored by the regular party apparatus. Hoover, MacArthur, and McCarthy were all scheduled to give major addresses, and Taft had every reason to expect that the nomination would be his.[45] Eisenhower's nomination was no sure bet. The convention was the scene of a massive battle between the party's anchor faction and moderates, with purists controlling the rules of the game. Had the Old Guard maintained control of the nomination process, Taft would have won. Eisenhower entered the Chicago convention over one hundred delegates behind Taft, who was himself less than one hundred delegates shy of the necessary 604 votes. Eisenhower's triumph had begun months earlier, with the shrewd handling of disputed delegates from Southern states such as Texas. There, the GOP was run by the party machine, and Texas GOP chairman Henry Zweifel took great pride in declaring that "I'd rather lose with Bob Taft than win with Eisenhower." To guard against an infusion of pro-Eisenhower Democrats at the party caucuses, the Texas state committee issued a resolution that participants had to sign an oath committing themselves to support the GOP in 1952, and declaring that "I am a Republican." Pro-Eisenhower forces were well-organized, however, and openly sought the support of Democrats such as *Houston Post* publisher Oveta Culp Hobby. The *Post* ran ads arguing that Democrats could participate "in BOTH Democratic and Republican elections—DO NOT BE

INTIMIDATED!" The "one-day Republicans" signed the pledge, and pro-Eisenhower Democrats and independents flooded GOP precinct meetings. At the state level, Taft forces refused to seat Eisenhower delegates, forcing them to hold their own rump convention. Rival state delegations from Texas headed for the national convention, where the Taft-controlled Republican National Committee would adjudicate between them, and presumably hand Taft the nomination. Similar incidents occurred in other states.[46]

The Eisenhower camp reacted masterfully to this threat. Eisenhower acted outraged in public, blasting corrupt politics and "rotten boroughs," and seeking "a clean, decent convention." The campaign claimed the moral high ground, crucial in a year in which the corruption of the governing party was a key issue. Signs appeared saying "Rob With Bob," "Graft With Taft," and "Texas Steal." Lodge turned aside offers by Taft forces to compromise on the issue of contested delegates, seeking what he called a "Fair Play Amendment" to the convention rules. The amendment denied the RNC the right to seat contested delegations on a temporary basis, a development that would have guaranteed Taft's nomination. Instead, Lodge wanted to allow the full convention to vote and choose between the disputed delegations. Then, Eisenhower forces would unite with favorite son delegations to stop Taft.[47]

Eisenhower forces locked down the support of other key players. Lodge and Dewey courted Richard Nixon, hinting that he might become Eisenhower's running mate. Nixon in turn canvassed California Republicans and released to the press the fact that they preferred Eisenhower should Governor Earl Warren, another 1952 hopeful, release his delegates. New Hampshire Governor Sherman Adams got all GOP governors to sign a manifesto for honor, fairness, and integrity at the convention, page two of which—unread by pro-Taft governors—supported the Fair Play Amendment. At the convention, Taft forces closed the deliberations to television, prompting the press to jump on Taft. When Taft won the delegate fights, his efforts appeared to be a steal, further reinforcing Eisenhower's moral stand. Taft lost control of the issue on the convention floor. The Fair Play Amendment won 658-548. The next day, Eisenhower forces were ready to challenge the disputed state delegations recommended by the Credentials Committee. His forces won the battle over Georgia's delegation, prompting Taft to give up Texas. When Eisenhower came up only nine votes short of the nomination on the first ballot, Stassen released his twenty to give Eisenhower the victory.[48] Eisenhower's personal popularity and the political skill of his allies took control of the convention away from GOP regulars. Eisenhower supporters waged a campaign that continued his nonpartisan style, working from outside the established party structure and rules and appealing to citizens who were not normal participants in Republican Party politics. In so doing, they broke the control of the established party leader over the delegates and foisted upon party purists a nonpartisan war hero.

1968: Richard Nixon

Given the magnitude of the problems facing the Democratic Party in 1968, one would think that the GOP would have attempted its own comprehensive redefinition of politics by running a true-blue purist, perhaps Goldwater again or California governor Ronald Reagan. Republicans had not forgotten the devastation of 1964, however, and were not about to rerun it, even if the context was appropriate. Several Republicans were mentioned as potential candidates in the mid-1960s, including Illinois senator Charles Percy, Michigan governor George Romney, New York City mayor John Lindsay, and wealthy New York governor Nelson Rockefeller. All were liberals, and all were to varying degrees not strongly partisan. All could have competed with the Democrats on Democratic terms. The problem they faced was that they would be pursuing the presidency on such terms just as the New Deal system began to break up.[49] At the same time, the party's anchor was too strong to permit an obvious return to what it derisively called "me too-ism." Facing the prospect of victory, yet wary of the ghost of 1964, the party played it safe and looked for someone every faction could live with—former vice president and 1960 presidential candidate Richard Nixon. It is certainly true that Nixon could not be called a blank slate in the sense of being a national unknown. Indeed, he tended to evoke rather powerful emotions from people. Nevertheless, the task of the blank slate candidate is to mask the central differences between the two parties rather than highlight them. He needs to retain enough ambiguity to allow voters to write their own vision of the candidate in their minds. That is precisely what Nixon did.

Nixon's personal history before 1968 made him a classic ambiguous centrist. Nixon was born in Yorba Linda, California, the son of a struggling grocer and a devout Quaker mother. Financial troubles prevented him from attending Harvard, so Nixon went to his hometown school, Whittier College. He graduated second in his class at Duke University Law School and served in the navy during World War II. His early political heroes were Lincoln, Wilson, and Robert LaFollette, the latter two hardly representative of Republican orthodoxy. In fact, Garry Wills refers to Nixon before 1946 as a political "blank slate."[50] Nixon entered politics as a Republican, and in many ways his record was a model of centrism. He supported Truman on foreign policy issues, against the desires of the Taft wing. He was aligned with Eastern liberal Republicans on many issues and supported Eisenhower in 1952, contrary to the Old Guard. Moderate Republicans pushed for Nixon as Eisenhower's running mate, and as vice president Nixon supported civil rights. He chose Eastern Republican Lodge as his running mate in 1960 and conferred with the bête noire of the Old Guard, Nelson Rockefeller, before the 1960 convention to come to agreement about platform language. The issue differences between Nixon and Kennedy in 1960 were not great, and he lost one of the closest races in history. Two years later the GOP right wing opposed Nixon in the primary race for the California governorship. He won, but then lost in the general election and seemingly walked away from politics forever.

If Nixon was such a moderate centrist, why did he evoke such powerful negative emotions from his opponents? As much as Nixon was moderate on most of his policy views, he was decidedly immoderate in his political tactics and stand on communism. In his first campaign in 1946, Nixon focused attention on accusations that incumbent Democrat Jerry Voorhis was a Communist. In 1948, while a member of the House Un-American Activities Committee, Nixon exposed then-State Department official Alger Hiss's involvement with the Communist Party in the 1930s, a case which brought Nixon great publicity. In his 1950 race for the Senate Nixon attacked incumbent Democrat Helen Gahagan Douglas as "pink right down to her underwear." It was Douglas who tagged Nixon with the label "Tricky Dick," but Nixon won the election, and it was his campaign style and choice of communism as a hammer to be wielded against all enemies that made him such a polarizing force for so many, despite his moderate voting record. Garry Wills refers to this style more broadly as "the denigrative method," a type of politics that is predicated on the assumption that people vote against something, not for it, and the smart campaigner will consistently attack his opponent's weak point and keep him on the defensive.[51]

Between 1962 and 1968, Nixon strove to be a good party man, working to reinvent himself. He sought party unity in the Goldwater campaign, getting Eisenhower to see the candidate and criticizing those who did not get behind the ticket. After the election, Nixon claimed the center by admonishing that neither extreme of the party could dominate but that "the center must lead." His work for the 1964 ticket won him the support of Goldwater and other conservatives as early as 1965. Conservatives did not like Nixon's views on domestic policy, but they appreciated his support, agreed with his strong stand on Vietnam, and liked Rockefeller and Romney even less. This early support from the right allowed Nixon to move quickly toward the center. He continued to play the part of exiled party leader by campaigning for numerous GOP candidates in the 1966 midterm elections, including Rockefeller, Romney, and Reagan, and seeking to expand the party base. Nixon recognized that the Democrats were the majority party and that the GOP needed to temper its image. He received much credit for the resurgence of the party that year, and many put him on their short list for 1968.[52]

Nixon's task was to kill off any liberal or conservative threat within the party while retaining his appeal to the center. Having held no office and cast no votes in eight years, he was relatively free of recent political baggage. The last office he had held was that of vice president under the immensely popular Eisenhower. Not only did he get Eisenhower's endorsement before the Miami convention but he also claimed the support of old congressional allies, much of the South, and many conservative notables. To avoid potential problems on issues, Nixon laid the early foundation of an indirect campaign by refusing to get into specifics about such things as Vietnam. Despite his anticommunist reputation, Nixon simply promised to "end the war and win the peace." He would not allow himself to be nailed down on anything more substantial than that vague prescription, saying he did not want to weaken his bargaining position if he became president, nor damage any current negotiations. He sounded like Johnson when he spoke of getting Vietnam to shoulder more of the burden and seeking negotiations, but once Johnson withdrew from the race, Nixon declared a moratorium on comments about Vietnam, allowing him to sit back and see how things developed without committing himself. This was the norm for Nixon's primary season. He consistently resisted efforts to coax him into spelling out the specifics of his position on Vietnam, choosing instead to focus on law and order and to begin his appeal to the "silent center"—the vast majority of Americans in the middle of the political spectrum.[53]

Nixon faced no significant opposition during the primary season. Romney dropped out early, and Rockefeller's hapless moves to rule himself out and then declare himself in won him few allies. Nixon worked to kill a threat from the right by meeting with Southern Republican leaders and promising to slow integration, resist busing, protect the textile industry, and seek a strong national defense. He promised Strom Thurmond a stronger national defense and continued resistance to communism if he kept South Carolina for Nixon and away from Reagan, the preferred candidate of the South. At the convention, Nixon had barely enough votes for the nomination. He walked a diverse line, saying publicly that he supported negotiations with the Communist bloc, but taking a harder line in private with delegates. To battle rumors that he would pick a liberal as his running mate, Nixon met again with Thurmond and Southern forces, promising them that his running mate would be "acceptable to all sections of the party" and that he would consult Thurmond before making his choice. He stressed his opposition to drugs and pornography and his support of military superiority and "strict constructionist" Supreme Court nominees. He supported integration but not through busing, and not at the expense of state and local rights. Matters were in doubt to the day of balloting, but Thurmond served as kingmaker, working hard to keep Southern delegations in line and prevent a bolt to Reagan that would have robbed Nixon of a first ballot victory and potentially thrown open the convention. Nixon won the nomination with 692 votes, only 25 more than was necessary.[54]

Nixon presented different faces to different audiences, much as Taylor forces had done in 1848 when they presented different visions of their candidate to the North and South. Nixon was vague or silent about many issues during the nomination battle and made a conscious decision to appeal to the center by adopting the law and order issue. He did what was necessary to nail down Southern and conservative support, but his historical affiliation with Rockefeller and endorsement by people as diverse as Eisenhower and Goldwater testify to the fact that the party as a whole treasured victory more than ideological purity in 1968. It was not the stuff of which redefinitions are made, but Nixon attempted to provide something for everyone. Considering his controversial background, it was a remarkably successful effort at wiping the slate clean and allowing many voters to write whatever they desired.

1992: Bill Clinton

In 1991 all eyes were on New York governor Mario Cuomo, the very embodiment of traditional Democratic liberalism. When he chose not to enter the race, Bill Clinton's opportunity became clear. Clinton was born William Jefferson Blythe III, a charter member of the baby boom generation. His father died before he was born, and Clinton was raised in Hot Springs, Arkansas, changing his name after his mother remarried an abusive alcoholic named Roger Clinton. His life was political from a very early age. Clinton was involved in student government at Georgetown University, and he worked both in the campaigns and in the office of Senator J. William Fulbright. When he won a Rhodes scholarship, Clinton met many of the people who would be involved in his administration in later years. Even while involved in the antiwar movement, Clinton was concerned that he remain "viable within the system," and he was reluctant to sacrifice that viability by openly resisting the draft. Clinton met his future wife Hillary Rodham while at Yale Law School, and the two quickly became partners in Democratic politics, campaigning for McGovern in 1972. Clinton failed in his 1974 attempt to run for Congress from Arkansas, but he was victorious in his race for attorney general in 1976, and for governor in 1978. Defeated in the Reagan surge of 1980, he retook the office in 1982. He came close to running for president in 1988, but held off until 1992.[55]

Clinton was hardly a blank slate candidate in the sense of being nonpolitical, but he was not well known nationally, and his status as a "New Democrat," a member of the Democratic Leadership Council (DLC), made him an ambiguous centrist. The DLC was founded in 1985 by a minority wing of the party as a counterweight to the Democratic National Committee. Formed by Sam Nunn and Charles Robb, it comprised a faction of moderates, many of them from the South, who wanted to shift the party's orientation back toward the center, toward the white middle class. The DLC sought to appear strong on foreign and defense policy and disciplined in the tax-and-spend arena. It marketed itself as a group that rejected liberal orthodoxy and pursued greater efficiency for federal programs. Clinton, who was chairman of the DLC in 1990, said the organization would create "a new middle ground of thinking on which someone can not only run for President but actually be elected." Cuomo confirmed the DLC's centrist position when he criticized its "implicit position that we have something we have to apologize for and now we have to move to the middle."[56]

Clinton's centrism was magnified by his status as a Southern governor who was not particularly liberal in his policies. He supported the death penalty, even going to Arkansas during the campaign to supervise the execution of a murderer. He supported a middle-class tax cut, paid for by higher taxes on the rich, thus preventing an increase in the deficit. He emphasized the need for personal responsibility and was noticeably more hawkish than mainstream Democrats on foreign policy. Clinton tried to run as an "agent of change" that balanced rights and responsibility and maintained the Democratic commitment to economic and social welfare while emphasizing the obligations of citizens. He marketed himself as an alternative to liberalism and conservatism, a consciously nonpartisan image typical of opposition candidates.[57] Clinton's difficulty in portraying himself as a blank slate candidate lay not in the ambiguity of his positions but in the notoriety of his private life. He was plagued early on by scandals involving sex, drugs, and the Vietnam-era draft. Still, Clinton's campaign consistently portrayed him as a moderate centrist unlike the traditional liberals who had held the Democratic banner. Once he secured the nomination, his consultants conducted focus groups to find out what people liked and disliked about him, attempting to learn how to effectively repackage Clinton in a more attractive form, using the right words and images to appeal to people. They emphasized his humble roots and stressed campaign phrases such as putting people first, opportunity with responsibility, reinventing government, and change. They also sought alternative methods of getting his message out, focusing on talk shows and hip pop-culture venues such as *The Arsenio Hall Show* and MTV. Clinton's sax-and-sunglasses stint on *Arsenio,* and other such endeavors, helped him appeal to the very voters he needed.[58]

The best example of this strategy was Clinton's run-in with Jesse Jackson at the 1992 Rainbow Coalition convention, where a Rap singer named Sister Souljah served as entertainer and participant. Following the Los Angeles riots that year, she had told the press that "if black people kill black people every day, why not have a week and kill white people?" Clinton had been looking for a way to distance himself from Jackson to appeal to white blue-collar voters in the South, so he told Jackson that Souljah's words were filled with "hatred." Comparing her to white supremacists, Clinton said, "If you took the words 'white' and 'black' and reversed them, you might think David Duke was giving that speech." Jackson defended Souljah, saying she deserved an apology, and that Clinton's remarks were designed to "contain" him and "appeal to conservative whites." Jackson was right, but Clinton made no apology. He had declared his independence from Jackson on Jackson's own turf, sending a clear signal that Jackson would enjoy no special treatment. Throughout the campaign Clinton took advantage of the fact that voters did not really know who he was and were uncertain regarding his beliefs. In the Reagan era, Democrats won by stealth—running someone from the South who had no national record and was not obviously liberal. That very ambiguity reinforced Clinton's blank slate status.[59]

Conclusions

Ideological purity is the wrong thing for the opposition party to seek in its campaign for the presidency, for it only calls attention to the core differences between itself and the governing party. The first move an opposition party can make to present a moderate front in the general election campaign is to choose a blank slate candidate over one from the anchor faction of the party, something that happened in every successful opposition party effort. Harrison and Taylor were both supported by Whigs who believed first Henry Clay and then the newer abolitionist wing of the party would lead the party to defeat. Cleveland was associated neither with the Tammany wing of the Democratic Party nor with the rising silver wing, and his good-government image served him well in an era in which such concerns enjoyed cross-partisan appeal. Wilson won the nomination over such party regulars as Champ Clark and Oscar Underwood, and he benefited from the cross-partisan dynamics of Progressivism. Eisenhower was supported strongly by GOP moderates who believed Taft could never win, and Nixon ensured his nomination in 1968 by appealing both to Reagan and Rockefeller supporters. Finally, Clinton's status as a moderate Southern "New Democrat" governor set him apart from previous liberal candidates such as McGovern, Mondale, and Dukakis.

Blank slate candidates who are nonpartisans or centrists are generally not ideologues who seek revolution, nor do the things that describe moderate campaign strategies lend themselves to movement politics. Thus, the same things that prompt opposition parties to seek blank slate candidates also tend to encourage indirect campaigns. All general election campaigns are battles to define the politics of the day in favor of one's desired candidate. On rare occasions, when the governing party has reached a moribund stage and is ripe for the kill, the opposition party can run a campaign repudiating the core beliefs and values of the governing party and establish itself as the new governing party. Jackson, Lincoln, Franklin Roosevelt, and Reagan accomplished this. Generally speaking, however, the opposition party is not well served by attacking the reigning governing philosophy, even if the governing party is in trouble. Assuming the trouble the governing party experiences is truly a short-term matter, as outlined in chapter 2, simple prudence demands that the opposition party avoid battle where the governing party is strongest. Instead of launching a frontal assault on the core principles of the governing party, the successful opposition party more often attempts to take advantage of the short-term difficulties experienced by the governing party, hammering on temporary problems to gain control of the executive branch, though not the long-term agenda. The opposition party does not avoid issues altogether in an indirect strategy—although sometimes this seems to happen—but it does avoid debate about the central questions that divide the two major parties. The blank slate candidate does not seek to repudiate the reigning governing philosophy. Instead, he seeks a more indirect route to power. How the blank slate candidate manages such a task is the subject of the next chapter.

Chapter 4

THE INDIRECT CAMPAIGN

Running in an election year in which the governing party is in trouble, and having selected a presidential candidate who seemingly has appeal beyond the anchor faction of the party, it is time to actually campaign for office. The basic strategy for a successful opposition party campaign is to mask the core differences between the two parties that the party purists would prefer to highlight. As explained in chapter 3, this process begins with the selection of the candidate—the individual who masks those core differences. It continues with other early campaign decisions, such as selection of a running mate and conduct of the national party convention. All of these moves culminate in the general election campaign, where the historical evidence suggests the opposition party has a wide range of specific strategies to choose from, depending on the dynamics of the particular contest. The opposition party may choose to avoid issues altogether in an effort to appeal to image over policy substance; it may focus instead on whatever principal weakness is afflicting the governing party; or it may move toward the governing party, actually reducing the ideological distance by embracing some of its own issues. Whatever the strategy, the common factor is that the opposition party avoids launching a frontal assault on the governing party, pursuing instead a more indirect avenue to victory. The party avoids core issues in favor of the temporary or peripheral and works to pacify and quiet the party purists who would prefer to attack the governing party where it is strongest at a time when its weaknesses lie elsewhere.

While the choice of a blank slate candidate does not necessarily satisfy party purists, the opposition party typically tries to pacify its anchor faction while maintaining its moderate front in the general election campaign. The most common method of pacifying an anchor faction is for the blank slate candidate to choose a running mate acceptable to that wing of the party. There is no surprise in this, for conventional wisdom states that presidential candidates should balance their ticket in some important way, usually geographically or ideologically. True to form, that seems to be the pattern for most successful opposition candidates. The general rule in choosing running mates has been to use that position to pacify party purists. Millard Fillmore was chosen as Taylor's running mate in 1848 because Fillmore was a Northerner who was billed as being antislavery and thus someone who might help retain purists who were dissatisfied with the nomination of Taylor. Indiana Governor Thomas Hendricks was a definite move toward Democratic Party regulars to balance Cleveland's outsider nomination in 1884, and eight years later Adlai Stevenson's soft money tendencies appealed to the party's growing silverite core. Indiana Governor Thomas Marshall, Wilson's running mate in two elections, was a move toward party regulars, as were Eisenhower's choice of Nixon and Nixon's choice of Spiro Agnew. Despite his moderate record, Nixon's reputation as a harsh anticommunist made him appealing to the conservative wing of the GOP in 1952. Then, when it was his turn, Nixon promised Southern conservatives that they would approve of his own choice for a running mate. True to form, it was party liberals who initially opposed Agnew's nomination. Thomas Dewey's choice of Ohio governor John Bricker as running mate in 1944 and Gerald Ford's choice of Kansas senator Robert Dole in 1976 are other examples of opposition party candidates appealing to their party core.

The two counterexamples to picking a running mate who appeals to the opposition party core are the choice of John Tyler in 1840 and Al Gore in 1992. Tyler's case is especially interesting. Because of his background as a Democrat, Tyler was a Whig in name only, a Southern Democrat by background, an antinationalist, and someone whom the Whigs expected to appeal to Southern slaveholders. In that sense, the choice of Tyler can be seen as a further move by the Whig party to mask the differences between Whigs and Democrats and inch even closer to the reigning governing philosophy. There is great evidence for this argument, considering the partisan trauma that resulted when Harrison died and Tyler took over as president.[1] By contrast, Clinton defied all conventional wisdom in 1992 by eschewing geographical, ideological, and generational balance by picking fellow Southern Baptist "New Democrat" baby boomer Gore as his running mate. The choice was in no sense an appeal to the liberal party core. Instead, the choice actually reinforced the moderate nature of the Democratic ticket—much as

Tyler did for Harrison—thus opening the door for disaffected Republicans of moderate cast to turn their backs on their own party. Other examples of this double-moderation strategy include Dewey's choice of California governor Earl Warren as running mate in 1948, Nixon's choice of Henry Cabot Lodge in 1960, and Ford's first choice for vice president, Nelson Rockefeller. While using running mates to pacify anchor factions tends to be the norm for the opposition party, it is not the only option to increase the chances of success.

Opposition parties also use party platforms and conventions to mask their core differences with the governing party. The best example of this was the Whig penchant for ignoring platforms altogether. In both of its victories, in 1840 and 1848, Whigs opted to draft no statement of party principles, focusing instead on the heroism and personal qualities of their military candidates. Again, by not calling attention to core issue differences between the two parties, Whigs diminished the distance between the two groups and were better able to market themselves as moderate alternatives to the governing party. Such a strategy would be unthinkable today, but in many cases the opposition party does the next best thing to not drafting a platform of principles, and that is drafting a platform that looks very much like that of the governing party. Cleveland's Democrats drew up platforms that were not dissimilar to those of the GOP in 1884 and 1892, focusing more attention on such things as good government than purist issues, and suppressing growing differences on the silver issue. In 1912, both Roosevelt and Wilson ran on progressive platforms, and by 1916 Wilson had made the 1912 Progressive Party platform his own. The Republican platform in 1968 supported civil rights and contained a Vietnam plank quite similar to Johnson's policy while the law and order stand of Democrats in 1992 recalled traditional Republican concerns. Both Nixon and Clinton appealed to the "forgotten" population of white, middle-class Americans. The one example in this group of a staunch partisan platform was the 1952 GOP document, and that year the opposition party had the fortune of running one of the most famous and honored men in the world.

Many other factors also work to lay the foundation for an indirect campaign. Sometimes a moderate image is fostered by the opposition party or candidate himself. For example, the forces behind Harrison and Taylor worked hard to stifle intraparty dissent and appeal to all while Eisenhower, despite the harsh tone of the GOP platform, served as a moderating force by drawing the support and participation of many Democrats and independents, thus breaking the control of the established party structure over the nomination and fall campaign. Candidates like Taylor in 1848, Nixon in 1972, and Clinton in 1992 made nonpartisan pleas for support to reach beyond their partisan base. Sometimes the state of affairs in the governing party serves the cause of the opposition. The perception of Republican excesses in the "Billion Dollar Congress" helped Cleveland gain leverage even on the core issue of the tariff in 1892. Democratic antics in 1972 could not help but make Nixon look moderate by comparison, while news media reports of a harsh and intolerant GOP convention in 1992 only helped Clinton's campaign. In the clearest example of party fortune, Wilson was able to sit in the moderate middle in 1912 as conservative and progressive Republicans tore each other apart. In this sense, the governing party problems analyzed in chapter 2 help lay the foundation for the indirect campaign.

Eventually the general election campaign begins, and the strongest example of the indirect campaign is one that is, generally speaking, devoid of issues. The original insight of Campbell and his colleagues was that the basic quality of deviating elections was that the opposition campaigns avoided the central issues of the day. The genuinely issueless campaign anchors this notion into place. Some campaigns focus almost totally on image and personality over substance, diverting attention from programs and issues to presumably less relevant things. At their worst, such campaigns are criticized for their character assassinations, demagoguery, and emotional pandering. The Whig Log Cabin campaign of 1840 is the prototype indirect campaign, focusing less on offering substantive policy alternatives to deal with Van Buren's economic mess than on mass entertainment, liquor, and image building. This was the campaign that created a false image of Harrison, a fairly wealthy aristocrat who was marketed as a poor, honest, humble, plain backwoodsman. This was the campaign that constructed a negative image of the incumbent Van Buren as an uncaring, wealthy aristocrat. This was the campaign of rallies, slogans, and war stories, and where issues threatened to intercede, Harrison effectively straddled them.

The Log Cabin effort is not the only example of a truly issueless campaign. Like "Tippecanoe and Tyler Too," the Whigs of 1848 relied more on the name recognition of "Old Rough and Ready" than any debate about core issues. Democrats in 1884 took advantage of the poor reputation of James G. Blaine to issue a stream of attacks on Republican scandals and corruption before capitalizing on the infamous "Rum, Romanism, and Rebellion" speech in New York. Cleveland's personal rectitude in the midst of the Maria Halpin scandal helped maintain the focus on personality. In 1952, Republicans had the advantage of running someone for whom support could be summarized in the slogan "I Like Ike," while "Nixon's the One" did the same in 1968. Nixon also manufactured crises in an attempt to create issues that favored him as the general election campaign grew tighter in the closing days. These were issues that did not really exist, a particularly odd form of indirect campaigning. Nixon's case is especially interesting because he has been criticized for packaging himself for mass consumption by creating a media image that did not reflect reality. Apparently there is nothing new in running a campaign of style over substance, especially for an opposition candidate. Clinton himself avoided most legitimate foreign policy issues in his 1992 campaign, and effectively sidestepped questions about his personal character. This type of issueless campaign is a logical development of the blank slate features analyzed in chapter 3.

The above account paints a fairly negative picture of the indirect campaign, but genuinely issueless efforts are not the only form such strategies take. There are times when the opposition party seizes the opportunity to campaign on some short-term issue on which the governing party is temporarily weak, perhaps on some foreign policy mishap or scandal. These short-term issues are precisely why the governing party is weak to begin with, as outlined in chapter 2. Such an attack represents not an assault on the core values of the governing party, for it would be foolish to focus on divisions that are not resonant in that particular election year. Instead, the opposition party simply defines the short-term issues in its favor, effecting a temporary redefinition of politics that allows it to claim control of the presidency. In a sense, all successful opposition campaigns do this, for the defining feature of indirect campaigns is that they strive to avoid comment on core values, whether tariffs and the bank in the nineteenth century or the fundamentals of the welfare state during the New Deal era. Republicans in the 1880s were weak on the issue of corruption, so it was only natural for Cleveland to focus on that issue in 1884, just as Eisenhower did in 1952 in response to charges of corruption in the Truman administration.

Eisenhower's campaign in 1952 focused eventually on the most impor- tant short-term issue of the day, the war in Korea. Eisenhower's vow that he would go to Korea, coupled with the credibility he enjoyed on national security, clearly defined the issue of "Truman's war" to his benefit. Eisenhower maintained his credibility on the foreign policy issue to such an extent that foreign policy crises in Hungary and the Middle East during the 1956 general election had no adverse effects on his campaign, and he walked away with the election. In the same vein, Nixon took advantage of the initial disarray of the Democratic Party on Vietnam in 1968. Similarly, with the possible exception of health care reform, Clinton's 1992 campaign did not constitute an appeal to return to the Great Society as much as it did an attack on the perceived inactivity of the Bush administration in dealing with the recession. Nothing Clinton campaigned on in response to this short-term problem called into question his "New Democrat" support of free trade, entitlement reform, and fiscal responsibility.

Sometimes important issues are discussed a great deal in a campaign, but the campaign remains indirect because, whether by chance or design, the issue differences between the two parties are greatly reduced, putting them on relatively common ground. Such a situation cannot help but serve the interests of an opposition party seeking to avoid debate about core matters. The clearest example of a campaign in which the issues disappeared into common ground is the 1912 case in which everyone claimed to be progressive. Issue differences there were important, to be sure, especially on the question of trusts, but there was much more in common between Wilson and Roosevelt, the two principal opponents. Both men sought change under the rubric of bureaucratic reform, and by being a Democratic progressive running against a Republican progressive Wilson reduced the distance between the two parties. Wilson's use of older tactics of indirect campaigns—such as questioning the legitimacy of his main rival by calling Progressives "irregular Republicans"—only furthered his cause. By 1916, the incumbent Wilson made it exceptionally difficult for the progressive Hughes to attack him.

Opposition party candidates do not have to rely on historical chance to enjoy Wilson's fortune. A skillful blank slate candidate can bring the two major parties onto relatively common ground by simply assenting to governing party principles. For example, Cleveland began his campaign in 1892 by attacking the tariff, a core principle for the GOP, but he quickly pulled back and declared that he would be no free trader, thus robbing the Republican party of an important issue. Similarly, and despite the tough stand of his party's platform, Eisenhower never repudiated the New Deal system. Instead, he expressed support for collective security, social security, unemployment insurance, and government action during economic depression. Democrats could not charge him with seeking to overturn Roosevelt's accomplishments. Nixon succeeded in avoiding controversy on Vietnam in 1968 by stating that he would not discuss such topics during the peace talks, and in so doing he reduced the ability of the governing party to attack him on that issue. When he expressed opinions on Vietnam policy, his stand was remarkably similar to that supported by Lyndon Johnson. Finally, after moving away from the center early in his first term, Clinton made a deliberate and carefully calculated shift back toward the right in 1995 and 1996, essentially stealing issues from the GOP through his support of budget balancing, welfare reform, and various middle-class values issues concerning everything from sex and violence on television to religious freedom and homosexual marriage. Stealing issues from the governing party is as effective an indirect strategy as not having any issues to begin with.

Having outlined the several options available to opposition party candidates, it is time to examine in greater detail how the successful examples executed effective indirect campaigns. Following are brief descriptions of each campaign, focusing specifically on what the opposition camp did to mask its core differences with the governing party.

1840: Log Cabin and Hard Cider

The Whig campaign of 1840 must go down in history as the quintessential indirect campaign. The Whig Party made a significant step toward an issueless focus by rejecting Clay as its candidate. Rather than nominating someone who exemplified everything that was different between Whigs and Democrats, Whigs nominated someone who exemplified very little of anything—an available politico who was not identified with the core Whig program. Whigs did not stop there, however. Recognizing that the heterogeneous nature of the party would make exceptionally difficult the creation of a platform on which all could unite, and not desiring to constrain their candidate beyond the specific issue of reversing the Jacksonian system, the Whigs simply chose not to write one, issuing no statement of party principles in 1840.[2] The real source for Harrison's views was his letters. There Harrison stated that he would serve only one term in office. He rejected the notion that the president had control over the public treasury. He promised to make no attempt to influence elections, nor would he use his office for partisan gain. He would also give reasons to the Senate for any removals of personnel. He promised to respect the representatives of the people, use the veto power only against unconstitutional bills, and never allow the executive to become a source of legislation. On the issues of slavery and anti-Masonry, Harrison promised to conciliate both sides in the party.[3] Harrison recognized very early the need for the anti-Democratic forces to be united in the coming election, and he made efforts to stifle and pacify dissent by the purists in the party, masking differences and avoiding extremist talk.

Given the self-inflicted disaster that awaited the Whig party, the choice of John Tyler as Harrison's vice president was the most problematic decision at the Whig convention. Tyler was a States' Rights Whig from Virginia who had been on the 1836 ticket with Hugh Lawson White. He had begun his career as a Jeffersonian Republican and Democrat who supported Jackson, not Clay, in 1828 and 1832. He was an antinationalist Democrat by heritage who had broken with Jackson over the nullification crisis, seeing Jackson's actions as abuse of executive prerogative. Tyler neither expected nor solicited a position on the ticket. Despite being a Clay supporter, he did not favor a national bank, which was the cornerstone of the Whig agenda, nor did he favor large-scale federal programs. His affiliation with the Whigs was tenuous at best, limited to similar theories about the use of executive power. With Harrison at the head of the ticket, Whigs believed they needed a running mate from a slaveholding state. Thurlow Weed attempted to get a Clay man, but all declined. The Tyler choice seems to have been a conscious effort by Whigs to further moderate the ticket. He was chosen as a peace offering to Clay followers, and in recognition of the Southern element in the Whig Party. He was also seen as a compromise gesture from National Republican Whigs to Southern States' Rights Whigs.[4] Presumably, he would help draw the South to Harrison. His background as a Southern States' Rights Democrat might also help Southern Democrats forsake the New Yorker Van Buren and support the Whig cause.

The general election campaign itself became the prototype of the image-over-substance operation, complete with emotional appeals, character attacks, and a variety of other diversions. Nothing like it had ever been seen before. Ironically, it was the Democrats who provided the Whigs with their first symbols. Perhaps because of their own weakness on the economy, Democrats began the campaign by scorning Harrison. The *Baltimore Republican* wrote, "Give him a barrel of hard cider and a pension of two thousand a year, and, our word for it, he will sit the remainder of his days in a log cabin by the side of a 'sea coal' fire and study moral philosophy." Whigs transformed the slur into a slogan of honest pride. The log cabin and coonskin with a barrel of hard cider became the emblem of the Whig campaign, seen as a symbol of the simple virtues of the people who supported him—farmers and backwoodsmen.[5]

The Whig Party itself was well-prepared to execute its campaign. Every state had a central Whig committee that controlled county committees, which in turn organized mass meetings. Whigs organized the electorate, polling voters and making sure they participated. Clay himself had argued that in a situation where parties were nearly balanced, the better-disciplined and better-organized party would win. Whigs published campaign papers like the *Hard Cider Press* and Horace Greeley's *Log Cabin,* the demand for which far exceeded expectations. Whigs organized conventions and massive meetings and rallies that featured spectacles such as the construction of log cabins and cider presses, cabins on steamboats, music and bands, flags, drinking, feasts and celebrations, and stump speakers. Playing up Harrison's war record was the campaign's slogan, "Tippecanoe and Tyler, Too." The party succeeded by copying the tactics employed by earlier Democratic campaigns. Instead of Old Hickory, the Whigs had Old Tip. Instead of Hickory Clubs, they had Tippecanoe Clubs.[6] This was politics as entertainment in an era in which there was not much else to entertain, and as such it was very successful. During this time, Harrison did his best to avoid discussion of domestic issues such as Clay's American System and to maintain his status as a blank slate candidate. His major issue focus, such that it was, remained curbing executive power. Harrison promised to restore the executive to its proper function, which was carrying out the people's will as expressed by Congress. Other than that, he concentrated on telling war stories. Democrats were reduced to bemoaning, "We have taught them to conquer us!"[7]

A measure of Harrison's success can be found in examining the nature of Democratic charges against him. Rather than attack Whig positions, Democrats chose to attack Harrison's Whig-created image, labeling him a Federalist and charging him with cowardice and incompetence in his military career. When Democrats did attack Harrison's issue positions, it was because of his own straddling of issues. For example, they accused Harrison of being an abolitionist. When Harrison refuted this charge in his letters, abolitionists threatened to defect to the Liberty Party. Harrison then equivocated, arguing that the people had an "unrestricted right to discuss any subject that to them may seem worthy of consideration." The people had the right to petition their legislature for redress of grievances and to adopt measures they thought "conducive to the Welfare of the Nation." However, Harrison deplored the exercise of that right in regard to slavery by citizens of other states. He saw this as interference in the concerns of a partner and believed that constant petition about slavery would impair the confidence that existed between the states. Democrats rightly regarded this as straddling the issue. Harrison tried to portray himself as a friend of slavery to the South and antislavery to the North. In fact, Harrison's record over the years showed him standing on both sides of many issues. In 1819 he believed the bank was unconstitutional; by 1838 he thought the bank and credit system was good. In 1828 he favored cheap lands; by 1836 he favored Clay's plan to distribute the revenue from the sale of public lands to the states in proportion to their population. He believed Congress had no power over slavery, but he phrased his language in such a way as to appear antislavery.[8] Even Tyler, a longtime foe of the bank, tried to equivocate on the issues, glossing over them for the sake of the campaign. Virginia Democrat John Winston targeted the odd pairing in a clever turn of phrase: "Tip was Bank, Ty was anti-Bank; Tip was Tariff, Ty was anti-tariff; Tip was Distribution, Ty was anti. In fact, Fellow citizens, Tip is Whig, Ty is Democrat."[9] Both sides seemed to understand that consistency on the issues was not important in this election.

Unlike the Whigs, the Democrats had a platform. Its planks included strict construction of the Constitution, separation of public money from the banking institution, and denouncements of the federal assumption of state debts, the national bank, internal improvements, and the protective tariff. The Whig campaign chose to ignore the Democratic platform and concentrate on building an image of Harrison as someone from poor stock, born in poverty in a log cabin, a man of humble beginnings who understood the world of the farmer and backwoodsman. The truth was that both Harrison and Tyler were born into well-established aristocratic families from Virginia and that only one wing of Harrison's spacious home in North Bend had been originally a log cabin. Nevertheless, the log cabin image became so powerful that even Daniel Webster mentioned it with affection, saying his older brother and sisters had been born in one. Instead of attacking the Democratic platform, therefore, Whigs used the log cabin image to attack Van Buren. They used the false but appealing image of Harrison as an alternative to Van Buren, whom Whigs portrayed as an aristocrat who lived in luxury and extravagance and used gold spoons. They vilified Van Buren as someone who was not the choice of the people but who had been "smuggled into the Presidential chair under the old general's popularity."[10]

The election of 1840 has been roundly criticized by many historians. It has been called "one of the greatest political shell games in American history," involving "unscrupulous demagoguery" and matchless in its emphasis on enthusiasm over thought.[11] To the extent that the Whigs focused on the issue of the "overmighty executive," the campaign of 1840 was not issueless. Opposition to executive tyranny was the most common Whig theme during the years the party existed. In that sense, Harrison ran on a "platform" of executive restraint.[12] However, the question of presidential power was an institutional issue more so than a policy one, and the primary locus of energy in the contest lay in the "Log Cabin and Hard Cider" marketing campaign of the mass public. The Whig campaign avoided domestic and economic issues and played up exaggerated images of its candidate. Perhaps the amazing thing in all of this is that the Whigs chose to conduct such a campaign despite the weakness of the Democrats on the economy. This archetypal indirect issueless campaign was conducted as such in spite of the fact that the Democrats were saddled with a ruinous depression.

1848: "Old Rough and Ready"

As in 1840, the rejection of Clay by the Whigs is evidence of the party's attempt to mask its differences with the reigning governing philosophy. In 1848, however, the party faced a hurdle even bigger than a Clay nomination. With Conscience Whigs arguing the antislavery issue with increasing vehemence, there was the potential for the Whig Party to be closely identified with the cause of abolition. That would signal the party's death in the South. At the Whig convention that June, Taylor was supported by slave states and opposed by the North. His success was hardly assured, but the hard work of his supporters paid off and he got enough votes for a majority on the fourth ballot. Taylor's victory caused a major stir as Conscience Whigs then bolted and helped form the new antislavery Free Soil Party. Massachusetts delegate Charles Allen summed up the feelings of the discontented when he said, "The Whig party is here and this day dissolved. You have put one ounce too much on the strong back of Northern endurance."[13] While the Barnburner bolt hurt the Democratic Party more than the Conscience Whig bolt hurt the Whigs, Taylor's nomination did not inspire great enthusiasm even among some of the major Whig leaders who remained. Clay himself never endorsed Taylor's candidacy, and other Whig leaders such as Daniel Webster and Horace Greeley were at best lukewarm. Formulating a party platform under such conditions would have been impossible, so the party repeated its 1840 decision not to issue one. Instead, the convention simply cheered Taylor's heroism and focused on his military victories. Even in his acceptance letter, Taylor said nothing about his principles.[14] The importance of these developments is that the Whig party as a whole moved against the Conscience Whigs, the group that was fast becoming the purist anchor faction of the party. In provoking them to bolt and not writing a platform of issues, the Whigs in essence moved their party closer to the reigning governing philosophy. They did not call attention to their own principles and instead masked their intraparty squabbles and interparty disputes with the Democrats under the shroud of Taylor's military stature.

The game continued with the battle over the vice presidential nomination. With a strong slaveholding Southerner as the party's standard-bearer, the logical move would have been to acquire a running mate who could soothe the hurt feelings of Northern Whigs. Taylor's managers, however, wanted Abbott Lawrence of New England for the job. Lawrence was not an antislavery man, and his nomination would have made for "cotton at both ends of the ticket." New York delegate John A. Collier sought to calm the adverse reaction of the Northern delegates by aligning himself with the antisouthern faction and identifying himself as a Clay delegate. He proposed fellow New Yorker Millard Fillmore as a peace offering to the disgruntled party men, and Fillmore won the nomination on the second ballot. Fillmore was a secondary figure on the national political stage, a former congressman from western New York who had served as chairman of the House Ways and Means Committee. He had gone to the Whig convention in 1848 with no inkling that he would leave as the party's vice presidential candidate. Fillmore was a rival to Thurlow Weed and William Seward in his home state, and that fact may have played a part in his nomination. Collier had identified Fillmore with Henry Clay, even though Fillmore had never been a Clay man. He had given the impression that Fillmore would appeal to the antislavery forces at the convention, even though Fillmore was not strongly antislavery. The nomination was seen as a compromise in which Taylor would be acceptable to the South and Fillmore to the North.[15] The party thus left the convention with a vice presidential candidate who was neither staunchly antislavery nor obviously proslavery. Given the inevitability of the Conscience Whig bolt, it was a deft way to handle the balancing of the ticket.

The 1848 contest was another example of an image-over-substance campaign. To be sure, Taylor had definite views about issues, which he revealed to his closest advisers. For example, he believed the bank issue was dead, the tariff should be increased only for revenue, internal improvements would continue, and there would be no slave states from the Mexican cession. Oddly enough, however, Taylor did not believe these issues were relevant to his quest.[16] Such an attitude could not help but make his an indirect campaign. Taylor was also still on active duty in the military, so he did not actively campaign for the presidency. Instead, the Whig forces relied on name recognition for motivation. Just as Whigs had chanted for Tippecanoe eight years earlier, so this time they shouted for "Old Rough and Ready." The Whigs conducted a low profile campaign in which they continually admonished their candidate to refrain from replying to any inquiries about his beliefs. The Whig focus remained on Taylor's character. He was honest, faithful, and full of good judgment, just like another general-president, George Washington. With Taylor himself consistently insisting that he did not care about the outcome of the election, there was little chance to engage him on the issues.[17]

The Whig Party would not leave the results of the election dependent upon the closed mouth of its candidate. The party engaged in a shrewd two-faced strategy to generate support for Taylor in the North and the South. In the North, Whigs stressed Taylor's commitment to the Whig doctrine of not vetoing congressional legislation. Thus, all Northerners had to do was elect Whigs to Congress who would vote for the Wilmot Proviso, and Taylor would be compelled by his own principles to sign it. In the South, Whigs stressed Taylor's status as a Southerner and a slaveholder, someone who would better defend the interests of the South than his opponent, Michigander Lewis Cass. In fact, Whig speeches in the South abused Cass and the Democrats, saying they were a danger to slavery and calling into question the trustworthiness of any Northern man. Van Buren was a prime example of this danger, for he was a Northern Democrat who had turned antislavery. Might not Cass do the same? Taylor was a slaveholder and a hero, and he would certainly oppose the Proviso. Whigs formed Rough and Ready Clubs, wrote Rough and Ready songs, and were able to draw many Southern Democrats into their column on election day.[18]

The biggest issue of the day was the extension of slavery, but on this matter neither major candidate took a clear stand. Cass never removed Southern uncertainty and fear that he would sign the Proviso, while Taylor's two-faced strategy was a rather indelicate attempt at fence-straddling. In fact, Taylor believed the Proviso unnecessarily agitated sectionalism, for climate and geography would not permit slavery in the new territories. Such a belief was never made public, however, due to Taylor's own sense of propriety. Taylor's opposition to excessive use of the veto was a consequence of his belief that the president had nothing to do with the making of laws. Such things should be left to the legislature. Consequently, Taylor believed his opinions in the campaign were "neither important nor necessary."[19] To a certain extent, the Whig issue of executive restraint got attention, but no more so than it did in 1840. The dichotomous campaign strategy of appealing to the different sections of the nation with divergent messages worked well, especially with a ticket that featured a popular war hero. The campaign never truly engaged the most divisive issue facing the country on a national level. Some observers questioned the extent to which there was any significant difference between the two major parties, as they were virtually indistinguishable on the basis of principles, and one historian compares Taylor and Cass to Tweedledum and Tweedledee.[20] It was enough to win the election.

1884: "Rum, Romanism, and Rebellion"

The 1884 Democratic convention worked to diminish the differences between the two parties and laid the groundwork for a campaign that focused on character, not core issues. Cleveland's opposition to Tammany and support from Bourbon Democrats fostered a moderate party image. Bourbon Democrats often pursued "good government" reform as the formula for electoral success. Thus, Cleveland's own principles of honest government appealed to both Bourbon Democrats and Mugwump Republicans. Tammany opposed Cleveland at the convention and did not endorse his candidacy until September 12. General Edward Bragg of Wisconsin said of Cleveland's anti-Tammany reputation, "They love Cleveland for his character, but they love him also for the enemies he has made." On other issues as well Democrats sought to minimize their differences with the GOP. The 1884 Democratic platform has been criticized by historians for being essentially the same as the Republican platform, straddling the fence on the currency issue, civil service reform, and even the tariff. Such stands would not have appealed to the more radical fringe of the party. George W. Curtis of *Harper's Weekly* said "the platforms of the two parties are practically the same."[21]

Ideological purity was not the aim of the Democratic Party. Cleveland did not try to pacify party purists represented by Tammany or agrarian Democrats. His adherence to his own principles enabled him and his allies to present a united front against Tammany, necessary if they were to attract dissident Republicans. By downplaying many of the traditional issues that divided Democrats and Republicans, Cleveland made it possible for the party to mask the differences between the two parties. By focusing on good and honest government and making direct appeals at the convention to Mugwumps, Democrats were able to give their traditional enemies a reason to leave their party and vote Democratic.

Any discussion of campaigns in the late 1800s must deal with the sectional dynamic facing the two parties. Ever since the Civil War the Republicans had successfully waved the "bloody shirt" to rally Northerners to the party. It was an emotional appeal to patriotism and the party that had saved the Union. Democrats had their own version of the bloody shirt, and it was stronger and more reliable than the Republican counterpart, reinforced as it was by the widespread denial of secure voting rights to freed slaves. Indeed, the

"Solid South" had its birth in the post war effort by Democrats to provide themselves with an electoral base that would not yield, and the party was remarkably effective. From 1880 to 1892, none of the fifteen Southern and border states gave a single electoral vote to GOP presidential candidates. This strength, based on an equally emotional appeal to patriotism and the party that opposed Northern aggression, aided by massive injustice, gave Democrats a solid base of about 135 electoral votes, needing only fifty more to win.[22] The GOP may have commanded the terms of political debate, but that command was sectional in nature, and the party faced as united an opposition in the South as one could imagine. In terms of sectional politics, neither side of the political battle focused its attention on issues. Instead, the mutual waving of the bloody shirt was an emotional rallying cry against the enemy in a war decades past. The aftereffects of that war, however, allowed the Democrats to profit more from an avoidance of issues.

Given the partisan dynamic in 1884, Democrats could not rest their appeal on issues. The party suffered internal weaknesses and disagreements on the tariff, so it could not focus on protection. It needed the alliance with the Mugwumps, so it could not humor Tammany and be pro-spoils. Localism and the currency question did not resonate that year, either. So, instead of issues, the party focused on character and personality. The natural target for Democratic attacks was the Republican nominee, James G. Blaine. Democrats were able to avoid major questions about issues by uniting on GOP scandals. The most persistent area of attack against Blaine was his reputation as a corrupt man, and here the Mugwumps aided the Democrats with more "Mulligan letters." The weekly comic *Puck* constantly castigated Blaine for "wallowing in spoils." Given the penchant of the politically active to compose amusing verse expressing their sentiments, Blaine inevitably ended up the target of abusive poetry. The most famous of these, although actually appearing after the election, was the following verse:

Blaine, Blaine, James G. Blaine,
The Continental Liar from the State of Maine!
Burn this letter!

Democratic attacks were not restricted to Blaine's political activities. His enemies also charged that his marriage was irregular and that he had fathered a child out of wedlock. Democrats accused Blaine of being anti-Catholic, even though his mother was a Catholic and his sister a nun. He was also portrayed as disease-ridden, a Know-Nothing, and anti-immigrant. Blaine toured the country in an effort to focus attention on the tariff, trade, and nationalism, and he attacked the Democrats for their silence on issues, but they simply responded by attacking Blaine's tour, saying it was unbecoming for a presidential candidate.[23]

Republicans were not innocent bystanders in this spectacle. The GOP used the Pensions Bureau for partisan gain, sending agents on government pay to convince Civil War veterans of Democratic threats to their pensions. The GOP also attacked Cleveland on a variety of points, including his hiring of a substitute during the Civil War, his supposed desire to reduce the tariff to end Civil War pensions, and his reported enjoyment of hanging criminals while serving as sheriff. The most notorious example of character attack was actually directed against Cleveland by unknown perpetrators. Democrats had discussed Cleveland's "woman trouble" at the convention before his nomination, but it was the *Buffalo Telegraph* that broke the story that Cleveland had produced an illegitimate child some years earlier by one Maria Halpin. The danger here was that Cleveland's reputation as a virtuous man would be blemished, but he skillfully defused the issue by responding to party leaders, "Whatever you do, tell the truth."[24]

The issueless politics of 1884 fittingly climaxed with the symbolic implosion of the Republican campaign. Blaine returned to New York City on October 29. Both sides saw New York as being the most important key to victory. Blaine went to a gathering of ministers where the Reverend Samuel D. Burchard extolled party loyalty and excoriated the Democrats as "the party whose antecedents have been rum, Romanism, and rebellion." Such sentiments were not new to the GOP, but the alliteration in the speech was inflammatory, and Blaine, perhaps tired from his tour or perhaps because he had not been paying attention, made no response. The *Associated Press* picked up the story, and a shorthand reporter who was shadowing Blaine reported the incident to Democratic headquarters. The opposition party spent the weekend printing handbills and wall posters advertising the remark and denouncing the implied bigotry. Irish Catholics, once thought to be behind Blaine, were now in danger of being lost. Blaine compounded the problem that evening by making a speech at the "prosperity dinner" at Delmonico's in front of some of the nation's richest men. The dinner was partially an appeal for funds, and the *New York World* was ready with its attack before the event even took place, with half of its front page devoted to a cartoon drawn before the dinner with headlines like "Mammon's Homage" and "Belshazzar Blaine and the Money Kings."[25] In an exceptionally close election, such stories only increased the difficulty of winning the crucial state of New York.

1892: The Quiet Men

Cleveland was the first opposition president to stand for reelection. While he lost that contest in 1888, his third nomination in 1892 was an act of moderation. Cleveland had not campaigned for fellow Democrats in the midterm elections, and in truth he was not that popular in his own party, but he was the only realistic candidate, representing as he did the party's center. Cleveland combined the party's previous themes of administrative honesty and tariff reform with conservatism in matters of business and finance. Only two years after the Republicans had passed the Sherman Silver Purchase Act in an attempt to address agrarian discontent, Cleveland remained anti-agrarian and anti-silver. No Southerner would win the party nomination, there was no Midwesterner of national stature, and Cleveland represented a unifying issue in tariff reform. Cleveland faced a challenge for the nomination from New York governor and senator David B. Hill. Hill was a much stronger party man than Cleveland, focusing his attention on party machinery, organization, and patronage. In this sense he was a much more traditional Democrat than Cleveland. Hill arranged an unusually early state convention—called the "snap convention" and "freezeout convention"—to stack the deck in his favor. He managed to get all of New York's delegates to the national convention pledged to him. He then traveled the country seeking support, touring the South while preaching the gospel of tariff reform, bimetallism, and spoils.[26]

During platform battles at the national convention, Easterners defeated free silver amendments, angering Democrats from the South and West. The party instead called for bimetallism in a coinage plank very similar to the stance of the GOP. Tariff reformers got a stronger tariff plank than Cleveland desired, calling the McKinley tariff "the culminating atrocity of class legislation" and labeling a high tariff as unconstitutional. Yet despite the tariff plank, the Democratic platform was not that different from the Republican. The GOP endorsed "free and unrestricted" elections, a position sure to inflame the South, and extolled Benjamin Harrison's administration of government, but Democrats succeeded in playing down the differences between the two parties on many issues.[27]

Once the party turned to the question of the nomination, Hill had no chance. Cleveland's enemies tried to call attention to his personalism and untrustworthiness as a Democrat, but Independents and Mugwumps again preferred him, seeking "any citizen in this United States who is a Democrat." Hill's ties to Tammany and his reputation as a spoilsman enhanced

Cleveland's reputation with non-New Yorkers, and Hill's efforts in the snap convention and subsequent tour of the South backfired, inspiring an "anti-snapper" movement as people saw through the transparency of his maneuvers. Without a single vote from New York, Cleveland won the nomination on the first ballot. Democrats threw a bone to the silverites by nominating Adlai E. Stevenson as Cleveland's running mate. Stevenson was not from the Bourbon wing of the party. Instead, he was a spoilsman who favored free silver. The fact that Stevenson was labeled a "sop to the silverites" is evidence that his addition to the ticket was an effort to appeal to a different wing of the party. Cleveland made no concessions to Tammany Hall, however. Despite his campaign chief's desire to patch things up with Hill, Cleveland kept his own reformers in line by steadfastly ignoring Hill and refusing to make any promises on the question of patronage. Tammany, having nowhere else to go, eventually fell in line.[28]

Cleveland was the same man in 1892 that he had been in 1884. Rather than choose a party regular who would emphasize patronage and partisan politics in the election, Democrats chose a man who retained his nonpartisan attitudes, even after four years in the White House. Rather than move toward the more radical free silver element of the party, Democrats played it safe with a man who adhered to the principles of sound money and who had the moral authority to challenge Republicans on the tariff without scaring away dissident Republicans. Cleveland and the Democrats were poised to attack the GOP where it was weakest.

There were no great moments of drama in the campaign of 1892. Both candidates were well known, both having served in the White House, and the campaign was relatively free of personal attacks. In fact, it was a relatively quiet contest. Blaine suffered from ill health and family tragedy, so he wrote only one public letter and made only one appearance. Harrison himself went on no speaking tour, refusing to leave the side of his ailing wife, who died on October 24. Cleveland engaged in some activity, writing letters about tariff reform and sound money and doing some fund-raising, but he made just one public appearance, at Madison Square Garden.[29] Harrison's only major contribution to the GOP campaign was his letter of acceptance, published September 5. The letter was a summary of the GOP platform, nearly half of it devoted to the tariff and reciprocity. Harrison called the Democratic stand on trade un-American, arguing that the traditional GOP position was patriotic and the key to prosperity. Harrison also called for international bimetallism on the currency question and made a pledge for free elections that involved neither force nor fraud. During the campaign itself, the GOP tried to downplay the Force Bill issue in order to keep attention on the tariff. GOP leaders also stressed the presumed dangers of letting Democrats control the government.[30] Otherwise, the campaign was lackluster and without inspiration.

Cleveland benefited from the backlash to the violent Homestead strike at the Monongahela River in Pittsburgh, which took place in July. The outbreak cost the GOP support, for union leaders blamed the strike on the protective tariff. Thus, while Cleveland's own letter of acceptance was only one-third the length of Harrison's, half of it dealt with the tariff. Cleveland defined the tariff as a moral issue, calling it class legislation that benefited a small group at the expense of the nation. He argued that it violated property rights when it was used for things other than maintaining the government. It was unjust and unfair, it invited corruption, and Cleveland blasted those "made selfish and sordid by unjust government favoritism." Cleveland pulled back from a radical denunciation of the tariff, however, adding that the nation need not fear free trade under his administration, for he was not an advocate of an "exterminating war against any American interests."[31] Cleveland felt free to interpret the Democratic plank as he saw fit, and while he criticized the tariff as a discriminatory tax paid by all for the benefit of the wealthy, he retreated from the more radical convention position. Thus he was able to temper any fear of Democratic irresponsibility by narrowing the gap between the two parties on the one issue the GOP decided to make its rallying cry.

In the meantime, Democratic leaders kept the South in line by focusing on the threat of federal supervision at the polls. This tactic helped eliminate the Populist threat in the region. The GOP had encouraged the Populists below the Mason-Dixon line. The new party had great appeal on currency, land, and transportation issues, and it had the potential to draw black voters to its cause. To prevent a defection of white farmers from the Democratic Party, leaders such as Adlai Stevenson recalled the evils of Reconstruction and emphasized the threat of black domination. Mobs shouted down Populist speeches and pelted the party's representatives with eggs, tomatoes, and rocks. "A vote for Weaver is a vote for Harrison" became the war cry. Southern Democrats controlled the ballot count in the cities and towns, and refused to lose the South.[32]

In the end, the personal habits of both candidates contributed to the quiet nature of the campaign, especially Harrison's White House vigil as his wife lay dying. The Democratic cause was served by the fact that Cleveland had credibility on the tariff issue and was able to draw back from the more radical statements of the Democratic convention. Still, it is difficult to arouse voters' passions when neither candidate chooses to do battle, and in the one section where Democrats may have lost key support, the party continued to wave its own version of the bloody shirt to retain Southern loyalties.

1912: Tweedledum or Tweedledee?

To understand the moderate nature of the Democratic Party in 1912, it must be compared to its principal opponent. Normally that would have been the GOP, but Roosevelt's bolt transformed the nature of electoral politics. After their rump convention, Roosevelt supporters agreed to meet again in Chicago in August. This was a full month after the Democratic convention, so although Democrats knew that the GOP had split, they did not yet know the nature of the new Progressive Party. The Progressive Party convention was a veritable religious camp meeting, a crusade of the righteous against an unholy system. Delegates sang "The Battle Hymn of the Republic" and "Onward Christian Soldiers." Roosevelt gave a speech called a "Confession of Faith," employing religious imagery and repeating the line he had used at the earlier rump convention, "We stand at Armageddon, and we battle for the Lord." The party's platform was called a "Covenant with the People" and included such items as support for women's suffrage, the use of the popular vote to overrule the court, a minimum wage for women, prohibition of child labor, health and safety standards for workers, a graduated income and inheritance tax, direct primaries, direct election of senators, the short ballot, the initiative, the referendum, the recall, an eight-hour workday and six-day workweek, commissions for business and tariff, and more.[33]

After Roosevelt's convention, progressive Democrats were positioned ideologically in the middle of the campaign. They were not as conservative as Taft's Republicans and not as radical as Roosevelt's Bull Moose Party. Because of the similarities in the two progressive platforms, Wilson could appeal to his party core as well as to unaligned progressives. On the other hand, Wilson could also appeal to those who were afraid of the Progressive Party agenda by claiming he was more in line with the American mainstream. Indeed, Socialist Party candidate Eugene Debs pointed out the similarity of many Progressive planks to his Socialist platform, saying that the "really progressive planks in the Progressive platform were taken boldly from the Socialist platform."[34] Such a statement would hardly reassure moderates and conservatives.

The campaign of 1912 was full of issues, but the battle took place in a context of partisan ambiguity. A reform movement with adherents in a large segment of the population crested at a time when all four major candidates—Wilson, Roosevelt, Taft, and Debs—could lay some legitimate claim to the progressive label. Instead of an "image over substance" campaign, what occurred was a campaign in which many of the issue distinctions that normally become associated with political parties diminished or disappeared. When issue distinctions become hidden, it does not matter if the issues have passionate adherents—the campaign will take on a more indirect quality. Wilson and Roosevelt became the primary contenders for the presidency, but their similarity on the issues forced them to focus on differences that many observers considered inconsequential.

Wilson began the campaign as a Jeffersonian progressive, believing federal power should be used only to eliminate special privileges and promote competition. Then, on August 28, Wilson met with progressive lawyer Louis Brandeis. Brandeis helped Wilson clarify his thoughts, to make the campaign shift from a focus on tariffs to trusts, and to make the case against big business. Wilson linked the two issues, claiming that high tariffs caused high prices and great profits for big business, hurting consumers, suppressing labor, and eliminating competition. Wilson sought regulated competition and economic freedom for small business. He wanted to set business free from the chains of monopoly and special privilege. Big business had become corrupt, and it in turn corrupted government to gain privilege and protection. Wilson proposed to restore competition by breaking up the trusts, using a federal commission to enforce antitrust laws and maintain competition.[35]

By contrast, Roosevelt took his inspiration from journalist Herbert Croly, who had written *Promise of American Life* in 1909, a treatise comparing Hamiltonianism with Jeffersonianism. The book armed the Hamiltonian Roosevelt with the intellectual ammunition to seek progressive goals through strong government. Like Wilson, Roosevelt supported a national commission to regulate trusts. Where the two men differed was on the details. Roosevelt did not see large combinations as inherently bad. He thought Wilson's notion that all trusts should be broken up, whether they were "good" or "bad," was unrealistic. The modern world was more sophisticated, and size was often needed to compete with other nations. Thus, economic consolidation could be good. Roosevelt wanted to regulate trusts that acted irresponsibly. He wanted his commission to regulate corporate conduct in order to aid workers and consumers. Accepting corporate power as a fact, Roosevelt would use an expanded, permanent, active bureaucracy to supervise it.[36]

Wilson saw Roosevelt's plan as paternalistic social welfare. He claimed that the "central purpose" of the Progressive Party plan for trusts was "a consummation of the partnership between monopoly and government, because when once the government regulates the monopoly, then monopoly will see to it that it regulates the government." Wilson said the choice between the two parties was a choice between attacking special privilege and restoring competition, or accepting "the established monopolies as inevitable and putting government in control of those it is supposed to regulate." Thus, Roosevelt's plan legalized monopoly and solidified the business-government relationship. Roosevelt responded to Wilson's charge by attacking Wilson's past support for limited government. He called Wilson's ideas more "outworn academic doctrine" and the "laissez-faire doctrine of English political economists three-quarters of a century ago." Progressives would "use government as the most efficient instrument for the uplift of our people as a whole." "What I am interested in," said the candidate, "is getting the hand of government put on all of them [business]—this is what I want."[37] Taft had his own position on the issue, which was to use the courts to enforce the Sherman Act. His record on this issue should have given him more credibility than Roosevelt, but Wilson ignored him and Taft himself did not actively campaign, playing golf and saving his thunder for Roosevelt, accusing the third party as existing "merely to gratify personal ambition and vengeance."[38]

The details of the issue differences between Roosevelt and Wilson were not unimportant in the context of American politics, but more interesting are the similarities between the two men. No one in the campaign supported a strict laissez-faire program. The rise of large-scale industry and private economic power narrowed the political options in 1912, pointing all parties toward an expanded regulatory state. *Change* became the dominant thrust. Wilson sought that change, but in doing so he also at times blurred the distinction between himself and Roosevelt. In his acceptance speech in August, for example, Wilson was not unlike Roosevelt in saying that the "organization of business upon a great scale of cooperation is, up to a certain point, itself normal and inevitable." Later in September, he drew a careful line between big business and trusts: "A trust is an arrangement to get rid of competition, and a big business is a business that has survived competition by conquering in the field of intelligence and economy. I am for big business, and I am against trusts." Roosevelt had his New Nationalism and Wilson his New Freedom, but they did not differ greatly in their approach.[39]

Wilson was not above using shrewd tactics to further his cause. He sought to define his principal opponent away from the progressive movement by referring to Roosevelt's Progressive Party as "the third party" or "the irregular Republicans," never by their chosen name. Also, when Roosevelt was shot in an assassination attempt in October, Wilson suspended his campaign and resolved not to speak of Roosevelt or the Progressive platform until Roosevelt was healthy. With only three weeks left before the election, this move effectively removed the major issues from the campaign for two weeks. Wilson's own remarks became less detailed and more vague and general as the campaign drew to a close.[40]

A decade later, William Allen White wrote that the difference between Roosevelt's New Nationalism and Wilson's New Freedom was that of Tweedledum and Tweedledee. This is perhaps unfair. Wilson and Roosevelt had fundamental disagreements on basic worldviews. Roosevelt was a conservative who was pessimistic about human nature, while Wilson was more liberal and optimistic. Nevertheless, Robert Wiebe argues that little separated the major candidates on many reform issues in 1912. They "reasoned from the same premises," assuming the responsibility of the national government for guidance and conceiving of that guidance in bureaucratic terms. Despite their differences, Roosevelt and Wilson had a common orientation—bureaucratic reform. Perhaps most important, as far as the issue of their similarity is concerned, all the major parties "claimed the privilege of completing the national progressive movement."[41] In the beginning, that national progressive movement had been Roosevelt's. Simply by being a progressive along with Roosevelt, Wilson moved closer to the GOP's best-known figure. To the extent that Wilson and his issues became identified with national progressivism, the campaign avoided a direct clash between competing core values.

1916: "He kept us out of war"

Following Cleveland, Wilson was the second opposition president to seek reelection. He was the first incumbent opposition president to win. As such, his actions as president would factor into the fall campaign. Like the 1912 contest, the 1916 presidential election was a case of ambiguous centrists fighting it out on progressive turf. Democrats understood that achieving an electoral majority required the capture of progressive votes. Given the central location of the progressive movement between both major parties, as well as the ambiguous loyalties of many of its adherents, this was the perfect strategy to move Democrats toward the middle. Progressives represented the swing vote that would turn to whichever party proved more faithful to their cause, and Wilson was well positioned to prove himself worthy of that support. Progressivism retained its influence in both major parties, and both parties sought the vote of the movement's adherents. Wilson did so by shifting his policy agenda strongly toward progressivism in 1916. The GOP, perhaps more reluctantly, did so by nominating a former progressive governor, Charles Evans Hughes, as its standard-bearer.

Wilson began his courting of the progressive vote by switching his public position and endorsing women's suffrage in 1915. Next, he won the confirmation battle over his nomination of Louis Brandeis to the Supreme Court. Wilson made the confirmation a partisan issue, personally intervening on Brandeis's behalf and even garnering the support of GOP insurgent Robert La Follette. Brandeis was confirmed by the Senate 47-22, with only one Democrat opposed. The Democratic national convention followed soon after, and the party platform was strongly progressive on domestic issues, supporting child labor legislation, rural credits, highway construction, workmen's compensation, a nonpartisan tariff commission, and much more. The keynote speaker stumbled upon what would become one of the fall campaign's biggest issues when he supported Wilson's diplomatic efforts to keep the nation out of war. The convention's enthusiastic response was unanticipated, but party leaders quickly adapted, and "He kept us out of war" became the campaign slogan. Bryan himself said, "I join with the American people in thanking God that we have a President who does not want this nation plunged into this war." Despite the party's historic isolationism, the platform also endorsed entrance into a postwar League of Nations.[42]

Wilson continued to move toward progressivism in July, courting the farm vote by supporting the Rural Credits Act, enabling farmers to obtain loans at lower cost. Wilson urged Southern Democrats to pass the child labor bill. He had been warned in mid-July that the bill was a progressive test, so the next day Wilson went to the Capitol to plead with party leaders, telling them that the party's fortunes depended on the bill's passage. The bill passed six weeks later. Wilson also took an issue from the GOP by supporting a nonpartisan commission to deal with tariff rates, reversing a historic Democratic policy and accepting what Roosevelt had proposed (and Wilson opposed) in 1912. In August, Congress passed a workmen's compensation bill for federal employees. In September, Wilson signed the Adamson Act, thus averting a railroad strike by giving workers an eight-hour workday and establishing a commission to study other related labor problems. Finally, Wilson worked with Democrats and progressives in both houses to pass an income tax bill that doubled the tax, raised the surtax, instituted a federal estate excise tax, and taxed the receipts of munitions manufacturers.[43]

Wilson identified with the swing vote by declaring, "We have in four years come very near to carrying out the platform of the Progressive Party as well as our own; for we are also progressives." Wilson encouraged comparisons to the Republican renegades, saying, "I am a progressive. I do not spell it with a capital P, but I think my pace is just as fast as those who do." Secretary of the Interior Franklin Lane commented on the new party position, saying, "The Republican party was for half a century a constructive party and the Democratic party was the party of negation and complaint. We have taken the play from them. The Democratic party has become the party of construction." In the summer of 1916, Democrats made the 1912 Bull Moose platform their own, enacting almost every important plank.[44] Wilson successfully masked any differences between his party and the progressive faction, exemplifying the political art of locking down one's base while reaching out to the swing vote in the electorate.

In this context, the GOP had the more difficult task from the very beginning. First, Hughes's domestic record as a progressive governor was quite similar to Wilson's record as president, so Hughes had much greater difficulty criticizing Wilson's legislation, a task essential when running against an incumbent. To compound the problem, the GOP platform had a progressive look, which placed Hughes and his party in a strategic dilemma. On domestic issues, should he repudiate Wilson and turn to the right or accept Wilson's reform goals but simply criticize his methods? On foreign policy issues, should Hughes endorse Theodore Roosevelt's prowar drum-beating, giving Democrats the peace issue and losing the German Americans, or hold fast to the German Americans and be open to attacks on patriotism?[45]

Republicans shot themselves in the foot every chance they got that fall. Hughes was a wretched campaigner, and his muted criticism of Wilson was seen as trivial. The party was not well organized, and the conservative-progressive split from 1912 still resonated. The two groups bickered with each other and remained attuned to every perceived slight, eventually costing Hughes California. Wilson was much better organized and took advantage of the progressive factor. The South was a lock for the party, as usual, but Wilson also sought votes from groups that had benefited from his legislation. He issued a public letter explaining to farmers how various measures would help the rural population. To labor he played up his support of the eight-hour day, claiming that the "workingmen of America have been given a veritable emancipation." To business Wilson explained that he had adjusted and reformed the system, not destroyed it. To progressives he portrayed himself as moving in their direction. Wilson received the support of eleven of the nineteen Progressives who had formed the Bull Moose resolutions committee in 1912. Organizations such as the Associated Progressive Committee, the Woodrow Wilson Independent League, and the Woodrow Wilson Progressive Leagues helped spread Wilson's appeal beyond the party. Wilson drew to his side virtually the entire leadership of advanced progressivism, transforming and recreating the Democratic Party and solidifying a progressive coalition against the GOP.[46]

In addition to mishandling the progressive factor, the GOP also stumbled on the war issue. Hughes knew he needed the German American vote, and he saw an opportunity to exploit the perception that Wilson was pro-British. German Americans retained some antagonism toward Wilson, so they supported Hughes. The Wilson campaign, however, had already defined itself as pro-peace, so it turned German American support for Hughes into an issue of patriotism, attempting to discredit Hughes by associating him with the Kaiser. The *New York World* wrote, "The followers of the Kaiser in the United States have set out to destroy President Wilson politically for the crime of being an American President instead of a German President. They have adopted Mr. Hughes as their candidate and made his cause their cause." Wilson saw an advantage in the German Americans being against him, and took every opportunity to paint Hughes as a friend to the Un-American. Replying to an anti-British agitator, Wilson wrote, "Your telegram received. I would feel deeply mortified to have you or anybody like you vote for me. Since you have access to many disloyal Americans and I have not, I will ask you to convey this message to them." Wilson won the support of the patriotic, even as Roosevelt worked to destroy the support of German Americans. Always vigorous in attacking Wilson's foreign policy, Roosevelt created large German American defections from the GOP by advocating action against Germany and attacking hyphenism.[47]

Wilson continued to play upon the war issue. His September 30 speech brought the slogan "He kept us out of war" into the campaign. In that speech, Wilson charged the GOP with being the war party and criticized Republicans for saying his foreign policy was wrong. The implication was that they would change it if they won the White House. Since Wilson's policy was one of peace, "the certain prospect of success of the Republican Party is that we shall be drawn, in one form or another, into the embroilments of the European War." In October Wilson said, "I am not expecting this country to get into war." Just before the election in November, the Wilson

Business Man's League ran an ad saying: "You Are Working—*Not Fighting!* Alive and Happy;—*Not Cannon Fodder!* Wilson and Peace with Honor? or Hughes with Roosevelt and War?"[48]

Wilson retained the enhanced power of the presidency to use rhetoric to good effect, raising fears of war and waving the flag. He retained the power of a unified party that had in many ways swung toward progressivism in its attempt to keep the GOP from reclaiming its 1912 deserters. The GOP, on the other hand, despite attempting to reclaim their lost sheep by nominating a progressive, appeared more conservative than progressive. Thanks to the efforts of the best-known former Progressive, Theodore Roosevelt, the GOP also looked like it wanted to plunge the nation into an unwanted war in Europe. The fact that the nation would be at war in less than a year did not matter in November.

1952: "I like Ike"

The 1952 campaign was a very partisan and bitter affair, with the GOP taking on a strong right-wing tone from the beginning. All aspects of opposition campaigns are not created equal, however. The 1952 campaign demonstrates that, if the other elements of an opposition campaign are present, an indirect campaign is not a requirement. The partisan nature of the campaign is simply further evidence of the exceptionally poor position of the Democratic Party and the great strength of Eisenhower's personal popularity. These factors overrode any tendency the GOP had to steal defeat from the jaws of victory.

Eisenhower's turn toward the Right was a matter of fence-mending and locking down his party base, but the extent to which he moved toward his anchor faction would have been foolhardy in any other candidate. He met with Taft immediately following his victory to patch things up. He chose Nixon as his running mate, a member of the Old Guard by virtue of his anticommunism but whose internationalism made him acceptable to moderates like Dewey. Eisenhower's appeasement of the purists did not end there. He expressed support for the "liberation of the satellite countries" of Eastern Europe, an implicit criticism of Roosevelt and Truman. Eisenhower appeared on stage with people who excoriated the United Nations, NATO, and the Marshall Plan. On September 12, Eisenhower met again with Taft, approving his statement blasting "creeping socialization," and pledging to cut federal spending and taxes and fight communism. Democrats, moderate Republicans, and the press labeled the meeting "the Surrender of Morningside Heights." In private, Eisenhower expressed impatience with the Old Guard, but he was committed to securing his base and maintaining a unified party, even if that required some hypocrisy by attacking a foreign policy he helped create. On domestic policy, there was little in the Old Guard positions that Eisenhower disputed.[49]

On the question of the indirect campaign, four points must be made. First, there was an aspect of Eisenhower's campaign that masked the central differences between the two parties. On the one hand, Eisenhower's campaign slogan was "It's Time for a Change." He opposed "paternalistic government" and the concentration of power in the federal government, and saw himself as someone who could "unseat the New Deal–Fair Deal bureaucracy in Washington." He was a traditional Republican in opposing the "whole-hog theory" of government. On the other hand, Eisenhower sought no wholesale repudiation of the New Deal. While focusing on lower taxes and a balanced budget, Eisenhower also advocated improving and extending Social Security, unemployment insurance, and public housing. He saw social welfare programs as necessary to serve the common good and promised to take action in the event of a depression. He made a commitment to collective security, promising to support NATO and the UN while being a more efficient manager of defense policy. Eisenhower accepted the political developments of the previous twenty years, and sought no great redefinition of American politics.[50] Eisenhower's rhetoric reinforced this ambiguity. In his acceptance speech at the convention, Eisenhower spoke of a "great crusade for freedom in America and freedom in the world," saying, "I know something of the solemn responsibility of leading a crusade. I will accept your summons. I will lead this crusade." The focus of this "great crusade," despite the warlike imagery, was not an attack on the fundamentals of the New Deal nor a long-term redefinition of American politics. Instead, it was on the "wastefulness, the arrogance and corruption in high places, the heavy burdens and the anxieties which are the bitter fruit of a party too long in power." The substance of the crusade was honesty and righteousness and a cleaner politics. It hit the Democrats on corruption and communism, taking advantage of short-term issues for immediate electoral success. Nothing about it indicated a threat to the New Deal itself.[51] Thus, in addition to being a nonpartisan war hero, Eisenhower was an ambiguous centrist.

Second, despite the often conservative tone of his campaign, Eisenhower continued to receive cross-partisan support. He decided to campaign in the solidly Democratic South, where he did very well. When Stevenson supported a Supreme Court decision giving the federal government "dominant rights" over the tidelands oil reserves, Eisenhower sided with the Southern states. When Stevenson campaigned as a liberal, Eisenhower appealed to Southerners by ignoring civil rights issues. Democratic governors in Texas, South Carolina, and Louisiana actively campaigned for Eisenhower while Democratic governors in Virginia and Georgia refused to endorse Stevenson and sat out the campaign. Thus, instead of a Dixiecrat revolt, the "Shivercrat" revolt had several Democratic state organizations working for Eisenhower.[52]

Third, Eisenhower was very effective in the public relations side of the campaign, both in speeches and on television. The 1952 campaign was the first one in which television played a significant role and it was the last time spending on radio was greater than spending on television. The GOP outspent the Democrats three to two and reached a larger audience. This disadvantage was compounded by Stevenson's difficulty in adapting to the new medium. His speeches, drafted by a group of intellectuals, were learned, articulate, and witty. They were also complex and better read than listened to by an audience. They were completely inappropriate for television, which demands an easier style and simpler structure. Stevenson could not speak to the "common man," unlike his predecessor Harry Truman, and he was accused in the press of speaking to "egg-heads." His focus on the written word also made it difficult for him to finish a speech for television on schedule, and he habitually ran over the allotted time, causing the television to fade out on him while he was still talking. This was in sharp contrast to Eisenhower, who came across as strong, assertive, and paternal. Eisenhower kept his television spots short and simple, and he avoided committing himself to specific answers. In his speeches he was much better at relating to an unsophisticated audience, making them think he was one of them, keeping his prose simple and plain, avoiding abstractions, and using clear illustrations, stories, and props. He even used self-deprecation by referring to himself as the one "not supposed to be the educated candidate."[53]

Finally, Eisenhower took advantage of the one short-term issue on which the Democrats were most vulnerable: Korea. It was the dominant national issue, and Republicans were effective in labeling it "Truman's war," even though Eisenhower and many Republicans had initially approved of Truman's policy. When Truman pressed Eisenhower to provide the nation with a remedy to the stalemate, Eisenhower made his dramatic statement: "I shall go to Korea." Even though he had no plan, the general was the one man in the nation who had credibility on the issue.[54] With that declaration, Eisenhower pounced on Democratic vulnerabilities and won the election.

1956: "New Republicanism"

Eisenhower was the second incumbent opposition president to win reelection. Where Wilson's actions late in his first term served to embrace the swing vote at a time when progressivism was present in both parties, Eisenhower's policies served to reassure a Democratic electorate that the basic accomplishments of the New Deal were not endangered. Nothing about Eisenhower's first term represented a general repudiation of the New Deal. The summer before the election, Assistant Secretary of Labor Arthur Larson published *A Republican Looks at His Party,* a work that popularized the term "New Republicanism" and placed Eisenhower's program at the ideological center of American politics. The book effected no genuine transformation of the essentially conservative Republican Party, but it served to cast Eisenhower in a moderate light. The president himself demonstrated a certain reluctance to run, but he believed the various governing party options to be "crackpot Democrats," and he saw no suitable Republican alternatives. When Eisenhower made his decision, he toyed with the idea of replacing Nixon as running mate with the Democratic governor of Ohio, recalling the success of the above-party Lincoln-Johnson ticket of 1864 (though not its disastrous end). Eisenhower retained Nixon, and he entered the 1956 contest in an exceptionally strong position.[55] He was not compelled to focus attention on the core differences between the two parties, and the election itself became a simple vote of confidence.

Eisenhower's position only became stronger as the campaign progressed. As stated earlier, Stevenson's reversal of long-standing Democratic Party positions on certain military and foreign policy issues created problems for the governing party. The coincidence of several important foreign policy crises at the end of the campaign also helped focus attention on Eisenhower's experience rather than on core issue differences between the two candidates. Great Britain, France, and Israel attempted to take control of the Sinai and Suez Canal while the Soviet Union invaded Hungary. Eisenhower acted patiently and prudently throughout the crises, which stretched through election day, and the handling of such troubles by an experienced hand factored into the president's success.[56]

1968: "Nixon's the One"

When examining the Republican effort in the tumultuous year of 1968, it is important to keep in mind the party's desire to avoid the specter of 1964.

Many of its actions and the actions of its candidate qualify as attempts to close the issue distance between the two major parties and avoid genuine discussion of fundamentals. Nixon's nomination was the most pragmatically moderate act of the convention, and Nixon attempted to continue in that vein with his vice presidential candidate. Southerners rejected liberals such as John Lindsay and Oregon senator Mark Hatfield, and Northerners rejected conservatives such as Ronald Reagan and Texas senator John Tower. Nixon preferred his friend Robert Finch, who was California's lieutenant governor and a Reagan rival, and thus hardly a right wing dream. When Finch rejected Nixon's overture, he shifted to Maryland governor Spiro Agnew. Nixon thought Agnew could be perceived as a blank slate himself, for he was an ethnic Rockefeller supporter from a border state. Agnew was a polarizing figure, however, for he had lashed out against black leaders in Baltimore after the riots following the King assassination, blaming them for the violence. Many viewed Agnew's selection as a payoff to the South, and the immediate reaction was one of incredulity. Although liberal forces challenged the nomination, Agnew easily prevailed. In an indication of how far Republicans were willing to go to preserve unity, Lindsay himself seconded the nomination.[57]

The effort to avoid the Goldwater experience continued with the platform. Everett Dirksen called it a platform "that any Republican can run on," and it was a model effort at seeking unity by avoiding issues. Its Vietnam plank was not that different from what Lyndon Johnson was pursuing at the time. The GOP sought a negotiated and honorable settlement while waging the war more effectively. This more effective warfare would be accomplished by escalating the conflict while also phasing out American troops in a "progressive de-Americanization of the war." The platform advocated allowing all parties to the peace table but also stressed that the war was still "winnable." The platform advocated "searching conversations" with Cold War adversaries, including China, and it stressed law and order, supporting civil rights while also seeking an all-out assault on civil disorder and crime. The platform was patched together by all GOP factions to give something to everyone and to walk a middle line by avoiding specifics on the harder questions.[58]

Nixon sealed the convention with a remarkable acceptance speech in which he again appealed to the middle. He reminded the nation of his tie to the last great popular president by referring to the support of the ailing Eisenhower. He appealed to those distressed by war by promising to seek an end to the Vietnam problem. He moved away from the right wing and his own anticommunist past by calling for an "era of negotiation" with Cold War enemies, ending in friendship. He split the difference on the race issue by supporting civil rights while opposing busing. He even made the inherently uncontroversial appeal to the American dream. Through it all, he appealed to "the great majority of Americans, the forgotten Americans, the non-shouters, the non-demonstrators," thus allying himself against the protestors and on the side of those who desired domestic tranquillity. It was an effective rhetorical technique that presaged his later appeal to the "silent majority." Nixon quickly received the support of liberal Republicans. The convention made him more appealing to conservative Democrats and independents, and he left Miami leading in the polls.[59] Nixon and the GOP were prepared to do nothing to attack the foundations of the New Deal democracy at a time when it seemed most vulnerable. There would be no talk of "extremism in the defense of liberty." They were well prepared to wage an indirect campaign that sought only a short-term redefinition of politics.

One of the more interesting aspects of Nixon's campaign was his media strategy. Packaging strategies are hardly new; Whigs had successfully marketed Harrison as a war hero in 1840, and Nixon's efforts were a natural descendant of that campaign. Beginning in the primary season, Nixon forces worked to prove that he was electable and to air his message unfiltered by the news media. The most famous book about Nixon's media strategy is Joe McGinniss's *The Selling of the President 1968*, written by a reporter who posed as a Nixon campaign worker. The title refers to the selling of a product rather than a dialogue about political issues. McGinniss asserts that Nixon's refusal to face the news media allowed him to present a false picture of himself to the world, a packaged image that did not reflect reality. From a marketing perspective, McGinniss argues that television is good for the politician who is "charming but lacks ideas." Ideas are better expressed in text, while on television it is personality that is important. Thus, "style becomes substance."[60] Nixon wanted to control the camera, so he employed experts to package him properly and create an image that hid his unattractive qualities and emphasized positive qualities that came across well on television.[61] He told his handlers, "We're going to build this whole campaign around television. You fellows just tell me what you want me to do and I'll do it."[62] The result was a series of one-hour television shows, aired live in front of a carefully screened studio audience prepped to cheer Nixon's answers to questions. The shows aired regionally, allowing Nixon to limit his topics and repeat his answers, and even vary them to appeal to local audiences. This allowed him to play to his strengths and avoid a hostile press by going over its head.[63] Nixon's media strategy extended to commercials as well, and McGinniss quotes his handlers as saying that "the radicalness of this approach is in the fact of creating an image without saying anything. The words are given meaning by the impressions created by the stills." As for the audience, "the public sits home and watches *Gunsmoke* and when they're fed this pap about Nixon they think they're getting something worthwhile."[64]

Some scholars dispute McGinniss's interpretation. Kathleen Hall Jamieson rejects McGinniss's argument that Nixon's handlers created his image, arguing instead that they simply chose the format in which he came across best, for the primary mission was to get the public to see Nixon as his friends saw him, and as he really was. Theodore White mirrors this argument, saying that Nixon's media strategy depicted the real Richard Nixon as a direct, spontaneous, and genuine individual.[65] Also, Nixon's strategy was hardly unique. Hubert Humphrey also taped question and answer sessions that were heavily edited for television, and McGinniss was reportedly very selective in his evidence, doing his own sort of packaging to support his argument.[66] Nevertheless, even if the motivation behind the media strategy was not as sinister as McGinniss claims, the strategy still allowed Nixon to play to his strengths, dialoguing with a few citizens in a controlled environment, editing and airing the best material for television and avoiding reporters while running a national campaign. Nixon outspent Humphrey two to one on television and appeared on a network news program less than a handful of times. It was not a strategy designed to foster debate about issues as much as it was to present the best possible picture of the candidate.[67]

Nixon's media strategy might not have been so important if debate about issues had been engaged in some other venue, but the campaign made no effort to be specific about the issues, sticking instead to general denunciations of Democratic policies and keeping the focus on "Nixon's the One." In this message, Nixon had a solution to what was wrong, even if he refused to actually propose one. Nixon ignored foreign policy, refusing to discuss Vietnam as long as negotiations continued, saying, "The pursuit of peace is too important for politics-as-usual." He consistently ignored Humphrey's proposal to debate, hiding behind the two-party system.[68] Nixon was aided by Humphrey's own problems, for as the administration candidate Humphrey was forced to support Johnson on the war, which meant he could not attack Nixon on that issue. In fact, Theodore White argues that on the issue of Vietnam, both candidates "engaged in variations of a fugue set by Lyndon Johnson."[69] Nixon could also afford to let George Wallace go his own way, for he focused on the alienation of people from their government, which was controlled by Democrats. Wallace's efforts were hampered by the comments of his running mate, General Curtis LeMay, who said the United

States could "bomb the North Vietnamese back to the Stone Age." LeMay's advocacy of nuclear weapons in Vietnam only served to make Nixon look more moderate. Nixon had Agnew attract Wallace voters in the periphery of the South, choosing not to fight him in his home territory. One week into October, he was still fifteen points ahead in the polls, and all he seemingly needed to do was run out the proverbial clock.[70]

In late September, Nixon criticized Johnson's plan to reduce American troop strength in Vietnam, even though the plan matched his own. Then, anticipating a Humphrey speech promoting peace, Nixon switched and praised the reduction, pledging to do the same more vigorously. On September 30, Humphrey finally made progress in healing intraparty wounds by proposing a halt to bombing, de-Americanization of the war, and an immediate cease-fire with United Nations supervision of the withdrawal of foreign forces. Nixon responded by appealing to the example of Eisenhower in Korea. He promised a "generous" peace and said he was even willing to rebuild North Vietnam. He promised to include Democrats in his cabinet and to seek Johnson's assistance to end the war. As the Humphrey surge continued, Nixon resorted to older tactics of dissembling, attacking the administration for a "security gap," akin to Kennedy's false missile gap charge eight years earlier. He argued that superiority, not "parity," should be the goal in national defense. Humphrey replied quickly, armed with numbers from the Department of Defense debunking Nixon's claims. In his growing desperation, Nixon proposed that the winner of the popular vote be declared the president, regardless of the electoral outcome. While Wallace's presence created the possibility of electoral problems, Humphrey rejected Nixon's unconstitutional suggestion.[71]

In mid-October Johnson joined Nixon in attempting to manipulate the election by trying to get both sides in Vietnam to agree to peace talks. He hoped North Vietnam would agree to the participation of the Thieu regime in South Vietnam and to respect the de-militarized zone (DMZ) and not attack South Vietnamese cities. Johnson would stop the bombing, and the prospect of peace would aid Humphrey. Nixon worked through fund-raiser Anna Chenault to stress the importance to Thieu of rejecting the proposal, arguing that he would do better with a Republican administration. Johnson knew of Nixon's maneuvering because he had his phones tapped, but that fact made him unable to assault Nixon in public. On October 26, Nixon accused administration forces of seeking a bombing halt for political purposes. North Vietnam agreed to Johnson's terms, and on October 31 Johnson announced a breakthrough on national television, ordering a halt to bombing and stating that talks would begin in Paris the day after the election. The announcement enjoyed massive public approval, and Humphrey passed Nixon in the polls with three days to go. The weekend before the election, Thieu announced that South Vietnam would not participate in the talks. Nixon had Robert Finch report that Nixon was surprised at the development, and that the administration must have made a hasty decision to help Humphrey. Nixon then rejected Finch's charge on *Meet the Press*, but in doing so made the point that behind the scenes diplomatic maneuvers were politically motivated. He then volunteered to negotiate for the administration to get Thieu to go to Paris. In one final attempt to affect the outcome of the election, Nixon reported on national television the day before the election that North Vietnam was "moving thousands of tons of supplies down the Ho Chi Minh Trail, and our bombers are not able to stop them." The report was false; Nixon had simply made it up.[72]

1972: Clandestine Tactics

Nixon continued the run of successful twentieth-century incumbent opposition presidents. He could not help but look moderate next to George McGovern, and the foreign policy triumphs of his first term only added to his presidential aura. Central to Nixon's reelection effort, however, was not a focus on partisan differences, but indirect clandestine activities. Nixon's Committee to Re-elect the President vigorously worked to sabotage the Democratic effort as early as the nominating season. The organization tapped McGovern's phone, investigated his finances, spread rumors and falsehoods about Hubert Humphrey and Henry Jackson, paid a girl to stand naked outside frontrunner Ed Muskie's headquarters and yell "I love Ed Muskie," planted a derogatory letter on Muskie stationery, and put out fake polls showing McGovern doing well in trial heats in an attempt to get the weakest opponent possible.[73] With McGovern as his opponent, Nixon targeted disaffected Democrats and independents, avoiding the term "Republican" and referring to McGovern supporters as "McGovernites." Nixon made an open appeal at his convention for Democrats to "come home." He identified himself with every president since Franklin Roosevelt, Democrat and Republican, on the issue of isolationism. In this way Nixon could act presidential, attack his enemies without attacking Democrats as a whole, and remain disassociated from the larger Republican campaign. Biographer Stephen Ambrose argues that Nixon became the politician "least interested in party and most concerned about personality," and in seeking a massive victory he tried to become, in nonpartisan fashion, the "president of all the people." Enemies and allies alike called it a "noncampaign," and McGovern complained that "for the first time in the history of this country, we have a Presidential campaign with only one candidate." Finally, although unknown at the time, Nixon covered up what would have been the biggest issue of the campaign, his own abuse of power.[74]

1992: "The economy, stupid"

Clinton began the final phase of his quest for the presidency by choosing fellow Southerner Al Gore as his running mate. It was not a conventional choice. Instead of balancing the ticket with a clear liberal from a region outside the South, Clinton gave it a moderate cast, picking another Southern Baptist, New Democrat baby boomer. Gore had the added advantage of being a Vietnam veteran (balancing Clinton's draft problem) and having a reputation as a good family man (to balance Clinton's morals problem). The convention itself reinforced the image of moderation. The platform advocated more police on the street, thereby removing from the phrase "law and order" the stigma that it was a codeword for racism, a common Democratic charge when used by Republicans. The platform also refuted "outdated faith in programs as the solution to every problem." While promising a health care plan that would provide "affordable, quality health care for all Americans," the plan was billed as a middle way between a single-payer government-financed system and more incremental, market-oriented reforms. Georgia governor Zell Miller referred to Clinton as a Democrat "who will move people off the welfare rolls and onto the job rolls." Mario Cuomo helped lock in the liberal core, and then Clinton made an appeal to the political center, focusing on "an expanding entrepreneurial economy" and pledging to work for "the hardworking Americans who make up our forgotten middle class." Nixon himself, in his own appeal to the silent majority, could hardly have done better. Clinton's appeal was explicitly nonpartisan, advocating "a new approach to government," claiming there was "not a program in government for every problem," and arguing that the choice in the election was "not liberal or conservative; in many ways, it's not even Republican or Democrat. It is different. It is new. And it will work." By the end of the convention, the New Democrat ticket was first in the polls.[75]

The contrast of the relatively unified and temperate Democratic meeting with the boisterous and troubled Republican national convention was stark.

The GOP platform was controlled largely by Christian Coalition forces and was very conservative on such issues as abortion, homosexuality, and America's Judeo-Christian heritage. Instead of focusing on the economy, Republicans attacked the Clintons. Pat Buchanan issued a jeremiad, saying, "There is a religious war going on in this country for the soul of America. It is a cultural war as critical to the kind of nation we shall be as the Cold War itself. . . . Clinton and Clinton are on the other side, and George Bush is on our side." Buchanan's sentiments were not unique. Christian Coalition founder Pat Robertson said "Bill and Hillary Clinton . . . are talking about a radical plan to destroy the traditional family and transfer its functions to the federal government." Such prime time speeches pushed television coverage of Ronald Reagan's address to eleven o'clock at night. The convention's theological tone replaced the Cold War with a religious war and made the Democratic Party the enemy, the propagator of a "guerilla war against American values." Against such rhetoric, Clinton and the Democrats could hardly help but appear moderate.[76]

The general election campaign did not lack for issues to debate, and at times Clinton veered close to a full-scale repudiation of the reigning governing philosophy. A closer examination of events, however, demonstrates that Clinton was not so ambitious. He faced two choices as the campaign began: he could either focus on Bush and the economy while allaying suspicions about his character, or he could "offer a policy-based frame" spelling out what he would do if elected. He chose the first option, "promising to be 'not Bush'" while offering enough policy proposals to give weight to his call for change.[77] Clinton's strategy centered on his campaign motto: "Change vs. more of the same. The economy, stupid. Don't forget health care." To the extent that Clinton advocated change, the campaign was issue-oriented. He attacked "trickle-down economics," blasting the 1980s as a "decade of greed" and comparing the economy to the previous GOP debacle, calling the Republican effort the "worst economic record since the Great Depression." His strategy for change revolved around his proposals to reform welfare and health care, raise taxes on the wealthy, and provide for more government investment in human capital. Such proposals satisfied every element of his campaign motto, but the "change" he campaigned for was a change from the current steward of the economy to himself more than it was from the idea of tax and deficit cuts to a new Great Society, and "the economy, stupid" easily became the best-known line from his campaign motto. Thus, Clinton's campaign was indirect in that he did not attack the roots of the Reagan system, just as Eisenhower refused to attack the New Deal. Clinton attacked the key short-term issue of Bush's weakness on the economy while adhering to his more conservative New Democrat base.[78]

The campaign had an indirect quality in three additional areas. First, Ross Perot's return to the race as an independent candidate muddied the waters. At one point both campaigns sent delegations to court Perot supporters, but the billionaire spurned their efforts and became a wildcard for both parties. Perot was famous for his witty one-liners and sometimes bizarre accusations, but his greater effect was in simply creating confusion about the real issue in the campaign. If at one time it was jobs and health care, Perot's return elevated the federal budget deficit. He forced everyone to focus on the deficit, for he believed neither campaign was dealing with this "crazy aunt locked in the basement." That was his top priority, and although he was more effective at keeping Bush on the defensive, his presence served to dilute the impact of Clinton's more direct attack.[79]

Second, while the issue of character was a legitimate one, the way it was handled was less than illuminating. The governing party attacked Clinton's draft record, his participation in antiwar demonstrations while at Oxford, and his 1969 visit to Moscow. The GOP even searched embassy files for information on Clinton. The implication in these efforts was that Clinton had committed treason. For the most part, Clinton did not answer the substance of the charges, choosing instead to deflect the attacks by maintaining his focus on the economy. Both campaigns degenerated into silliness at times, with Bush referring to the Democratic ticket as "two bozos" and to Gore as "ozone man," and the Clinton camp sending hecklers dressed as chickens to Bush campaign stops saying "Chicken George Won't Debate."[80]

Finally, Clinton joined his criticism of Bush to a reassurance that he would not be like previous Democrats. He stayed relentlessly on message, promising to relieve economic suffering while also demonstrating that he was not a traditional Democrat on the death penalty, that he wanted to "end welfare as we know it," that he approved of spending cuts, and that he wanted to seek a "third way" between the two political sides. In other words, Clinton seized every opportunity to minimize the distance between his proposals and the Reagan regime. With few exceptions, he avoided foreign policy, keeping the focus on domestic issues. He aligned himself with Bush on free trade, thereby removing another issue from the campaign. Even on health care, Clinton claimed the middle ground "beyond partisan political debate." He portrayed his plan as "a private system" that "does not require new taxes," asserting that the funding would come from the elimination of waste and thus acknowledging the continuing power of the Republican antitax message. His commitment to universal coverage assumed the plan would be deficit-neutral, thus acknowledging the continuing power of the Republican antideficit message. To avoid charges that the plan would become a new big government program, Clinton emphasized its market aspects, thus acknowledging the continuing power of the Republican anti–big government message. In fact, Clinton gave only one speech outlining his plan. His message remained a largely rhetorical one of change without specifics.[81]

Clinton proved to be effective in relaying his message in a variety of venues that enabled him to bypass the traditional news media. He remained comfortable with details and comfortable talking to people in such a way that they believed he cared for and understood them. This was in stark contrast to Bush's admission during one debate that he was not sure he "got" the question, reinforcing the public's notion that Bush lacked the requisite understanding of and attention to their problems.[82] Given this dynamic, Clinton saw no reason to be too risky in his own campaign. With the character question irrelevant, the people endorsed a change in management.

1996: Running as a "Semi-Republican"

Clinton suffered a near-death experience with the 1994 Republican takeover of Congress, but he completed the perfect record of successful elected twentieth-century incumbent opposition presidents by moving sharply in the direction of the governing party in the second half of his first term. Part of Clinton's success was due to his control of campaign finances. Immediately following his 1994 midterm loss, Clinton understood his status as an opposition leader facing a robust governing party. His response was to become a voracious fund-raiser, all in an effort to prevent the GOP from getting too far ahead. In a variety of forums, including White House dinners, coffees, and overnight stays in the Lincoln bedroom, Clinton courted wealthy donors for money. He was eventually able to control millions of dollars in campaign funds, much of it "soft money" managed by the Democratic National Committee. During the 1995 budget battle with Congress and 1996 election season, Clinton retained effective control of how soft money would be used in issue advocacy ads that were nominally independent of his presidential campaign.[83] Clinton's fund-raising efforts demonstrated his understanding of his constrained position. His early use of advertising placed him at a great advantage in terms of getting the message out that he was a centrist. Despite his best efforts, Dole was never able to paint Clinton as a liberal.

Clinton began his political shift to the right by changing his focus from the economy to values, a traditionally Republican strength. In an effort to reclaim the loyalty of voters who were conservative on values issues, Clinton began to avoid talk of redistribution and the economy and instead focused on moral decline. Despite Clinton's own vulnerabilities on morals issues, he began appealing to middle-class suburban parents by criticizing pop culture and television violence. Out of this strategy came a variety of policy proposals, including support for the television V-chip, more educational television for children, regulations against pornography on the Internet, a voluntary television ratings system, school uniforms, teen curfews, a college tuition tax credit, expansion of family leave, standardized tests, tax credits for adoption, tracking of former sex criminals, and much more. Some of these were Republican issues, some Democratic, but all were couched in the language of values. Clinton signed an executive order mandating that teen mothers on welfare live at home and either work or go to school. He appealed to religious conservatives by outlining where and how religion and moral values could be promoted in public schools. He even signed the Defense of Marriage Act, a Republican measure that allowed states to ban homosexual marriage. The act placed into federal law a definition of marriage stating that it was "a legal union between one man and one woman as husband and wife." Clinton's support was clearly reluctant—he signed the law after midnight, with no publicity—but a better example of co-opting the GOP agenda could not be found.[84]

Clinton hinted at his electoral strategy in his campaign manifesto *Between Hope and History.* There he outlined a nonpartisan "third way" in policy, writing about people being "forced to choose between two wrong arguments. One seemed to argue for the government to spend more money on the same bureaucracies working in the same way. The other argues that government was inherently bad." Clinton sought "a new and bold course for the future."[85] This "bold course" was to eliminate as many differences between himself and the GOP as possible. Clinton began with his 1995 shift toward deficit reduction and continued with his Reaganesque 1996 State of the Union declaration that "the era of big government is over." Next on his list was welfare reform. Aid to Families with Dependent Children had been an entitlement for sixty years. It had also long been targeted by conservatives for change. Reagan had advocated turning over the program to the states and ending the federal entitlement, and the GOP's 1994 "Contract with America" sought to repeal this symbol of the New Deal. Most of the early welfare reform debate consisted of the administration wrestling with the GOP, and Clinton vetoed some version of welfare reform twice. By the summer of 1996, he believed he could not afford a third veto. GOP efforts had solidified into a plan that ended the federal guarantee of cash benefits to the poor by transferring control of the program to the states. Recipients were required to work within two years, and there was a five-year eligibility limit. The plan also cut food stamps and aid to legal immigrants. On July 31, Clinton announced that he would sign the bill, against the opposition of congressional Democrats, led by Dick Gephardt, and of liberals within his own administration.[86]

Supported by Vice President Al Gore and First Lady Hillary Clinton, the president cooperated with Newt Gingrich in reversing sixty years of domestic policy, rescinding a key part of the Social Security Act of 1935 that had helped inaugurate the New Deal era. Clinton believed that appearing as a centrist was essential to his reelection, but in a rather perverse argument, he followed up welfare reform by appealing for his own reelection so that he could fix the problems in the bill he had just signed. The bill won strong support in Congress, but all twenty-one senators and all but two of the 101 representatives who voted against the bill were Democrats. Marian Wright Edelman, Clinton friend and head of the Children's Defense Fund, called the bill "an act of shame," and her husband Peter Edelman, an assistant secretary of Health and Human Services, along with other top HHS officials, soon resigned.[87]

Welfare reform was only the most notable example of Clinton's move toward the reigning governing philosophy. He and the Republican Congress took additional steps to eliminate a variety of issues from the fall campaign. Both sides collaborated on the Kennedy-Kassebaum Health Insurance Portability and Accountability Act, which required health insurance companies to offer continuing coverage to employees who lose jobs or switch employment. Clinton also won passage of legislation requiring health insurance plans to cover forty-eight hours of hospitalization for new mothers. He even won passage of a raise in the minimum wage. Clinton can be seen in these instances as achieving modest accomplishments—less ambitious than in his first two years—that trimmed the edges of the GOP's agenda. More important, these actions removed from the presidential race many of the issues about which Dole could have campaigned. The Democratic national convention portrayed Clinton as a nonpartisan leader not strongly identified with his party, and a frustrated Dole complained that Clinton's strategy was "to run as a Republican." Clinton moved even further toward the governing party by reappointing Alan Greenspan to a third term as chairman of the Federal

Reserve. By moving toward the right, Clinton co-opted Republican issues and blurred the distinctions between his goals and those of the GOP. In one of his columns, David Broder quoted political scientist Gary Jacobson's assessment that Clinton ran as a "semi-Republican." The political debate was still defined in GOP terms, with Clinton differing from those terms only in degree, not in kind. He had shifted to the right for political survival, and he succeeded.[88]

Conclusions

Opposition parties do not always pursue issueless campaigns, and it is when they pursue the alternative strategy of strongly repudiating the reigning governing philosophy in an attempt to redefine fundamentally American politics that they are most spectacularly unsuccessful. Sometimes opposition party candidates appeal to their anchor factions and engage in open warfare against the governing party agenda. Prime examples of such efforts include Bryan's three campaigns in 1896, 1900, and 1908, Landon's 1936 campaign against Roosevelt, Goldwater's 1964 attack on the New Deal, and Mondale's 1984 assault on Reagan's conservative agenda. Republicans Landon and Goldwater are perhaps the best examples of spectacular electoral catastrophes, running vigorous campaigns repudiating the reigning governing philosophy only to suffer the worst two popular vote defeats in American history. All were campaigns in which the opposition party candidate attempted to make as the central issue in the campaign the supposed deficiencies of the reigning governing philosophy. All were campaigns in which the opposition party candidate attempted to spell out and delineate clearly the principal differences between the two major parties. All were campaigns in which the opposition party candidate attempted to increase the ideological distance between the two major parties in an attempt to redefine politics and draw public support toward the opposition party. The result in 1896 was a realignment that strengthened and solidified Republican control over the national agenda. The results in 1936, 1964, and 1984 were resounding victories for the governing parties and devastating defeats for the opposition.

Of the three elements present in most successful opposition party campaigns, this last is the most difficult to pin down, and it appears on the surface to have much greater variation than the other two, calling into question Campbell's assertion that this feature—rather than short-term forces or blank slate candidates—provides the basic quality of opposition victory. In fact, some features of the indirect campaign build upon the foundation laid by the other two elements of successful opposition party campaigns, making this element at least partially derivative of the others. Nevertheless, whether the focus is on image and personality, or short-term issues, or on the effort to eliminate troubling differences between the two parties, the common denominator—indeed, the intersection point for all three of these strategies—is that the opposition party succeeds in reducing the distance between the two candidates. By shifting attention away from the central issues that define the core ideologies of the two parties, the opposition party prevents the governing party from playing to its strengths, from appealing to the public on the basis of the core issues that allowed it to become the governing party and to define the reigning governing philosophy. The shrewd opposition party eschews the temptation to attempt a long-term redefinition of politics when the time is not ripe—for that would inevitably fail—in favor of defining one specific election in its favor.

Chapter 5

FROM CAMPAIGNING TO GOVERNING

The Electoral Connection

When laying out the model for the successful opposition party's presidential campaign in chapter 1, I suggested that the prescription might end up being a twist on the 1964 Republican injunction to seek "a choice, not an echo." Instead, in order to be successful, opposition parties might want to seek "an echo, not a choice." The historical evidence appears to bear out this advice. By their very nature opposition parties are oriented to run against the grain of history. They seek to undo what has been done and set the nation on a different path. To win, however, it seems that the best prescription for opposition party victory is to run with the grain of history. Doing so is simply a matter of the opposition party's understanding and acknowledging that it is playing by rules established by the governing party. It must, in essence, beat the governing party at its own game. The success of opposition party campaigns is candidate-centered, lacking strong ideological content, and not grounded in the core partisan divisions of the day. It takes advantage of short-term forces that temporarily afflict the reigning party, and uses that dynamic to claim the presidency. This is true not only in the current candidate-centered system but throughout American history.[1]

Nothing in these various strategies guarantees the opposition party victory, however. There are numerous examples of some of these conditions being met without such a result. In 1872 Liberal Republicans formed their own party, but Grant still won. In 1924 Republican renegade LaFollette led another Progressive Party effort, but Coolidge still won. Many blank slate opposition party candidates have gone down to defeat, including a number of military heroes. The 1948 election is the best example of a classic opposition party campaign that did not succeed. With the governing party facing two different factional bolts (although added together the Dixiecrats and Progressives did not break 5 percent of the popular vote), the GOP fielded centrist Thomas Dewey against a weakened Harry Truman, putting forth a moderate party front with liberal Republican Earl Warren as running mate and seeking no broad repudiation of the New Deal. The race is famous for its nail-biting finish, so close at least in part because of the opposition campaign, but Truman took the day.

It is clear that each of the three factors that are involved in opposition victory is not present in every campaign with the same intensity or power. What is not clear is whether one of the three factors is consistently more important to victory than the others. In an effort to summarize and clarify the historical analysis thus far, table 5-1 lists the twelve successful opposition party elections. There is no easy way to quantify levels of blankness or indirection, so I have taken on the mantle of movie reviewer to evaluate and rate these three features and compare their relative importance on the probability of victory. The ratings are based on my sense of the historical record. In all three cases I employ a three-star system of ranking. For the governing

TABLE 5-1:
Summary Rating of Winning Opposition Campaign Features

Year	Winning Candidate	Governing Party in Trouble	Blank Slate Candidate	Indirect Campaign	Total
1840	Harrison	*	**	***	6
1848	Taylor	**	***	***	8
1884	Cleveland	**	**	***	7
1892	Cleveland	**	*	**	5
1912	Wilson	***	**	*	6
1916	Wilson	**	*	*	4
1952	Eisenhower	**	**	**	6
1956	Eisenhower	*	**	**	5
1968	Nixon	***	*	**	6
1972	Nixon	**	*	**	5
1992	Clinton	***	**	**	7
1996	Clinton	**	*	**	5
	Average:	2.08	1.67	2.08	5.83

party in trouble, I give one star for incumbent status—the presence of a weak governing party incumbent or an opposition party incumbent. I give one star for internal party tension, on the order of the Mugwump or Shivercrat bolts of 1884 and 1952 or the intraparty challenges of 1912 and 1992, and one star for full-scale third-party threats, either stemming from within the governing party or without. For the blank slate candidate, I award one star to each of them for their status either as a war hero, an unknown, or a centrist/cross-partisan. If the candidate combines two of these qualities, such as Cleveland and Wilson as unknown centrists or Eisenhower as war hero centrist, I award two stars. If the candidate combines all three qualities, he gets three stars. The indirect campaign category is the most subjective of the three. There I award stars based on my sense of how indirect the campaign was in terms of avoiding core issue differences. For example, the efforts in 1840 and 1848 appear to be the purest examples of image-over-substance campaigns. The two-star campaigns worked to avoid core differences and decrease the ideological distance between the two parties, even while highlighting, perhaps, the short-term problems of the governing party. Other campaigns, particularly that of 1912, are more arguable, and my case for the indirection of the one-star elections is made in chapter 4. To evaluate the relative importance of these three elements, I have averaged the ratings at the bottom of each column. I have also added the total number of stars per campaign in the far right column, giving us an idea of how strong each campaign was in matching these three elements. Finally, I have applied this same analysis to the twenty-nine (to date) unsuccessful opposition party campaigns in table 5-2.

Unquestionably there is room for debate about these ratings, but one thing seems clear: there is no rigidly uniform prescription for opposition party victory. As table 5-1 indicates, each campaign is unique. Sometimes the strongest factor in an opposition party victory is the indirect campaign. Sometimes the various factors seem evenly weighted. It appears that victorious opposition candidates have become less of a blank slate in recent years, though we have only the example of two individuals to set that trend. The short-term forces that create problems for the governing party are important features in all opposition victories, though they range significantly in terms of intensity. Although one should be cautious about interpreting too much in factors that are measured quite differently from each other, the three averages in table 5-1 indicate that the governing party in trouble and indirect campaign factors may be slightly more important than the blank slate candidate factor. This is somewhat contrary to the argument of Campbell and his colleagues, who

TABLE 5-2:
Summary Rating of Losing Opposition Campaign Features

Year	Losing Candidate	Governing Party in Trouble	Blank Slate Candidate	Indirect Campaign	Total
1832	Clay	—	—	—	0
1836	3 Whigs	—	*	*	2
1844	Clay	—	—	*	1
1852	Scott	—	*	**	3
1856	Fremont	—	*	—	1
1864	McClellan	—	*	—	1
1868	Seymour	—	—	—	0
1872	Greeley	*	*	**	4
1876	Tilden	—	—	**	2
1880	Hancock	—	*	**	3
1888	Cleveland	*	*	—	2
1896	Bryan	—	—	—	0
1900	Bryan	—	—	—	0
1904	Parker	—	**	**	4
1908	Bryan	—	—	*	1
1920	Cox	—	—	—	0
1924	Davis	*	**	*	4
1928	Smith	—	—	—	0
1936	Landon	—	*	—	1
1940	Willkie	—	**	**	4
1944	Dewey	—	*	**	3
1948	Dewey	**	*	**	5
1960	Nixon	—	*	**	3
1964	Goldwater	—	—	—	0
1976	Ford	*	*	**	4
1984	Mondale	—	—	—	0
1988	Dukakis	—	—	*	1
2000	Gore	—	—	—	0
2004	Kerry	—	—	*	1
	Average:	0.21	0.62	0.90	1.72
	Difference:	1.87	1.05	1.18	4.11

stated that the indirect campaign provides the basic quality of opposition victory. This table indicates that the presence of governing party difficulties is at least as important, setting the stage for what is to come.

A comparison of the ratings in table 5-1 with those in table 5-2 further draws out these distinctions. Here the differences between successful and unsuccessful opposition party campaigns become rather stark. The averages for the three campaign features in successful efforts are markedly higher than those for the unsuccessful efforts. We can also get a clearer notion of the relative strength of the three factors by comparing the differences between successful and unsuccessful efforts, depicted in the final row of table 5-2. The difference between successful and unsuccessful opposition party campaigns when looking at the governing party in trouble is much larger than the difference between successful and unsuccessful campaigns in either of the other two factors—nearly ten times the average in the first, as opposed to between two to three times the average in the latter two. In fact, although the differences between successful and unsuccessful campaigns are clear in all three categories, the lack of a governing party in trouble constitutes the most dramatic difference between results. This fact lends further support to the notion that it is the governing party in trouble that lies at the foundation of opposition party success, not the indirect campaign. That does not make the other two factors unimportant or optional. It does suggest, however, that the three factors build upon each other. The governing party in trouble is a necessary but not sufficient ingredient for opposition party success. The decision to run a blank slate candidate and wage an indirect campaign is a strategic one that must be based on the existence of the first feature. Although hardly a guarantee of success, as 1948 demonstrates, this model can be taken as a kind of formula for what ingredients are necessary for opposition party victory. The precise measurements of each variable vary from election to election, but they build naturally upon each other.[2]

Finally, it is interesting to note the numbers in the far right column in both tables, which give us an idea of how strong each campaign was in matching these three elements. It would seem that the campaigns of Taylor (1848), Cleveland (1884), and Clinton (1992) are the strongest exemplars of the model, while that of Wilson (1916) is the weakest of the successful group. Among the unsuccessful campaigns, only a handful match the numbers of the lowest successful race, that of Wilson in 1916. Indeed, the close race of Dewey against Truman in 1948 stands out again as the single clear example of an unsuccessful opposition party campaign that adhered to the model.

The importance of all three ingredients can be better understood by comparing the opposition party victories with other elections. A brief glance at the elections of the Reagan era will serve this purpose. In 1980 the governing Democrats were clearly in major trouble. Carter was a weak incumbent who drew a significant primary challenge from the liberal wing of his party in the person of Senator Ted Kennedy. Then, in the general election, he faced a threat from the center in the third-party candidacy of renegade Republican John Anderson. These problems put Carter's position in the three-star category. However, Reagan was hardly a blank slate candidate, and he waged a campaign that directly challenged core New Deal principles. His victory, then, was no deviation, but a genuine reconstruction of politics—the transformation of the GOP into the new governing party. In 1984 the GOP faced no significant threats—Reagan was a popular incumbent who faced no challenge from within his party and no third-party danger from without. Opposition leader Walter Mondale, Carter's vice president, was hardly in a position to pose as a blank slate candidate, and his pledge to raise taxes represented a direct challenge to core conservative doctrine. This makes the resulting electoral slaughter easy to understand. In 1988, there was an open race in the GOP, giving the opposition party some room for hope, but there was no significant intraparty factionalism and no third-party threat. Michael Dukakis's status as a northeastern liberal Democrat counteracted his attempt to pose as a competent manager, and Republicans were successful in playing up various cultural and social issues that had become resonant during the Reagan era. Skipping forward to 2000, the GOP did not control the White House, but neither did it face an incumbent president. Gore may have been able to pose as a blank slate candidate in 1988 or 1992, but he would have to work harder to do so following eight years of Clinton, and his choice to run a more populist campaign of "the people versus the powerful" represented a more direct assault on conservative principles than the warm embrace of the Clinton economic record would have been.

As with the opposition party victories, the governing party victories also vary in strength. The 1980 experience constitutes an echo of earlier similar elections, such as 1860 and 1932. The governing party victory in 1984 bears a close resemblance to 1964, when Lyndon Johnson's governing party Democrats began in very solid shape, then faced Barry Goldwater, the very definition of a fully defined candidate running a campaign targeting core issues. Perhaps the most intriguing elections of the past half-century are those involving the third-term understudies of opposition presidents.[3] Like 2000, the governing party in 1960 and 1976 did not control the White House. Ford, like Gore, was handicapped to some extent by the sins of his former boss; Nixon, perhaps, suffered by comparison to Eisenhower. All three opposition candidates were individuals who had cultivated moderate images at various points in their career. Where Gore veered away from an indirect campaign strategy, however, both Nixon and Ford avoided a direct confrontation with the New Deal system, their minor differences with Kennedy and Carter a stark contrast to that presented by Goldwater and Reagan just four years later, respectively. All three of these races ended up being exceptionally close contests, in contrast to the one example of a third-term understudy from the governing party during this period—George H. W. Bush in 1988. As an exercise in counterfactuals, it is interesting to speculate about what sort of success Gary Hart—the relatively unknown "new ideas" guru—would have had against Bush had he not self-destructed. The strength of the governing party in 1988 indicates that Hart would have had no easier a time than Dukakis.

It would be premature to end an analysis of presidential elections without exploring their effect on presidential leadership. The interpretation of election results is the first thing that goes into the construction of that most ephemeral of political phenomena, the mandate for action.[4] In the next section, I examine the nature of opposition party victories, beginning with a brief overview of the results of these twelve elections, then continuing with an evaluation of the political capital these new presidents acquired from their elections. I conclude with a final section examining the larger consequences of these types of victories for leadership in general, both of the president's party and its agenda, and of the nation as a whole.

Evaluating the Results

There was a huge increase in voter turnout in 1840, proving the efficacy of Whig campaign tactics. Harrison won the election in an electoral landslide, 234 to Van Buren's 60, and captured nearly 53 percent of the popular vote. Van Buren carried only two states north of the Mason-Dixon line and Ohio River (New Hampshire and Illinois), while Harrison embarrassed the Democrats by taking both New York (Van Buren's home) and Tennessee (Jackson's home). At the same time, the Whigs took control of both houses of Congress—the only time in its history the party would enjoy such a position. The Whigs were marvelously successful in ousting the governing party, but to do so they had to suppress many of the elements of their own governing philosophy. There was no sense in which the Democrats were beaten on the issues. They were simply out-organized and out-hustled during a poor economy.[5] The Whigs redefined politics for the short-term without effecting a long-term redefinition that would place them in the position of controlling the larger terms of political debate. The Whigs had learned how to play the game of politics better than the party that had originated it, but they would take power with no mandate for their own policies.

By contrast, the election of 1848 was no landslide victory for Taylor. He won 163-127 in the Electoral College, but the presence in the campaign of the Free Soilers was critical. The party took no states, but in seven states its vote exceeded the margin by which the state was won by the major party. Both Whigs and Democrats were harmed in various states, but Democratic loyalty to Van Buren made the Free Soil split especially bad for the Democrats in New York, which was carried by the Whigs.[6] The continuing status of the Whigs as an opposition party remained crystal clear at their moment of triumph, however. For the first time in history, the new president's party did not control either house of Congress. There were more Democrats than Whigs in the new Congress, with Free Soilers holding the balance of power. Once again the Whigs were successful in ousting the governing party, but once again they did so by suppressing many of the elements of their own governing philosophy. The Democrats were not beaten on the issues. The Whigs had redefined politics for the short term by focusing attention on an image. They had sold that image in different packaging to two different sections of the country. The problem now was to find a way to govern effectively without the imprimatur of an issue-based victory.

Cleveland won the presidency in 1884, beating Blaine 219-182 in the Electoral College. His plurality of the popular vote was only 30,000. The Democrats also took control of the House, but the GOP retained the Senate. Various explanations have been given for Cleveland's victory. Burchard's alliteration stands at the top of the list, but the GOP was hampered by a number of other self-inflicted wounds, most of which hurt its cause in New York. Black and rural Republicans stayed home from the polls because of bad weather. Blaine's rival, former senator Roscoe Conkling, never gave his support to the party ticket, which may have cost Blaine two thousand votes in Conkling's home county. Temperance supporters gave 25,000 New York votes to their candidate, and many may have supported Cleveland, contrary to expectations. Finally, the Mugwump defection certainly hurt the GOP in New York. Cleveland won the state by only 1,149 votes, and anti-Blaine Mugwump petitions contained thousands of signatures. Contemporary

Republicans blamed Mugwumps and attacked them, while Cleveland himself believed they contributed to his victory.[7] The narrowness of Cleveland's victory is testimony to the strength of the governing party, even when faced with great adversity. Democrats used strategies developed by the Whigs to claim the presidency for the first time in twenty-four years, taking advantage of a party that was temporarily weak, running a candidate with cross-partisan appeal, avoiding a focus on what separated the two parties, and running a campaign based on personalities instead of issues. Like the Whigs, however, the Democrats had to suppress many of the elements of their own governing philosophy to win. They did not beat the GOP on the issues. Instead, they won a battle of character attack and took advantage of GOP stupidity in the closing days of a very close campaign. They redefined politics for the short term by focusing on the personal foibles of James G. Blaine, but they in no sense effected a long-term redefinition of politics. There would be no mandate for the Democratic governing philosophy.

Cleveland captured the White House for a second time in 1892 with a strong electoral win of 277-145. He won the South, performed well in the mid-Atlantic states, and even drew strong support in the Midwest. He won a plurality of the popular vote, drawing 400,000 more than Harrison. More important, the Democrats took control of Congress, making 1892 the first time since before the Civil War that the party controlled both legislative and executive branches. Party leaders expressed the thought that a fundamental change had taken place, a revolution that had swept the GOP from power for years. What Democrats ignored by making such statements was the fact that Cleveland remained a minority president, winning only 45.8 percent of the popular vote. Populists won twenty-two electoral votes, and just over one million popular votes. All of their electoral votes were west of the Mississippi, in more traditionally Republican states. A variety of factors influenced the Populist victories, including dislike of GOP personalities and policies and emotional apprehension over the economy.[8]

The 1912 election was not even close. The Republican split made Democratic victory inevitable. An opposition candidate could not have asked for a more fortuitous situation. Wilson won over 6 million popular votes, 435 electoral votes, and forty states. Roosevelt won 4 million popular votes, 88 electoral votes, and six states. Taft came in third, with 3.5 million popular votes, eight electoral votes, and only two states. Democrats took both houses of Congress for the first time in two decades. Reform candidates Wilson and Roosevelt ran strong, seemingly creating a mandate for change. The trouble for Wilson and the Democrats was that the election results, as strongly in their favor as they were, did not represent any essential change in voting patterns. Wilson votes came from the normal Democratic constituency, just as Taft and Roosevelt together received the normal GOP vote. In fact, Wilson received just 42 percent of the popular vote, making him a minority president. As proof of the continuing GOP reign, Taft and Roosevelt together received just over 50 percent of the popular vote. Wilson's national ticket got clear majorities in only the eleven Southern states, and in twenty-five states that Wilson won he was actually beaten by the combined GOP-Progressive vote. Wilson failed to make his party the majority party in the country. He was able to take advantage of the GOP internal difficulties to define things in his favor for the short term, but in no way did he redefine politics for the long term. Republicans seemed to understand that fact most of all. The GOP Old Guard believed from the beginning of the campaign that a GOP loss under split-party conditions would not be permanently damaging. They were willing to lose in order to save the party from Roosevelt. They realized that there was a gap between the support of Roosevelt and the support of the Progressive Party. If they could let the progressive storm blow over, things would return to normal again. It was still a Republican era, and Wilson would have to govern with that in mind.[9]

In spite of the horrendous performance of the Republican Party in 1916, the GOP nearly won the race. The election was so close that it took two days for the results to be known. It appeared at first to be a GOP victory, and Wilson went to bed on election night thinking he had lost. In fact, Wilson beat Hughes by half a million popular votes, winning thirty states to Hughes's eighteen. The electoral vote, 277-254, was the closest in thirty years. The election was much closer than the electoral vote indicated. Democrats stayed strong in the Senate but barely retained control of the House, where the balance of power lay with third parties and independents. It was more a personal success for Wilson than a party success, for he ran ahead of most Democratic senatorial and gubernatorial candidates. Wilson also did not win a majority of the popular vote. Because of the presence of third parties and because the major parties finished the race so close to each other, Wilson received the support of only 49.3 percent of the voters, making him once again a minority president. Finally, Wilson won the key state of California by only 3,773 votes. Had Hughes and Johnson found a way to work together, the state would have gone Republican, and Wilson would have lost. It was an election the GOP could have won had it not been for its internal problems. Progressive Republican James R. Garfield, son of the former president, said, "The defeat of Mr. Hughes was wholly unnecessary.

Had courageous action been taken in every State and had both Mr. Hughes and the Eastern Committeemen understood the Progressive spirit of the West, we would have won an overwhelming victory."[10] Wilson remained a minority president in a Republican age. His partisan majority in Congress was gravely weakened, and his progressive allies were about to split on the issue of war.

The 1952 election was a great personal triumph for Eisenhower. He won almost 34 million popular votes, 442 electoral votes, and all but nine states, including Texas, Tennessee, Virginia, Florida, and Oklahoma. Stevenson won 27.3 million votes, 89 electoral votes, and nine states, all in the South. Eisenhower won over 55 percent of the popular vote, and the GOP took control of Congress, ensuring Eisenhower a united government for his first two years. However, Eisenhower's victory was larger than his party's victory, and he ran ahead of his party everywhere, lending credence to the suggestion that his victory was due more to personal appeal than any new loyalty to the GOP. In no way did Eisenhower weaken the partisan position of the Democratic Party. The new Republican majority was exceptionally slim. The party controlled the House by only a ten-vote margin, and the Senate by only one vote. Given that the president's party normally loses ground in midterm elections, it was likely that Eisenhower's control of Congress would not last longer than two years.[11] Eisenhower is a perfect example of candidate selection by an opposition party. Over one hundred years later, he perfected the Whig strategy of seeking a nonpartisan war hero who had a "continental reputation." As such, the 1956 results were no surprise. Eisenhower improved on his 1952 performance, getting 57 percent of the popular vote and adding Kentucky and Louisiana to his list of Southern victories. However, Eisenhower did little campaigning for GOP congressional candidates, and his party lost two additional House seats and one Senate seat. The party of the popular president failed to retake Congress, making Eisenhower the first president since Zachary Taylor—another nonpartisan war hero—to be elected to office without at least one house of Congress on his side. The election was more a vote of confidence in Eisenhower than an endorsement of the GOP.[12]

In 1968, Nixon won one of the closest elections in history, capturing 31.8 million popular votes, compared to Humphrey's 31.3 million and Wallace's 9.9 million. He won only 43.4 percent of the popular vote, virtually no gain in support since the beginning of his campaign, despite his indirect strategy, and less than a percentage point higher than Humphrey. It was the smallest percentage of the popular vote for a president since Wilson in 1912. Nixon did better in the Electoral College, ending with 301 votes to Humphrey's 191 and Wallace's 46, but he could claim no mandate, and he would take office with the support of neither house of Congress. For the first time since Taylor, a new president failed to carry either chamber. Republicans gained a handful of seats in each house, but it was not enough to end the Democratic reign. Meanwhile, the South rejected the Democrats, splitting its vote between Nixon and Wallace and giving Democrats only 31.1 percent of its vote. The combined Nixon/Wallace vote of 56.9 percent indicated a turn toward the right, but such a turn needed to be solidified by a leader willing to present choices to the population, and that did not happen in 1968. There was never a real confrontation with core issues.[13] Despite the vulnerability of the governing party, Nixon did not run a campaign that redefined politics in any fundamental way. Like the Whigs of 1840, he chose not to run an issue-based campaign. At a time of opportunity, he played it safe and even then came close to losing it all. Nixon understood the potential of making 1968 a realigning year. But the GOP learned the lessons of 1964 too well, and Nixon did not repudiate the New Deal Democracy, so he entered office as a minority president without the political capital and institutional support necessary to effect such a fundamental change. Taking into account the low popular vote percentage and lack of congressional support, Nixon entered office as the weakest of all elected opposition presidents. By contrast, Nixon won his 1972 reelection bid by a mammoth margin, winning 60.7 percent of the popular vote, beating McGovern by 18 million votes, and winning every state except Massachusetts. He won the Catholic vote, the blue-collar vote, and split the labor vote. Again, however, Nixon failed to bring either house of Congress into the GOP fold. The party gained slight ground in the House but lost two seats in the Senate, making Nixon the only president in history, to date, to win two elections without once enjoying a partisan majority in either house of Congress.[14]

In 1992, Bush suffered the worst popular defeat of an incumbent since Taft, winning eighteen states, 168 electoral votes, and just 37.4 percent of the popular vote. Perot had the best third-party showing in terms of the popular vote since 1912, claiming 18.9 percent of the vote and placing third in history for third-party performances, behind Roosevelt and Fillmore. As for the winner, Clinton won thirty-two states and 370 electoral votes, but claimed only 43 percent of the popular vote, the narrowest base for a winner since 1912, and the third-smallest since 1828. There were no Democratic gains in either chamber of Congress, and the GOP actually gained ten seats in the House, and within six months added two in the Senate. So, although

Clinton's party controlled Congress, he remained a minority president with no congressional debts to cash in.[15] The parallels with 1912 are striking. In a three-way race, an ambiguous centrist whose focus was domestic policy won a minority victory over the one-term successor to a dynamic two-term national leader, enjoying the temporary advantage of a Congress controlled by his party. Clinton ran as a "New Democrat" who sought a "third way" between polarized parties but who did so by affecting a centrist posture. He faced three difficulties with a victory of this type. First, the election was more a negative judgment of Bush than a popular endorsement of Clinton, a fact demonstrated by his low popular vote. Second, Clinton had said the election was about "change" but it was unclear what exactly constituted his mandate for change. Was it health care reform? Budget-balancing? Job creation? Clinton faced the task of finding a moderate middle at a time when the Democratic Party was becoming more liberal and the GOP more conservative. Finally, because Clinton enjoyed unified government, the public expected effective governance. Given that difficult and severely constrained context, it was imperative that Clinton choose a governing strategy that would allow him to work with Congress without appearing to repudiate what remained a fairly robust governing party.

Clinton won reelection handily in 1996, winning 379 electoral votes to Dole's 159 and thirty-one states to Dole's nineteen. However, the election saw the lowest turnout since 1924, falling below 50 percent of the voting age population, and Clinton obtained only 49 percent of the popular vote, compared to 41 percent for Dole and 8 percent for Perot. The GOP lost nine House seats, but it gained two in the Senate. Clinton remained a minority president, the first since Wilson to win two terms with a majority voting against him both times and the first Democrat in history to be elected facing a GOP Congress. The political debate was still defined in Republican terms, with Clinton differing from those terms only in degree, not in kind. He had shifted to the right for political survival, and he succeeded.[16] Clinton came to power on the strength of a classic opposition president campaign, but misunderstood his electoral victory by presuming to employ a power—that of redefining the terms of political debate—that he did not possess. Once his limitations became apparent to him, Clinton chose to redefine himself. His deliberate step to the right enabled him to steal core issues from the governing party, and the sometimes excessive actions of the governing party allowed Clinton to pose as the moderate defender of what were often Reaganite virtues. Clinton's strategy helped him become the fourth twentieth-century opposition president to win reelection. His strategy did not bode well for his party, however, which endured three successive congresses as the minority, its worst long-term performance since the 1920s.

Given this narrative summary of results, a more systematic analysis is necessary to make comparisons easier. The larger question concerning these victorious opposition party campaigns is the strength of the winning candidate's political base, and that in turn points to their relative political weakness. Taylor was the first president to win an election with both houses of Congress controlled by the other party, a feat matched only by Eisenhower, Nixon, Bush, and Clinton. All but Bush were opposition presidents. Nixon remains the only president to have won two elections without ever enjoying a partisan majority in either house of Congress. Cleveland, Wilson, and Clinton are the only twice-elected presidents never to capture a majority of the popular vote. What do such performances say about the mandate for action all new presidents covet? Tables 5-3 through 5-6 represent an attempt to describe the constrained context opposition presidents face at the beginning of their terms, constraints in many ways reinforced by the conduct of opposition campaigns. Table 5-3 lists, in descending rank order, the highest and lowest quintiles of winning presidential candidates by percentage of popular vote, based on the forty-five presidential elections since 1828. Table 5-4 lists the popular vote advantage enjoyed by the top and bottom winning candidates over their nearest rivals, also in descending rank order. Tables 5-5 and 5-6 describe the same information for the electoral vote results. Opposition presidents are listed in italics.[17]

Presidents love to declare mandates for action, usually based on election results. The practice is at best suspect, but if political and media elites focus attention on such things, then the definition of election results becomes an important part of a president's political capital. Tables 5-3 through 5-6 present four different possible measurements of presidential mandates, focused in this case on the extremes—those who enjoyed the strongest claim to a mandate and those who enjoyed the weakest. In terms of both popular vote victory and electoral vote victory, opposition presidents are underrepresented in the highest quintile. Twelve of the forty-five surveyed elections—27 percent—resulted in opposition party victories, but victorious opposition party candidates comprise only two of the highest quintile of popular vote results and electoral vote results, a slightly lower rate of just 22 percent. In both cases, the top-performing opposition candidates were Nixon in 1972 and Eisenhower in 1956. Both represent reelections of incumbent presidents, one an extremely popular war hero and the other an incumbent running against a governing party in crisis. The same two opposition victories appear in the

TABLE 5-3:
Highest and Lowest Quintiles of Popular Vote Results, 1828–2004

Year	Winning Candidate	Percentage of Popular Vote	Rank
1964	Johnson	61.1	1
1936	Roosevelt	60.8	2
1972	*Nixon*	*60.7*	*3*
1920	Harding	60.3	4
1984	Reagan	58.8	5
1928	Hoover	58.2	6
1932	Roosevelt	57.4	7
1956	*Eisenhower*	*57.4*	*8*
1904	Roosevelt	56.4	9
.	.	.	.
.	.	.	.
.	.	.	.
2000	Bush	47.9	37
1888	Harrison	47.8	38
1848	*Taylor*	*47.3*	*39*
1892	*Cleveland*	*46.1*	*40*
1856	Buchanan	45.3	41
1968	*Nixon*	*43.4*	*42*
1992	*Clinton*	*43.0*	*43*
1912	*Wilson*	*41.8*	*44*
1860	Lincoln	39.8	45

Source: Jerrold G. Rusk, *A Statistical History of the American Electorate*, p. 132; adapted and updated by author.

highest quintile of electoral vote margins, but only 1972 (Nixon) appears in the highest quintile of popular vote margins, a rate of just 11 percent. By contrast, three of the highest quintile of popular vote winners and five of the highest quintile of electoral vote winners are reconstructors at various stages of their careers.

Opposition presidents are overrepresented in the lowest quintile of three of these measures. Victorious opposition party candidates comprise five of the lowest quintile of popular vote results (56 percent) and four of the low-

TABLE 5-4:
Highest and Lowest Quintiles of Popular Vote Margins, 1828–2004

Year	Winning Candidate	Popular Vote Advantage*	Rank
1920	Harding	26.2	1
1924	Coolidge	25.2	2
1936	Roosevelt	24.3	3
1972	Nixon	23.2	4
1964	Johnson	22.6	5
1904	Roosevelt	18.8	6
1984	Reagan	18.2	7
1932	Roosevelt	17.8	8
1928	Hoover	17.5	9
.	.	.	.
.	.	.	.
.	.	.	.
1976	Carter	2.1	37
1844	Polk	1.5	38
1968	Nixon	0.7	39
1884	Cleveland	0.3	40
1960	Kennedy	0.2	41
1880	Garfield	0.02	42
2000	Bush	–0.5	43
1888	Harrison	–0.8	44
1876	Hayes	–3.0	45

*Percentage point difference between winning candidate and nearest rival.

Source: Jerrold G. Rusk, *A Statistical History of the American Electorate*, p. 132; adapted and updated by author.

est quintile of electoral vote results (44 percent). Due to varying outcomes caused by the differences between popular vote and electoral vote totals, the identities of these lower-ranking winners differ slightly according to criteria. The multiparty races of 1892 (Cleveland), 1912 (Wilson), and 1992 (Clinton), which resulted in low popular vote victories, appear on the popular vote list but not on the electoral vote list. On the other hand, the extremely close elections of 1848 (Taylor) and 1968 (Nixon) appear on both. When considering the electoral vote margins enjoyed by the winners, three of the

TABLE 5-5:
Highest and Lowest Quintiles of Electoral Vote Results, 1828–2004

Year	Winning Candidate	Percentage of Electoral Vote	Rank
1936	Roosevelt	98.5	1
1984	Reagan	97.6	2
1972	*Nixon*	*96.7*	*3*
1980	Reagan	90.9	4
1864	Lincoln	90.6	5
1964	Johnson	90.3	6
1932	Roosevelt	88.9	7
1956	*Eisenhower*	*86.1*	*8*
1852	Pierce	85.8	9
.	.	.	.
.	.	.	.
.	.	.	.
1960	Kennedy	56.4	37
1848	*Taylor*	*56.2*	*38*
1968	*Nixon*	*56.0*	*39*
1976	Carter	55.2	40
1884	*Cleveland*	*54.6*	*41*
2004	Bush	53.2	42
1916	*Wilson*	*52.2*	*43*
2000	Bush	50.4	44
1876	Hayes	50.1	45

Source: Jerrold G. Rusk, *A Statistical History of the American Electorate*, p. 132; adapted and updated by author.

same four opposition presidents appear in the lowest quintile as appear in the lowest quintile of electoral vote winners, with 1968 (Nixon) just missing the bottom quintile. In terms of the popular vote margins, however, there is some variation. The elections of 1848, 1912, and 1992 do not appear in the lowest quintile of popular vote margins, but 1892 and 1916 just miss the list. The election of 1884 also ranks in the bottom quintile of popular vote margins. To present these differences more clearly, table 5-7 lays out

TABLE 5-6:
Highest and Lowest Quintiles of Electoral Vote Margins, 1828–2004

Year	Winning Candidate	Electoral Vote Advantage*	Rank
1936	Roosevelt	97.0	1
1984	Reagan	95.2	2
1972	*Nixon*	*93.5*	*3*
1980	Reagan	81.8	4
1864	Lincoln	81.6	5
1964	Johnson	80.7	6
1932	Roosevelt	77.8	7
1956	*Eisenhower*	*72.3*	*8*
1852	Pierce	71.6	9
.	.	.	.
.	. .	.	.
.	.	.	.
1880	Garfield	16.0	37
1960	Kennedy	15.6	38
1848	*Taylor*	*12.4*	*39*
1976	Carter	10.6	40
1884	*Cleveland*	*9.2*	*41*
2004	Bush	6.5	42
1916	*Wilson*	*4.3*	*43*
2000	Bush	0.9	44
1876	Hayes	0.3	45

*Percentage point difference between winning candidate and nearest rival.

Source: Jerrold G. Rusk, *A Statistical History of the American Electorate*, p. 132; adapted and updated by author.

the four measurement options for all of the winning candidates who appear somewhere in the lowest quintiles of these criteria. Candidates are listed in chronological order; opposition party winners are listed in italics.

It would seem that very few opposition presidents enjoy even the option of proclaiming a mandate. Eisenhower's 1952 election merits consideration as a strong victory since it ranks above average on all four measures, but

TABLE 5-7:
Winning Candidate Appearances in Lowest Quintile Mandate Measures

Year	Winning Candidate	Popular Vote Results	Popular Vote Margins	Electoral Vote Results	Electoral Vote Margins	Total Appearances
1844	Polk	X				1
1848	Taylor	X		X	X	3
1856	Buchanan	X				1
1860	Lincoln	X				1
1876	Hayes		X	X	X	3
1880	Garfield		X		X	2
1884	Cleveland		X	X	X	3
1888	Harrison	X	X			2
1892	Cleveland	X				1
1912	Wilson	X				1
1916	Wilson			X	X	2
1960	Kennedy		X	X	X	3
1968	Nixon	X	X	X		3
1976	Carter		X	X	X	3
1992	Clinton	X				1
2000	Bush	X	X	X	X	4
2004	Bush			X	X	2

Source: Calculated by author from Rusk, *Statistical History,* p. 132.

that means just three opposition party victories to date—1952, 1956, and 1972—can be considered truly strong, and two of those belong to the popular general. Harrison's 1840 election ranks better than the midpoint on three measures, while Clinton's 1996 reelection is slightly lower. As table 5-7 indicates, the other seven opposition party victories all fall into the lowest quintile in some respect, with the elections of 1848, 1884, and 1968 faring the worst. From a simple numerical perspective, seven of twelve opposition party victories falling into this low range constitute a rate of over 58 percent. By contrast, only ten of thirty-three governing party victories fall into this range, a rate of just 30 percent, about half that of the opposition party. Clearly, opposition presidents are much less likely to be able to claim a mandate for action than governing party presidents.

TABLE 5-8:
Divided Government as Institutional Constraint, 1828–2008

	President of Governing Party	President of Opposition Party
United Government	88 of 128 years–69%	14 of 52 years–27%
Divided Government	40 of 128 years–31%	38 of 52 years–73%

The problem of political capital and the limitations on freedom of action for opposition presidents is only compounded by the issue of institutional control.[18] Governing and opposition party presidents face different experiences in the area of partisan control of institutions. Divided government tends to be one artifact of oppositional status. It exacerbates the problem of mandates outlined above and serves as a convenient symbol of the constraints faced by opposition presidents. Table 5-8 demonstrates that fact, indicating how often governing party and opposition party presidents experience divided government. Governing party presidents have been in power for 128 of the past 180 years (counting from 1828 through 2008). In that time, governing party presidents have experienced united government for 69 percent of their terms and divided government for 31 percent of their terms. The situation is almost the mirror image for opposition presidents, who experience united government for only 27 percent of their terms and divided government for 73 percent of their terms. While divided government has become much more of a problem for governing party presidents in the Reagan era, the situation for opposition presidents remains similar to that experienced in earlier eras. This dramatic difference is an indication of the constraints opposition presidents face by not commanding the power to define politics.

Political Strategies, Political Agendas, and Political Time

As titular party leaders, opposition presidents should be as concerned with the core agenda of their party as any other president, and it is here that the consequences of the electoral strategy outlined in this book become all too apparent. Having won the electoral game playing by rules not of its own choosing, the opposition party often finds that it does not get what it was hoping for. It is often faced with a leader not wholly committed to the party's core agenda, coming to power in a context that would not allow for a strong mandate even if the new opposition president *did* want to pursue the party's core agenda.

To a certain extent, this problem is not as troubling as it might first appear. All opposition presidents face a choice between two governing strategies. For the advocate of the party's core agenda, the natural inclination is to launch a full frontal assault on the governing party in an attempt to achieve ideological and policy victory. The problem with this strategy is that, however weak the governing party is due to short-term factors, the long-term grain of history still runs in its favor. We can think of such notions as realignments or regime reconstructions as national conversations during times of crisis during which the people recreate their political world. Presidents are most free to exercise energetic national leadership at these times, and their actions tend to set the direction of American politics for the long term. The agenda-setting aspect of national leadership remains with the governing party. Opposition presidents are constrained by the fact that the political system does not require a change in course when they are elected, and seeking dramatic change often leads to negative consequences. Thus, the second governing strategy is the preferred option for the opposition president—pursue a more indirect approach in favor of moderation, usually through tempering the party's ideological agenda by trimming the edges of the reigning governing philosophy or even finding grounds for compromise.[19] This governing strategy seems to be tailor-made for presidents who run as blank slate candidates in campaigns that avoid the core issue differences between the parties.

The problem is that history is not so neat and simple. Matching personalities and leadership agendas to historical context is a complex process that often depends on events beyond anyone's control. Even the wisest party sage may have difficulty discerning the difference between a governing party that is in short-term trouble and one that is collapsing—but when comparing 1980 to 1992, it is exceptionally important to figure out that the first scenario provides for the opportunity for reconstruction while the second does not. Add to that the fact that party purists are most resistant to compromise, and the delicate leadership challenge that awaits the opposition president becomes clear. To clarify this dynamic, a brief sketch of the leadership experiences of these elected opposition presidents is in order.[20] This account highlights the cross-pressures and conflicting incentives that face all opposition presidents and their parties.

In the area of obtaining office, the Whigs were the model for future opposition leaders. They understood that, even in an electoral era that did not favor their party, there were certain years that simply were not good "Democrat years," and the party took advantage of them. Whether the governing party faced the misfortune of being in power during an economic downturn or dealing with recalcitrant factions that would not toe the line, the opposition Whigs were quick to seize their opportunity. They understood that highlighting their differences with the governing party was not the best strategy for achieving power, so they nominated military heroes whose issue positions were either restrained or unknown. They were nonpartisan blank slates upon which voters could write their own visions of the candidates. The party sought to suppress ideological purity through the absence of party platforms, and it often chose to focus its campaign efforts on personalities and character, not on traditional Whig doctrines. The success of this strategy is evidenced by the lack of success of the one man who could lay legitimate claim to being the true opposition leader of the Jacksonian era—Henry Clay. Clay failed to obtain the nomination of the Whig party as many times as he failed to win the presidency as a candidate. The major reason for this failure lies in the fact that Clay never commanded the terms of political debate, yet he always fought against them. Clay was a true believer who could never be portrayed as a blank slate candidate, nor could he be seen as someone who would simply tinker at the edges of the reigning governing philosophy. He was too closely associated with his own American System and opposition to the Jacksonian way. He had an ambitious agenda that ran counter to the reigning governing philosophy.

Clay is the political figure who demonstrates the constrained leadership dynamic that accompanies opposition leadership. After waging the paradigmatic indirect campaign in 1840, the Whig party greatly desired to enact important measures, and winning both the White House and Congress seemed to enable them to do just that. However, the election of 1840 was won by stressing Harrison's personal virtues—his honesty, integrity, courage, and public spirit. After a campaign based on his qualifications, he was then expected to allow Congress and Henry Clay to seize the initiative. Harrison, of course, was not in office long enough to lead much of anything, but he seems to have had some understanding of his constrained historical context, and in his short month he succeeded in antagonizing his principal Whig ally in Congress. Clay expected to serve as a type of prime minister, acting as the energizing force behind the Whig agenda, with Harrison following his lead. He failed to realize that it is the president who is the leader of his party, and he retains an inherent constitutional power even if he is seen as a cipher. There are indications, however, that Harrison was not prepared to allow Clay to run things from Congress. Harrison's death leaves the question open, but his successor, John Tyler, was in office only a few months before he reverted to his Democratic roots and repudiated his party's program. Most of his cabinet resigned and his party expelled him. The "president without a party" ended up supporting the rival Democrats. The Whigs were the first party to learn how difficult it is for opposition parties to effect change despite electoral success. This problem was self-inflicted. After running a campaign that avoided the core issue differences that divided the parties, the Whigs chose to govern as though they had the power to reconstruct politics—forgetting that the individuals they put in power to win the election were not inclined to move in that direction.

Things were little better with Taylor. The general who wanted independence in a campaign free of party doctrine got a presidency free of party control of Congress. His personal candidacy became a personal presidency. Like Harrison and Tyler, Taylor experienced tremendous tension with Whig leaders, including Clay. In working out the Compromise of 1850, which sought to settle a variety of issues arising from the Mexican War, Taylor and Clay engaged in fierce intrapartisan war, allowing the issue to be defined and managed by Democrats. At one point Vice President Millard Fillmore was forced to inform his boss that, should the vote end in a tie in the Senate, he might support Taylor's enemies. Taylor's own willingness to consider renaming the Whigs the "Republican" Party testifies to his self-image in his party. When Taylor died prematurely, Fillmore helped resolve the crisis, but his own support of the Fugitive Slave Act exacerbated the partisan rifts that soon destroyed the Whigs. In both cases, then, Whig presidents were elected who were generally free of long-standing commitments to the party's core agenda. Although this enabled the party to capture the White House, it created significant tension with congressional partisans who actually wanted to move on their policy agenda. The party seemingly forgot the constrained nature of its own victory. The Whigs were the first to learn that electoral success does not guarantee partisan good fortune.

Grover Cleveland was certainly successful in electoral politics, remaining one of only three men to win the popular vote in three successive elections. Following the example set by the Whigs, Cleveland ran a classic opposition campaign to take office and then managed to conduct a fairly successful first term as president. Although he experienced some tensions with his party, he charted a fairly moderate course at a time when moderation was rewarded. The historical context changed when he won his second term in 1892. Whenever a party wins both elective branches of the government after a long drought, there is a temptation to assume more from the election results than is actually merited. Without exception, success for a party or president depends on an accurate understanding of the political context of the victory. In 1840, victorious Whigs took control of both branches, assumed they had the political power to effect dramatic change, and soon found themselves chastened when the governing party had other ideas. In 1892, the Democrats faced a more ambiguous situation. The presence of a third-party movement in the West pointed to an opportunity for Cleveland and the Democrats to redefine politics and seize control of the long-term agenda-setting power of the government. Discontent was there, the Republican base was threatened, and soon an economic depression would change the rules of the game. To take advantage of such an opportunity, however, the party would need a leader who could adapt to such a situation through imagination and flexibility, preferably running a campaign that called for dramatic change.

Cleveland would not prove to be such a man. He was, after all, essentially the same man who ran as a blank slate candidate in 1884—a moderate centrist with little vested in the long-term interests of the party. Cleveland's primary rift with his party came with the issue of currency. At a time when free silver was growing in importance in Democratic circles, Cleveland remained a staunch supporter of the gold standard. After fighting some battles over gold and silver in his first presidency, Cleveland fell on his sword over the issue in his second. Offered a compromise by his own party leaders in Congress on the question of repeal of the Sherman Silver Purchase Act, Cleveland stubbornly refused, effecting the repeal with Republican help against the core of his own party. He had an opportunity to mend party fences the following year by supporting a moderate measure authorizing a small amount of silver coinage. Congressional Democrats personally appealed to Cleveland to sign the measure as a gesture of party unity. Instead, Cleveland angrily vetoed the measure, prompting Democrats to charge that he had violated Democratic precepts of executive power. Cleveland's exercise of executive power against the Pullman strikers further embittered his fellow partisans. Things deteriorated to the point that Senate Democrats rejected two of Cleveland's Supreme Court nominations. He was referred to as "Judas Iscariot" by more than one party leader, and his party utterly repudiated him in 1896, prompting him to support a third-party movement that would ensure his own party's defeat.

The twentieth-century opposition presidents did not experience quite the level of conflict evidenced by their nineteenth-century predecessors, but their actions still generated significant tension with their coalitions in Congress and often frustrated their parties' policy agendas. For example, much as Clay's Whigs sought significant policy achievements when they enjoyed united government in 1841, so Old Guard Republicans envisioned ambitious moves when Eisenhower led united Republican government in 1953. Harrison's reputation as a war hero in many ways had been manufactured. Taylor had the virtue of demonstrating physical courage, but he did not have broad appeal in every sector of the country. In terms of having a continental reputation, Eisenhower was the genuine item. However, despite his strong electoral victory and despite his party's control of Congress, Eisenhower resisted a direct frontal assault on Roosevelt's achievement. He understood the dangers of such a move and stood firm in the face of pleas for more bold action. His moderate policies were derided by conservatives as "Just a Republican New Deal," and on national security issues such as the proposed Bricker Amendment, which would have placed limits on the president's power to make treaties and executive agreements, Eisenhower required the assistance of Democrats to defeat his own party. Although personally conservative, Eisenhower constantly experienced tension from his right, and his talk of "New" or "Modern" Republicanism was an attempt to remake his party along more moderate lines. The general consensus by scholars is that Eisenhower helped consolidate the transformation in politics brought by the New Deal, making it part of the national consensus. Ultimately he failed to lead his party in a new direction, and upon his departure the GOP began its shift toward Goldwater and Reagan.

Clinton is the twentieth-century opposition president most similar to Eisenhower in terms of context. Both men began their presidencies with two years of united government, losing control for the duration at the first midterm election. After running a campaign that in many ways adhered to the principles outlined in this book, Clinton began his presidency pursuing a largely purist policy agenda that fit well with core Democratic elements—liberalized abortion policies, public works projects, and an ambitious health care reform effort. At the same time, however, Clinton exacerbated relations with labor, one of his core constituencies, with his support of the North American Free Trade Agreement, passage of which required congressional Republican help against a majority in his own party. To salvage his reelection prospects following the disastrous midterm election in 1994, Clinton shifted to the right, supporting deficit reduction, welfare reform, and a number of traditional values issues, including the Defense of Marriage Act. In his 1996 State of the Union Address he stated that "the era of big government is over," a rhetorical flourish that could have come from the lips of Reagan himself. He was excoriated by many Democrats for what they perceived to be an abandonment of principle on welfare reform, he ratcheted up tensions with his party leaders in Congress when he cut budget deals with Republicans in 1997, and those same leaders repudiated his effort to secure "fast track" authority to negotiate trade agreements. Just as some argue that Eisenhower furthered the New Deal agenda, so disgruntled cabinet official Robert Reich argued that Clinton had "fulfilled the Republicans' own unfinished agenda."[21] Like other opposition presidents, Clinton's electoral strategy conflicted with his and his party's policy agenda. When he recognized his political danger, Clinton shifted back to the normative strategy outlined above—classic moderation—but that only succeeded in exacerbating relations with both sides of the aisle. Clinton's pursuit of a tempered agenda did not always bode well for his political fortunes. One can make a strong argument that by claiming key GOP agenda items as his own and taking credit for them, Clinton only served to anger the governing party more, making him continually susceptible to attack.

The presidential election of 1968 had the potential to be a great reconstruction. Another Republican candidate might have attempted to join a redefinition of politics to the change in partisan systems and become the next Lincoln or Roosevelt, but not Nixon, and not the GOP. Republicans remained haunted by the specter of 1964, so they ran an opposition campaign. Nixon's campaign strategy, and the subsequent results of the election, caused him to enter office without the political capital or institutional support necessary to repudiate the reigning governing philosophy. He was forced into the position of opposition leader, and a very constrained version of one at that, for unlike the Whigs in 1840 he did not even command a majority in Congress. Yet for Nixon to transform politics, he would have had to govern in a manner different from the way he had campaigned, for tempered pursuits are not the stuff of which redefinitions are made. It would have required an open strategy of party strengthening, policy development, and ideological leadership, all of which would have been very difficult given the context of Nixon's victory. Nixon himself claims to have been interested in the notion of an "emerging Republican majority," and he writes that he was interested in using his power to enhance the electoral prospects of the GOP and "revitalize the Republican Party along New Majority lines." Apparently, strengthening the party was one of his top reform items for his second term.[22]

Instead, of the twentieth-century opposition presidents, Nixon did the most damage to his party and its agenda. His claims were at odds with his actions. Although Nixon did make moves to appeal to Wallace supporters, his campaign in 1968 made a reconstruction project very difficult. Rather than pursue an open strategy of partisan change, Nixon pursued a clandestine one. In his first term he proposed a mammoth expansion of the New Deal state through a negative income tax. He uttered the heretical statement "I am now a Keynesian in economics" and then instituted wage and price controls. He established a large number of new federal regulatory programs, including the Environmental Protection Agency. He flabbergasted his anti-communist allies by opening the door to China and instituting détente with the Soviet Union. Finally, he essentially abandoned his role as party leader in the elections of 1970 and 1972, proving unwilling to support his party in the former and focusing more on personal victory in the latter. Biographer Stephen Ambrose argues that Nixon became the politician "least interested in party and most concerned about personality."[23] At the same time Nixon was warmly embracing the New Deal system, he pursued a secret agenda to undermine it through illegal means.[24] Assuming his interest in strengthening the GOP was genuine, Nixon's actions during the Watergate scandal greatly harmed his party in the next two election cycles.[25]

The one seeming outlier of all the opposition presidents is Wilson, but we must remember the circumstances surrounding his victories. Twice he received a minority of the popular vote, and twice he benefited from facing a divided opponent. Wilson was uncommonly well matched for electoral victory. He came to political prominence at a time when a progressive strain ran through both parties, one identified with the best known politician of the day, Theodore Roosevelt. By running as a progressive Democrat against Roosevelt, Wilson could not help but appear moderate. The cross-partisan pressures placed on both parties allowed Wilson to play the part of the ambiguous centrist, letting the governing party self-destruct while masking the historic differences between the two major parties with a progressive cloak. Wilson did not alter the basic electoral alignment that had been forged in the 1890s, nor did he change the essential nature of the successful opposition candidacy. He simply put a new spin on how to pursue it. As president Wilson proved to be an adept party leader in his first term, forging significant domestic achievements as the leader of his team in Congress. Despite his successes, however, Wilson never succeeded in strengthening his party's electoral position, losing significant ground in 1914 and barely winning reelection in 1916. He accomplished his second victory by promising to keep the country out of war, but he was unable to keep that promise. When the institutional context turned against him in 1918, he retained the loyalty of most of his party in Congress but failed to listen to their counsel in the disastrous debate over the Treaty of Versailles. Wilson forged what became an intensely personal presidency, leading to policy failure and a huge electoral defeat in 1920.

The central issue remains that of context. While presidents such as Taylor, Cleveland, Wilson, and Nixon had no claim to a mandate in various years, Harrison, Eisenhower, and Clinton fared little better. The reason lies not so much with numerical measurements of mandates as it does with the context and conduct of campaigns. The historical data suggest that opposition parties that want to win elections when governing parties are still resilient must follow the prescriptions laid out in this book. Such a victory requires first and foremost some temporary crisis in the governing party, but it must be followed with a strong effort to reduce the distance between the two parties, and even then victory is not assured. Victory in the election then positions the new opposition president to succeed at a strategy of moderation, which is precisely the governing strategy recommended for a president in this context. The problem with this prescription is that while it makes electoral victory more likely for the opposition party, it does not lend itself to the type of governing and leadership most chief executives desire. Few presidents relish the notion that their policy options are limited and their leadership constrained, especially if they are presidents who want to push their party's core agenda. Yet opposition party candidates from Harrison to Clinton—blank slate candidates who seek an image of moderation and avoid core issue differences—run campaigns that by their very nature limit their policy options once they are in office. Everything about successful opposition party campaigns hampers the opposition president's ability to pursue his party's ideological objectives. The campaigns are run by individuals who do not highlight the long-term core issues that divide the parties, and they tend to result in narrow victories. This dynamic eliminates any pretense that a mandate for change exists, even in landslide victories like those of Eisenhower and Nixon. The way the campaigns are conducted prevents the president from obtaining the political capital necessary for dramatic change. Thus, parties and their candidates are faced with a catch-22. If the opposition president decides to pursue significant policy success, he will not win. The pursuit of policy success on core issues will come at the expense of stability, system energy, and success itself. If the opposition president decides to pursue moderation instead, as the context of his victory requires, he may achieve tempered success, but that success will often come with intrapartisan tension.

The opposition president is not to be blamed for this conundrum. It appears that the only way for opposition party candidates to win is to play the game according to the rules established by the governing party. When running against the grain of history, successful opposition party candidates must run *with* the grain. Yet by playing the game according to governing party rules, the opposition party only reinforces those rules. Thus, having been shrewd enough to understand what is required for electoral victory, the new opposition president must now be wise enough to recognize what is possible for his time and what is not. The party and its leader must think strategically. Sometimes the purists seize the agenda and try to achieve long-term victory, to their detriment. The Whigs in 1841 forgot that Harrison's election constituted no repudiation of Jacksonian politics. They overreached, and paid the price. Clinton did the same thing in his first two years of office, and the consequences for him and his party were severe. The less ideological opposition presidents guard against the natural tendency to overreach in their ambition for policy success, but the result is inevitable tension with the party's core. Despite his distaste for the New Deal system, Eisenhower suppressed goals he knew were unattainable at the time and sought a more tempered agenda, but he constantly battled the conservative anchor of his party and never succeeded in transforming the party into his image.

There is one alternative to this prescription, and that is to pursue from the outset a purist campaign like that of Goldwater in 1964. The lesson of this analysis is that electoral victory is possible for opposition parties under certain circumstances, but that victory tends to be a very short-term one that expires when the opposition president leaves the scene, if not before. The Goldwater strategy points to a different model for a different kind of success. By highlighting the core differences between the parties and running a vigorous campaign based on those principles, Goldwater hid nothing. It should be no great mystery why immediate partisan victory was out of the question. However, the Goldwater campaign laid the foundation for future long-term victory by setting the stage for Ronald Reagan. Goldwater helped mobilize a new movement of conservative Republicans who organized for future elections, gaining in strength in the 1970s until circumstances allowed them to come to power with Reagan's victory. No history of Reagan's success would be complete without dealing with the foundation laid by Goldwater. Of course, Goldwater's heirs had to wait sixteen years before they achieved victory. Rarely are political parties or presidential candidates willing to look several election cycles into the future for success. In the short-sighted world of instant gratification that often seems to be associated with the quest for power, such a long-term perspective must seem like an eternity. Thus, the parties fall back to the time-honored Whig model for opposition success. Perhaps a deeper understanding of its dangers and consequences will lead to greater practical wisdom, on the part of both the opposition president and his fellow partisans.

AFTERWORD ON
THE 2004 ELECTION

The analysis in this book sheds light on the question of how candidates from the disadvantaged party in a specific electoral era win the office. Its use of history helps illuminate the patterns and cycles many scholars perceive in American politics. The true test for any model of politics, however, is how that model looks when applied to new cases. This model explains how Whig candidates won during the Jacksonian era and how Republican candidates won during the New Deal era. It could just as easily be applied, in a reverse analysis, to determine why opposition party candidates do *not* win. If the analysis of regime cycle theorists is correct, we currently live in a conservative "Reagan era." Just as this account explained what Bill Clinton had to do to win as a Democrat in 1992, so we can use this analysis to understand later elections. The most recent test of this model was the presidential election of 2004. The argument in this book allows us to place that election into a broader context to understand the difficulties faced by Senator John Kerry as he sought to defeat the Republican incumbent, President George W. Bush. Kerry's defeat should be explainable, at least in part, by a failure to meet the standards established by previously successful opposition presidents.

The first key to opposition party victory is that the governing party should be in political trouble. There should be some preexisting weakness in the governing party that gives the opposition party its opportunity. Certainly 2004 did not look like the 1920s (when Democrats had no realistic chance to win) or the 1930s (when Republicans had no realistic chance to win). Republicans were hardly invulnerable. A brief recession early in Bush's presidency transitioned into sometimes anemic and at best staggered progress in job creation that seemed to indicate possible weakness on the economic front. Nevertheless, the economic situation hardly compared to the recession that hammered Van Buren in 1840 or even the recession that harmed Bush's father in 1992. In fact, the economic data were solid enough that most elections forecasters predicted a Bush victory.[1] Complicating matters was the fact that Bush was a war president. In this area he joined an interesting list of previous regime managers who presided over wars—a list that should not have given Bush great comfort. James Madison, heir to the Jeffersonian regime, won reelection in 1812 but had some difficulty, in large part because of the unpopularity of the War of 1812. James K. Polk, manager of the Jacksonian system, engaged in an adventure in Mexico that helped cost his party victory in 1848. Harry Truman and Lyndon Johnson, operating in the shadow of FDR, both opted out of reelection bids due to unpopularity over wars in Korea and Vietnam. Even Bush's father, serving a type of third Reagan term, failed to extend his post–Gulf War popularity to the domestic arena. Clearly the penchant for foreign adventures some regime managers seem to possess places them on shaky electoral grounds. In Bush's case, however, the war in Iraq was tied to the larger war on terror, itself inaugurated by the terrorist strikes of September 11, 2001. Although the war in Iraq remained very controversial, it did so in a very partisan way without splitting the GOP. Bush maintained credibility on the larger war on terror throughout the election contest.

In fact, Bush's principal weakness was his placement within the Reagan regime.[2] Bush was a late-regime manager, coming to power twenty years after the regime's founding, after the governing party had already lost control once. In historical context he looks most similar to Polk, Benjamin Harrison, Harding, and Kennedy—all presidents who attempted to apply the orthodoxy of the regime founders to new circumstances. Although Reagan faced a Democrat-controlled House, he was in a stronger position politically than Bush because he was able to play off of the stagflation of the 1970s, the Iranian hostage crisis, the Soviet invasion of Afghanistan, and the growing controversies over values issues. At best, Bush could promise to return the nation to the right path, both in the area of policies and "restoring honor and dignity" to the White House. He could not promise to change Reagan's direction. Reagan came to power on the strength of three major policy arenas. In the area of foreign policy, he was a fierce anticommunist. By 2000, however, communism was all but dead. History gave a tragic gift to Bush in the 9-11 attacks, allowing him to transform a vigorous foreign policy designed to end the Cold War into a new foreign policy designed to combat international terrorism. Reagan's second policy strength was in the area of economics, broadly defined as the combination of tax cuts to rejuvenate the economy and program cuts to reduce the size of government. By 2000, however, deficits had been conquered and the nation faced surpluses for the foreseeable future. Bush's 2001 tax cut plan can be considered the capstone of the Reagan economic revolution while his attempts to create an "ownership society" continued the effort to transform New Deal institutions in Reaganesque ways. The problem for Bush was that his efforts to complete the Reagan revolution took place when the baby boom generation was twenty years closer to retirement than they were when Reagan himself first fought these battles, and it remains unclear which party will benefit more politically from the swift return of large deficits. Finally, Reagan derived strength from the mobilization of social conservatives, highlighting one of the major fault lines of American society in the area of moral values.

Having said all of that, it must be noted that Bush benefited greatly by enjoying one thing that most other governing party presidents who fall victim to opposition candidates do not—a party lockstep in his camp. Vermont Senator Jim Jeffords's defection from the GOP in 2001 was the only real intrapartisan problem President Bush faced in his first term. Unlike most of the cases outlined in chapter 2, he faced no internal threat to the nomination and no significant third-party threat from the center. One would have thought that the context of his disputed election victory in 2000 would draw potential challengers out into the open, but the president led Republicans to increased congressional strength in the midterm elections of 2002, enjoyed stratospheric approval ratings from his own partisans (in the face of hellish ratings from Democrats), and was remarkably successful at managing the various stress points listed above to secure renomination by acclamation. There was no Theodore Roosevelt, Eugene McCarthy, or Pat Buchanan threatening him from within the party, and no Martin Van Buren, George Wallace, or Ross Perot assaulting him from without. No one would deny that Bush had some weaknesses in 2004, but a divided home base was not one of them, and that worked to Kerry's disadvantage.

The second key to opposition party victory is that the opposition party standard-bearer should be a blank slate candidate. That is, he should be a candidate who is ambiguous enough in his political beliefs and policy agenda that he allows voters from a variety of perspectives to write their own image of the candidate in their minds. He should not be readily labeled a purist candidate. For a Democrat in 2004, it was important not to be easily labeled a liberal in a conservative age. Very clearly one of Kerry's critical weaknesses was the ease with which Republican forces could label him a Massachusetts liberal. The February 28, 2004, *National Journal* feature ranking Kerry as the most liberal senator for 2003 (and running mate John Edwards as the fourth-most liberal senator) gave the Bush campaign fuel that lasted until election day as it consistently compared Kerry to Massachusetts' more "conservative" senator, Edward Kennedy. Much ink has been spilled demonstrating that the *National Journal* rankings are more ambiguous in interpretation—but those nuances were utterly irrelevant from a political perspective.[3] One demonstration that the 2004 election was still part of the Reagan era was Kerry's response to the *National Journal* story. Instead of embracing the label, as any conservative senator would have done in a similar circumstance, Kerry called it "a laughable characterization" and "the most ridiculous thing I've ever seen in my life."[4] When President Bush leveled the charge that Kerry was a liberal in the second presidential debate, Kerry responded by saying, "Labels don't mean anything."[5] In fact, labels mean a great deal when they serve as short-hand descriptions of political philosophies and policy agendas, and Kerry's instincts were right to try to avoid or smother the charge.

One method Kerry employed to try to compensate for his obvious political baggage was to flirt seriously with the notion of putting Republican senator John McCain on the ticket.[6] This type of bipartisan ticket has not been seen since the nineteenth century, when Harrison selected John Tyler and Lincoln tapped Andrew Johnson to serve as running mates. Apparently, however, there was substantial swooning over the prospect of a Kerry-McCain ticket, despite the accurate description by one columnist that McCain was a "pro-life, pro-gun, pro-death penalty, pro-Iraq war defense hawk"—hardly a description of a unified administration.[7] The fact that Kerry's first instinct was to overlook his own party in his search for a running mate says something about his self-awareness of the constraints historical context had imposed upon him. One can hardly think of a better way to mask the central differences between oneself and the governing party than to pick a running mate from Reagan's camp.

Kerry's most obvious strategic move to inoculate himself against the liberal charge, however, was his adoption of one of the more venerable icons of successful opposition efforts—the nonpartisan war hero. General Wesley Clark had tried to run under that banner during the primary season but proved to be a less than stellar candidate. Kerry's decision to focus the Democratic national convention on his four months of service in Vietnam rather than his many years in the Senate was a clear attempt to cast himself in the mold of the traditional military hero, directing attention to nonpartisan qualities such as selfless service, duty, and heroism. By choosing to pose as a war hero rather than a Washington politician with a twenty-year voting record, Kerry tried to embrace the standard set by Harrison and Taylor over a century and a half earlier, and Eisenhower in the 1950s. Presumably Kerry could purge the party of the antiwar and antimilitary strains that had plagued it since McGovern's run, while also avoiding the draft evasion problems that faced Bill Clinton.

Several problems prevented Kerry from taking advantage of this strategy. First, it is possible that Kerry's rank as a junior officer was insufficient to elevate him to the heroic status of war generals such as Taylor and Eisenhower. Second, Kerry's public disavowal of his actions in the early 1970s, captured on film, prevented him from picking up the war hero banner decades later. It is hard to run as a war hero when you are on record opposing your own actions. Third, to his great misfortune, Kerry found that groups such as the Swift Boat Veterans for Truth were far more capable of calling into question important aspects of his service than Harrison's Democratic counterparts in 1840. If a candidate is going to run as a military hero, he has to make sure that the label will resonate with the electorate and not provoke a fierce backlash. With gadflies like Michael Moore traveling the country on Kerry's behalf, the candidate's efforts to close the ideological gap were bound to fail. Ironically, one of the reasons Democratic voters sided with Kerry over Vermont governor Howard Dean in the party nomination battle was that Kerry was perceived as more electable. In the end, however, Kerry was unsuccessful in his attempt to employ the blank slate model.

The third key to opposition party victory is to run an indirect campaign—one that does not highlight the core ideological differences between the opposition party and the governing party. One of the things that made Howard Dean so dangerous to the Democratic Party—and why many Republicans were licking their chops at the prospect of running against him—was that he put a spotlight on the differences between the two parties and bragged about them.[8] As laid out in chapter 4, the philosophical purity of a campaign is more or less relevant depending on the party's position in historical context, and the better strategy for the opposition party is to focus on things other than the core issue differences. Kerry was in a difficult position on this front. As a long-time veteran of the Senate, he had taken positions on many issues, and the ambiguity behind some of those votes made it easy for the White House to brand him a "flip-flopper." At the same time, Democratic partisans clearly loathed President Bush and nearly everything he was about, but if the election focused on Reagan-era issues, Kerry would be in trouble.

The Kerry campaign seemed to have some understanding of this dynamic, which helps explain why the Democratic national convention was so pro-military and pro-religion in tone. A sharper focus on Kerry's Senate record and the many issues he voted on over the years would have raised inconvenient questions for the candidate. When the campaign began in earnest after Labor Day, Kerry continued to attempt to elide the differences between the parties in his policy positions and rhetoric. Kerry and Bush disagreed over the wisdom of requiring six-nation talks with North Korea instead of bilateral moves, but such nuances were likely lost on most voters. In other areas it was difficult to perceive clear battle lines. Despite Kerry's retrospective negative judgment of the president for his conduct of the war in Iraq, he never made it clear what precisely he would do differently in the future. In the second presidential debate, when challenged by a citizen to pledge not to raise taxes, Kerry parroted Bush's father's "no new taxes" pledge sixteen years earlier, stating emphatically that he would "not raise taxes."[9] Of course, Kerry (and the questioner) exempted anyone making more than $200,000 a year, a qualification that certainly made him a villain in tax-cutting circles. Nevertheless, the fact that Kerry spoke in terms of tax cuts and was willing to pledge no new taxes for the vast majority of Americans testifies to the fear he had of that issue. In other areas the campaign engaged in hyperbolic language to try to win the issue war. Accusations that Bush planned to cut Social Security benefits as much as 45 percent if he won or that he was planning to reinstate the draft were followed by indelicate references to the vice president's daughter's sexuality and suggestions that a Kerry presidency would save the lives of such beloved screen icons as Christopher Reeve.[10] The Social Security and draft charges were throwbacks to earlier Democratic campaigns while comments concerning sexual preference and embryonic stem cell research sought to split the conservative base.

Therein lay the problem for Kerry, however, for it is the social issues that have assumed greater importance over the years. The Bush campaign understood the importance of motivating social conservatives on such issues as abortion, gay marriage, and embryonic stem-cell research. In addition to some over-the-top rhetoric, Kerry attempted to pick that lock by qualifying his positions with such phrases as "personally pro-life but" and "oppose gay marriage but"—but the ambiguous issue of "moral values," represented by eleven successful state ballot measures concerning gay marriage, helped make the campaign very much centered on core issue differences. There was considerable discussion following the election about the importance of "moral values" on the outcome. Certainly a poorly crafted poll question that conflates the whole panoply of hot-button cultural issues while separating such foreign policy issues as the war on terrorism and the war in Iraq obscures as much as it illuminates. However, there is no doubt that the issue of "moral values," broadly defined, was an important factor in the election outcome, and it helped mobilize a key element of Bush's conservative base. Despite the emphasis on religion at the Democratic national convention, some party leaders interpreted the election results as a message to work even more vigorously to reach out to religious traditionalists. Leon Panetta remarked, "The party of FDR has become the party of Michael Moore and 'Fahrenheit 9-11,' and it does not help us in big parts of the country."[11] Despite winning all three presidential debates—where issues are presumably most central—Kerry was unsuccessful in running from his image, demonstrated in those *National Journal* rankings, as a liberal icon.

At the time of this writing, presidential candidates seeking the 2008 nomination are in the midst of the most wide-open race since 1928. Democrats are presented with an opportunity in 2008, for there will be no incumbent Republican on the ballot. That has led to a hotly contested primary battle in the GOP, with no way to predict how the losing factions may respond. A factional bolt by any group to a third party would certainly help Democratic chances. At the same time, the presumptive pre-season favorite in the Democratic Party was New York senator Hillary Clinton, who hardly fits the bill as a blank slate candidate. Indeed, it is hard to imagine a candidate more likely to provoke stark comparisons on key Reagan-era issues. Clinton seems to understand this problem, for she is reportedly working hard to craft a more moderate image. At the same time, former North Carolina senator and vice presidential candidate John Edwards tried to craft a staunchly progressive platform. While Edwards was able to run as a relative unknown in 2004, he could not retain that quality four years later, and a campaign highlighting a return to New Deal-style programs was hardly an example of an indirect campaign. From the perspective of the historical model, Illinois senator Barack Obama appears to represent a more ideal opposition party candidate. The first-term senator is a political newcomer who certainly qualifies as a blank slate candidate of the "unknown" variety who is attempting to use rhetoric and personal charisma to mask the issue differences he has with the core Reagan-era program—differences highlighted by his February 2008 *National Journal* ranking as the most liberal senator in 2007. However, Obama's status as a "fresh face" means he is disconnected from the political battles that have marked the current era, including those associated with the most recent Democratic president, Bill Clinton. It is certainly possible for a purist ideologue from the opposition party to win, and Republicans would be well-served to be careful what they wish for. Jimmy Carter looked forward to facing off against right-wing ideologue Ronald Reagan in 1980, seeing him as an easy mark in the vein of Barry Goldwater. Times had changed, however, and in 1980 the opposition party candidate became a governing party president. The success of a strongly liberal campaign will depend on whether 2008 presents a similar opportunity to the Democratic Party. In the absence of those elements, history has been fairly consistent in what it requires for opposition party victory.

NOTES

Preface

1. Fred I. Greenstein, "George W. Bush and the Ghosts of Presidents Past," 77.
2. For the best analysis of this argument, see Sidney M. Milkis, *The President and the Parties: The Transformation of the American Party System since the New Deal.*
3. See David K. Nichols, *The Myth of the Modern Presidency.*
4. Stephen Skowronek, *The Politics Presidents Make: Leadership from John Adams to George Bush.*
5. David A. Crockett, The *Opposition Presidency: Leadership and the Constraints of History;* Richard E. Neustadt, *Presidential Power and the Modern Presidents: The Politics of Leadership from Roosevelt to Reagan,* 167.
6. See Marc Landy and Sidney M. Milkis, *Presidential Greatness,* for a deeper exploration of reconstructive presidents.
7. Alexander Hamilton, James Madison, and John Jay, *The Federalist Papers,* 379–83.
8. My apologies to George Lucas and the *Star Wars* franchise.
9. Skowronek, *Politics Presidents Make,* 44.

Chapter 1: Campaigns and Elections in Historical Context

1. E. E. Schattschneider, *The Semisovereign People,* 66.
2. See Crockett, *Opposition Presidency,* 17–23, for a fuller discussion of this dynamic.
3. This is best evidenced by the elections of 1876 and 2000—two virtual dead heats that ended in Republican victories in part because of long-term Republican control over key institutions.
4. For a cogent and concise discussion of how historical context ought to shape leadership, see Herbert J. Storing, "The Creation of the Presidency," 371–72, and "A Plan for Studying the Presidency," 392–94.
5. Charles O. Jones, *The Presidency in a Separated System,* 2.
6. Neustadt, *Presidential Power,* 167.
7. An excellent history of this scholarly project can be found in Theodore Rosenof, *Realignment: The Theory that Changed the Way We Think about American Politics.*
8. To say there is a "rough consensus" on this point does not mean there is unanimity. Attacks on realignment theory persist. Most recently, David Mayhew's treatise

Electoral Realignments: A Critique of an American Genre sought to dismantle realignment theory root-and-branch. Much of his book, however, focuses its attack on questioning the existence of a realigning election in 1896. At times, his language becomes hyperbolic, mirroring the more exaggerated claims of some realignment specialists. For example, no one would seriously argue that "voters could not or did not do anything effective or consequential" between realigning elections (30). Mayhew also proposes alternative cut-points in American history and presents alternative stories of the American political experience—but the presence of realignment periods does not preclude other methods of dividing American history into eras, nor do realignment specialists deny that there are other interesting stories to be told. Indeed, Skowronek layers his own form of cyclical analysis on top of a model of secular change. Perhaps Rosenof's remarks in his scholarly history say it best: "realignment theory remains useful as a concept, guide, and tool. It should not be treated as the key to the future; nor should it be viewed as a recipe or formula to be discarded if each ingredient or facet of each realigning era fails to fit an allotted slot" (166–67).

9.   Walter Dean Burnham, *Critical Elections and the Mainsprings of American Politics.*

10.   Samuel Lubell, *The Future of American Politics.*

11.   Edward G. Carmines and James A. Stimson, *Issue Evolution: Race and the Transformation of American Politics.*

12.   Walter Dean Burnham, "Critical Realignment: Dead or Alive?"

13.   For a small taste of the other literature on this topic, see the following: V. O. Key Jr., "A Theory of Critical Elections"; Angus Campbell, Philip E. Converse, Warren E. Miller, and Donald E. Stokes, *Elections and the Political Order;* Paul Kleppner, *The Third Electoral System, 1853–1892: Parties, Voters, and Political Cultures;* James L. Sundquist, *Dynamics of the Party System: Alignment and Realignment of Political Parties in the United States;* Bert A. Rockman, *The Leadership Question: The Presidency and the American System;* John E. Chubb and Paul E. Peterson, "Realignment and Institutionalization"; Walter Dean Burnham, "Realignment Lives: The 1994 Earthquake and Its Implications."

14.   See Barrington Moore, *Social Origins of Dictatorship and Democracy,* 111–55.

15.   See Rosenof, *Realignment,* 164–66.

16.   Garry Wills, *"Negro President": Jefferson and the Slave Power,* 2–5, 234.

17.   Potentially the most important difference is the location of the most recent partisan transformation. Realignment specialists tend to point to 1968–1972, though not universally. Skowronek sees Reagan and 1980 as the better cut-point. The two perspectives are not mutually exclusive if one understands the 1968 era as one that began a critical partisan dealignment without providing for a redefinition of the terms of debate in American politics. That redefinition had to await the Reagan era. See Crockett, *Opposition Presidency,* 24–32, as well as the chapters on Nixon and Clinton, for my attempt to reconcile these arguments.

18.   Gary King and Lyn Ragsdale. *The Elusive Executive: Discovering Statistical Patterns in the Presidency,* 426–29.

19.   Debate about the true state of the contemporary era is fierce. For the argument that American politics is typified by dealignment in a candidate-centered system that began in the 1960s, instead of realignment, see John H. Aldrich and Richard G. Niemi, "The Sixth American Party System: Electoral Change, 1952–1992"; Martin P. Wattenberg,

The Decline of American Political Parties, 1952–1988; John H. Aldrich, *Why Parties? The Origin and Transformation of Party Politics in America;* and Burnham, "Critical Realignment: Dead or Alive?" For the argument in favor of ideological realignment and the resurgence of partisanship, with debate over whether the appropriate cut-point is 1968 or 1980, see Bruce E. Keith et al., *The Myth of the Independent Voter;* Alan I. Abramowitz and Kyle L. Saunders, "Ideological Realignment in the U.S. Electorate"; and Marc J. Hetherington, "Resurgent Mass Partisanship: The Role of Elite Polarization."

20.　James MacGregor Burns, *The Deadlock of Democracy: Four-Party Politics in America.*

21.　See Richard Hofstadter, *The Idea of a Party System: The Rise of Legitimate Opposition in the United States, 1780–1840.*

22.　For an explanation of this lexicon, see Campbell et al., *Elections and the Political Order,* 63–64.

23.　I use the terms "majority party" and "minority party" in this section because they are Campbell's terms. In general, I prefer the terms "governing party" and "opposition party." Although the former terms are easier to define, they are dependent on survey research data. The latter terms more clearly indicate political reality. No one would suggest that the Republican Party in 1860 had majority support in the nation, but it certainly redefined the nature of political debate. Similarly, the persistent Democratic advantage in partisan identification in the contemporary era makes explaining Republican advances difficult. The "governing-opposition" dichotomy allows for this ambiguity.

24.　Campbell et al., *Elections and the Political Order,* 69–72.

25.　See especially the history of these efforts in Rosenof, *Realignment,* chapter 8.

26.　See Alan Abramowitz, *Voice of the People: Elections and Voting in the United States,* 180.

27.　Campbell et al., *Elections and the Political Order,* 69.

28.　Campbell et al., *Elections and the Political Order,* 73–74.

29.　Campbell et al., *Elections and the Political Order,* 71–73.

30.　Of course, in 1966 the three war heroes comprised 60 percent of the field of deviating victors.

31.　Campbell, *The American Campaign: U.S. Presidential Campaigns and the National Vote.*

32.　Campbell, *American Campaign,* 103–108.

33.　See Crockett, *Opposition Presidency,* for a full exploration of these differences in leadership style.

34.　Ceaser, *Presidential Selection,* 153–57, 324–25; Harry V. Jaffa, "The Nature and Origin of the American Party System," 60–63.

35.　Campbell et al., *Elections and the Political Order,* 73.

36.　Anthony Downs, *An Economic Theory of Democracy.*

Chapter 2: The Governing Party in Trouble

1.　I begin each of the next three chapters with an analysis of historical data. For specific citations of sources, see the detailed case studies in the second half of each chapter.

2. If we add Lincoln's victory in 1860 to the data, the opposition party victory rate is still only 26 percent.

3. For a fuller discussion of the incumbency advantage, see Campbell, *American Campaign*, 102–10.

4. If we add the three reconstruction victories to the data, the opposition party victory rate rises to 35 percent.

5. See Steven J. Rosenstone, Roy L. Behr, and Edward H. Lazarus, *Third Parties in America: Citizen Response to Major Party Failure*, for a full explanation of this dynamic.

6. For the purposes of clarity, to distinguish third-party movements from factional politics, I do not include the elections of 1824 and 1836. Both of those elections were multiple-candidate contests in which several individuals captured more than 10 percent of the popular vote. However, the four-way contest in 1824 was due to competing personal factions in the one-party "Era of Good Feelings," not to true third-party movements. The four-way race in 1836 occurred because of the Whig strategy of running three sectional candidates in an effort to prevent Van Buren from achieving a majority of electoral votes. The election remained a two-party race.

7. As with 1856, 1860, and 1980, however, one could argue that the Progressive Party presence in 1924 was also an early precursor to the New Deal realignment sequence, not yet strong enough to harm the GOP, but an indication of where politics was heading within eight years.

8. See the argument in chapter 3.

9. Rosenstone, Behr, and Lazarus, *Third Parties in America*, 57–58, 117–19.

10. Rosenstone, Behr, and Lazarus, *Third Parties in America*, 103–10.

11. Michael F. Holt, *The Rise and Fall of the American Whig Party: Jacksonian Politics and the Onset of the Civil War*, 61–64; William R. Brock, *Parties and Political Conscience: American Dilemmas, 1840–1850*, 10–11; Norma Lois Peterson, *The Presidencies of William Henry Harrison and John Tyler*, 21–24; Glyndon G. Van Deusen, *The Jacksonian Era, 1828–1848*, 116–17; John Steele Gordon, *Hamilton's Blessing: The Extraordinary Life and Times of Our National Debt*, 59–64.

12. Michael F. Holt, *The Political Crisis of the 1850s*, 32–34; Holt, *American Whig Party*, 65–67; Van Deusen, *Jacksonian Era*, 118–22.

13. Peterson, *Presidencies of Harrison and Tyler*, 21–24; Robert Seager II, *And Tyler Too: A Biography of John and Julia Gardiner Tyler*, 129.

14. Elbert B. Smith, *The Presidencies of Zachary Taylor and Millard Fillmore*, 13–15; Van Deusen, *Jacksonian Era*, 240–41.

15. Brock, *Parties and Political Conscience*, 180–83, 241–42; Holt, *Political Crisis of the 1850s*, 50–56.

16. Brock, *Parties and Political Conscience*, 215–18; Holt, *Political Crisis of the 1850s*, 59–61; Holt, *American Whig Party*, 319; Van Deusen, *Jacksonian Era*, 246–50.

17. Van Deusen, *Jacksonian Era*, 257–59; Brock, *Parties and Political Conscience*, 225–27; Holt, *American Whig Party*, 342.

18. Lewis L. Gould, "The Republican Search for a National Majority," 179; John A. Garraty, *The New Commonwealth, 1877–1890*, 281–84.

19. Gerald W. McFarland, *Mugwumps, Morals and Politics, 1884–1920*, 2–14;

Richard E. Welch Jr., *The Presidencies of Grover Cleveland*, 30; Mark Wahlgren Summers, *Rum, Romanism, & Rebellion: The Making of a President 1884*, 24.

20. McFarland, *Mugwumps, Morals and Politics*, 18–58; Summers, *Rum, Romanism, & Rebellion*, 198–205.

21. H. Wayne Morgan, *From Hayes to McKinley: National Party Politics, 1877–1896*, 66–69, 137–56, 210–11; Allan Nevins, *Grover Cleveland: A Study in Courage*, 160–62; Welch, Presidencies of Grover Cleveland, 40–41; Summers, *Rum, Romanism, & Rebellion*, 62–67, 206–209; McFarland, *Mugwumps, Morals and Politics*, 15–16.

22. R. Hal Williams, "Dry Bones and Dead Language: The Democratic Party," 139.

23. Kleppner, *Third Electoral System*, 328–42; R. Hal Williams, *Years of Decision: American Politics in the 1890s*, 46–53; George Harmon Knoles, *The Presidential Campaign and Election of 1892*, 125–27.

24. Williams, *Years of Decision*, 53; Morgan, *From Hayes to McKinley*, 349–56; Gould, "Republican Search," 181–82.

25. Paul W. Glad, *McKinley, Bryan, and the People*, 37–48; Garraty, *New Commonwealth*.

26. Morgan, *From Hayes to McKinley*, 367–91, 423–24.

27. Knoles, *Presidential Election of 1892*, 34–68; Morgan, *From Hayes to McKinley*, 395–403.

28. Lewis L. Gould, *Reform and Regulation: American Politics, 1900–1916*, 25–34, 63–76; Arthur S. Link, *Woodrow Wilson and the Progressive Era, 1910–1917*, 2–3; John Milton Cooper Jr., *Pivotal Decades: The United States, 1900–1920*, 149; James Chace, *1912: Wilson, Roosevelt, Taft & Debs—the Election that Changed the Country*, 18.

29. Gould, *Reform and Regulation*, 89–95; Cooper, *Pivotal Decades*, 147–56; Francis L. Broderick, *Progressivism at Risk: Electing a President in 1912*, 32–35; Chace, *1912*, 14–17; Link, *Wilson and the Progressive Era*, 3–5.

30. Chace, *1912*, 57–58, 95–100; Link, *Wilson and the Progressive Era*, 6–7; Gould, *Reform and Regulation*, 99–103; Broderick, *Progressivism at Risk*, 38–41; Cooper, *Pivotal Decades*, 150–61; John Milton Cooper Jr., *The Warrior and the Priest: Woodrow Wilson and Theodore Roosevelt*, 150–56.

31. Cooper, *Pivotal Decades*, 161–71; Gould, *Reform and Regulation*, 108–12; Broderick, *Progressivism at Risk*, 41; Chace, *1912*, 104–106.

32. Gould, *Reform and Regulation*, 115–18; Chace, *1912*, 112–13; Cooper, *Pivotal Decades*, 172–75; Link, *Wilson and the Progressive Era*, 14–17; Broderick, *Progressivism at Risk*, 45–56.

33. Campbell, *American Campaign*, 102–10.

34. Gould, *Reform and Regulation*, 165; Link, *Wilson and the Progressive Era*, 230–31.

35. S. D. Lovell, *The Presidential Election of 1916*, 34–35, 40–55.

36. Lovell, *Presidential Election of 1916*, 126–47; Cooper, *Pivotal Decades*, 253–54.

37. John Robert Greene, *The Crusade: The Presidential Election of 1952*, 11–13; Gary W. Reichard, *Politics as Usual: The Age of Truman and Eisenhower*, 73–74.

38. Sundquist, *Dynamics of the Party System*, 337–39; Greene, *Crusade*, 13–16; Alonzo L. Hamby, *Liberalism and Its Challengers: From FDR to Bush*, 81–91; Reichard, *Politics as Usual*, 60–71.

39. Hamby, *Liberalism and Its Challengers*, 69–70; Reichard, *Politics as Usual*, 47–51; Greene, *Crusade*, 11–12, 140–43.

40. Greene, *Crusade*, 63–70, 123–29, 157–68; Reichard, *Politics as Usual*, 78.

41. Reichard, *Politics as Usual*, 123–24; Chester J. Pach and Elmo Richardson, *The Presidency of Dwight D. Eisenhower*, 126–35.

42. William E. Leuchtenburg, *In the Shadow of FDR: From Harry Truman to Ronald Reagan*, 142–50; Hamby, *Liberalism and Its Challengers*, 258–63.

43. John Morton Blum, *The Progressive Presidents: Roosevelt, Wilson, Roosevelt, Johnson*, 192–99; Hamby, *Liberalism and Its Challengers*, 268–71; Lewis Chester, Godfrey Hodgson, and Bruce Page, *An American Melodrama: The Presidential Campaign of 1968*, 21–31, 53–57; Leuchtenburg, *In the Shadow of FDR*, 153.

44. Theodore H. White, *The Making of the President 1968*, 23–29, 199–210, 214–23; Chester et al., *American Melodrama*, 513–15; Sundquist, *Dynamics of the Party System*, 382–84.

45. Sundquist, *Dynamics of the Party System*, 363–64; Chester et al., *American Melodrama*, 271–85; White, *Making of the President 1968*, 345–48.

46. White, *Making of the President 1968*, 76–90, 122–25, 161–66; Chester et al., *American Melodrama*, 78–100, 153–55, 414–15; Ronald Radosh, *Divided They Fell: The Demise of the Democratic Party, 1964–1996*, 83–105.

47. White, *Making of the President 1968*, 275–310; Chester et al., *American Melodrama*, 532–37, 569–91; Radosh, *Divided They Fell*, 118–31.

48. Radosh, *Divided They Fell*, 134–82; John Robert Greene, *The Limits of Power: The Nixon and Ford Administrations*, 158–62; Theodore H. White, *The Making of the President 1972*, 23–33, 159–66, 187–92; William Manchester, *The Glory and the Dream: A Narrative History of America, 1932–1972*, 1282–86; Stephen E. Ambrose, *Nixon: The Triumph of a Politician, 1962–1972*, 579–86.

49. Jack W. Germond and Jules Witcover, *Mad as Hell: Revolt at the Ballot Box, 1992*, 46–51, 81–91; Hamby, *Liberalism and Its Challengers*, 392–94; Paul R. Abramson, John H. Aldrich, and David W. Rohde, *Change and Continuity in the 1992 Elections*, 15–17.

50. Peter Goldman, et al., *Quest for the Presidency 1992*, 310–17; Hamby, *Liberalism and Its Challengers*, 392–94; Germond and Witcover, *Mad as Hell*, 47–61; Abramson, Aldrich, and Rohde, *Change and Continuity*, 173–75, 199–212, 315.

51. Hamby, *Liberalism and Its Challengers*, 392; Germond and Witcover, *Mad as Hell*, 28–46, 132–33, 475–76; Goldman et al., *Quest for the Presidency*, 324–26, 348–49; Abramson, Aldrich, and Rohde, *Change and Continuity*, 26–30, 44.

52. Germond and Witcover, *Mad as Hell*, 221–23, 371; Goldman et al., *Quest for the Presidency*, 422–23; Abramson, Aldrich, and Rohde, *Change and Continuity*, 39–41, 167–70, 325.

53. Elizabeth Drew, *Whatever It Takes: The Real Struggle for Political Power in America*, 44–45; Evan Thomas et al., *Back from the Dead: How Clinton Survived the Republican Revolution*, 82, 177–78; Bob Woodward, *The Choice*, 418–20.

54. Woodward, *The Choice*, 289–311, 377–99; Thomas et al., *Back from the Dead*, 24–30, 103–108, 193–94; Drew, *Whatever It Takes*, 1–2, 97–98, 217–19.

55. See Campbell, *American Campaign*.

56. Lonna Rae Atkeson, "From the Primaries to the General Election: Does a Di-

visive Nomination Race Affect a Candidate's Fortunes in the Fall?" 285–312; Campbell, *American Campaign*, 113–17.

Chapter 3: The Blank Slate Candidate

1. In fact, Jackson could very reasonably be labeled a military hero blank slate candidate who not only won election but also succeeded in transforming American politics. The other reconstructors—Lincoln, Franklin Roosevelt, and Reagan—have much less claim to the blank slate label. Although Lincoln had minimal political service in his background, his status as a Republican candidate—the antislavery party—in 1860 made diminishing the ideological distance between the new party and the Democrats impossible. Although FDR paid some lip service to balanced budgets in his campaign, he was a former vice presidential candidate and governor of the largest state in the union, and he pulled no punches in excoriating the ruling Republicans. Similarly, Reagan was the natural heir to Barry Goldwater, the conservative purist from 1964.

2. Some of these candidates could be called political amateurs. For an interesting study of political amateurs in Congress, see David T. Canon, *Actors, Athletes, and Astronauts: Political Amateurs in the United States Congress.*

3. Because the American political system rewards appeals to the ideological middle, one might think that the blank slate model can apply just as well to the governing party as to the opposition. Some of this is due to the natural aging of an electoral era. For example, aside from the fact that he was an unknown, Jimmy Carter's campaign as a moderate Southern Democrat placed him in the ambiguous centrist role—a shrewd move considering the teetering state of the New Deal coalition. However, Polk's dark horse status in 1844 is diminished by the fact that he was also known as "Young Hickory"—an explicit rhetorical link to Andrew Jackson. In general, the advice to run to the center can work for both parties. This analysis suggests that it is one possible option for the governing party, depending on historical context; if the opposition party desires victory, however, this advice is decidedly not optional.

4. Andrew E. Busch and William G. Mayer, "The Front-Loading Problem," 22–28.

5. It should be obvious that not all purists are created equal. Clearly candidates like Clay, Bryan, and Goldwater provide a very strong anchor to the notion of what ideological purity can look like. Two of these more unfamiliar names bear brief explanation. I place Horatio Seymour in this category because he was a two-term governor of New York who became a leading Democratic Party critic of Lincoln's administration. He was not a military hero or an unknown, and to the extent that he vigorously and openly opposed the policies of the founder of the new Republican regime, he can hardly be considered a centrist. Similarly, James Middleton Cox served two terms in Congress and three terms as governor of Ohio before running for president. Neither a military hero nor an unknown, Cox was a progressive reformer who also strongly supported Wilson's foreign policies, perhaps the central issue at dispute in the 1920 election.

6. Given this record, one could easily ask why the opposition party would ever run someone other than a blank slate candidate. Perhaps optimists in the party always hope

that any specific election year is their big opportunity to effect one of Skowronek's recon-structions. Given the influence purists have on the nomination—whether ideologues or interest groups—it may be difficult for the party as an organization to submerge its ideal inclinations in favor of raw electability. After all, the Whigs were not always successful in denying Henry Clay the nomination.

7. It should be noted that eight of these seventeen elections also involved signifi-cant third-party efforts, with 1948 an arguably ninth example. As argued in chapter 2, the presence of strong third parties tends to make life difficult for the governing party, includ-ing driving down the total vote for the winner. Although more blank slate candidates are involved in these close races than third parties, there is clearly an overlap in categories that is difficult to separate completely.

8. Dorothy Burne Goebel, William *Henry Harrison: A Political Biography*, 324–25; Peterson, *Presidencies of Harrison and Tyler*, 8–14; Holt, *American Whig Party*, 93–96.

9. Merrill D. Peterson, *The Great Triumvirate: Webster, Clay and Calhoun*, 289; Goebel, *William Henry Harrison*, 337–39.

10. Peterson, *Great Triumvirate*, 282–83.

11. James A. Green, *William Henry Harrison: His Life and Times*, 328; Van Deusen, *Jacksonian Era*, 141–42.

12. Peterson, *Great Triumvirate*, 290.

13. Goebel, *William Henry Harrison*, 342–343; Freeman Cleaves, *Old Tippecanoe: William Henry Harrison and His Time*, 317–18; Holt, *American Whig Party*, 101–105.

14. Goebel, *William Henry Harrison*; Cleaves, *Old Tippecanoe*.

15. Green, *William Henry Harrison*, 312–25; Goebel, *William Henry Harrison*, 306–10, 326–43; Cleaves, *Old Tippecanoe*, 315–18; Holt, *American Whig Party*, 90–91, 100–101; Van Deusen, *Jacksonian Era*, 110–111, 142–43.

16. Holman Hamilton, *Zachary Taylor: Soldier in the White House*, 56; Holt, *American Whig Party*, 269.

17. Brainerd Dyer, *Zachary Taylor*, 265; Van Deusen, *Jacksonian Era*, 251.

18. Smith, *Presidencies of Taylor and Fillmore*, 25–28; K. Jack Bauer, *Zachary Taylor: Soldier, Planter, Statesman of the Old Southwest*, 94–95, 223–24; Dyer, *Zachary Taylor*, 207–42; Van Deusen, *Jacksonian Era*, 229–30; Holt, *American Whig Party*, 269–70.

19. Holt, *American Whig Party*, 270–75; Bauer, *Zachary Taylor*, 219–48; Dyer, *Zachary Taylor*, 267–73.

20. Hamilton, *Zachary Taylor*, 56.

21. George Rawlings Poage, *Henry Clay and the Whig Party*, 157.

22. Holt, *Political Crisis of the 1850s*, 62; Bauer, *Zachary Taylor*, 215–16; Dyer, *Zachary Taylor*, 266.

23. Bauer, *Zachary Taylor*, 217–21; Dyer, *Zachary Taylor*, 268–71; Holt, *American Whig Party*, 269, 285–91.

24. Brock, *Parties and Political Conscience*, 185–89; Van Deusen, *Jacksonian Era*, 252.

25. Bauer, *Zachary Taylor*, 232–33; Dyer, *Zachary Taylor*, 278–81; Hamilton, *Zachary Taylor*, 77–83; Holt, *American Whig Party*, 275–82, 307–10; Van Deusen, *Jacksonian Era*, 251–55.

26. Bauer, *Zachary Taylor*, 243–44; Dyer, *Zachary Taylor*, 286–87; Holt, *American Whig Party*, 351–53, 361.

27. Hamilton, *Zachary Taylor*, 42–44.

28. Nevins, *Grover Cleveland*, 112–44; Summers, *Rum, Romanism, & Rebellion*, 116–22, 146–53; Horace Samuel Merrill, *Bourbon Leader: Grover Cleveland and the Democratic Party*, 17–31; Morgan, *From Hayes to McKinley*, 192–200; Welch, *Presidencies of Grover Cleveland*, 21–28.

29. Summers, *Rum, Romanism, & Rebellion*, 149; Morgan, *From Hayes to McKinley*, 208.

30. Morgan, *From Hayes to McKinley*, 208–11; Summers, Rum, *Romanism, & Rebellion*, 161.

31. Woodrow Wilson, *Constitutional Government in the United States*, 32–33; John Morton Blum, *Woodrow Wilson and the Politics of Morality*, 13–22; Robert H. Wiebe, *The Search for Order, 1877–1920*, 216–17; Broderick, *Progressivism at Risk*, 62–63; Cooper, *Warrior and the Priest*, 134–36; Blum, *Progressive Presidents*, 62–63.

32. Gould, *Reform and Regulation*, 134; Link, *Wilson and the Progressive Era*, 9–10; Cooper, *Warrior and the Priest*, 165–76; Broderick, *Progressivism at Risk*, 67–68; Blum, *Politics of Morality*, 38–49; Chace, *1912*, 51–52, 61–65.

33. Gould, *Reform and Regulation*, 135; Link, *Wilson and the Progressive Era*, 10; Broderick, *Progressivism at Risk*, 61–77; Chace, *1912*, 128–32.

34. Broderick, *Progressivism at Risk*, 78–84; Link, *Wilson and the Progressive Era*, 11–12; Chace, *1912*, 125–28; Cooper, *Warrior and the Priest*, 179–181.

35. Chace, *1912*, 141–42, 148–58; Broderick, *Progressivism at Risk*, 92–101; Blum, *Politics of Morality*, 54–57; Cooper, *Warrior and the Priest*, 183–86; Gould, *Reform and Regulation*, 139–41.

36. Greene, *Crusade*, 24–27; Clinton Rossiter, *The American Presidency*, 228.

37. Stephen E. Ambrose, *Eisenhower: Soldier, General of the Army, President-Elect, 1890–1952*.

38. Leuchtenburg, *In the Shadow of FDR*, 51; Greene, *Crusade*, 50–53; Pach and Richardson, *Presidency of Dwight D. Eisenhower*, 5–6; Ambrose, *Eisenhower: President-Elect*, 96.

39. Ambrose, *Eisenhower: President-Elect*, 268–69.

40. Ambrose, *Eisenhower: President-Elect*, 413–14, 459–64, 477–78; Leuchtenburg, *In the Shadow of FDR*, 46.

41. Ambrose, *Eisenhower: President-Elect*, 465–69, 510–16; Leuchtenburg, *In the Shadow of FDR*, 52–54.

42. Ambrose, *Eisenhower: President-Elect*, 490–99, 515; Richard Norton Smith, *Thomas Dewey and His Times*, 553–57; Herbert S. Parmet, *Eisenhower and the American Crusades*, 33–36, 49–50.

43. Ambrose, *Eisenhower: President-Elect*, 514–22; Theodore J. Lowi, *The Personal President: Power Invested, Power Unfulfilled*, 73–75; Smith, *Thomas Dewey*, 577–79; Parmet, *Eisenhower*, 47; Greene, *Crusade*, 75–79.

44. Ambrose, *Eisenhower: President-Elect*, 522–28; Greene, *Crusade*, 80–85; David W. Reinhard, *The Republican Right since 1945*, 81–82.

45. Parmet, *Eisenhower*, 97–98; Ambrose, *Eisenhower: President-Elect*, 530–43; Reinhard, *Republican Right*, 84.

46. Greene, *Crusade*, 91–93; Ambrose, *Eisenhower: President-Elect*, 535–37; Parmet, *Eisenhower*, 75–77; Smith, *Thomas Dewey*, 586–87.

47.   Ambrose, *Eisenhower: President-Elect*, 536–37; Greene, *Crusade*, 93–94; Reinhard, *Republican Right*, 82–83.

48.   Greene, *Crusade*, 89–91, 103–17; Smith, *Thomas Dewey*, 584–97; Parmet, *Eisenhower*, 79–93; Ambrose, *Eisenhower: President-Elect*, 537–41.

49.   Garry Wills, *Nixon Agonistes: The Crisis of the Self-Made Man*, 181–206, 226–27.

50.   Wills, *Nixon Agonistes*, 84.

51.   Stephen E. Ambrose, *Nixon: The Education of a Politician, 1913–1962;* Chester et al., *American Melodrama*, 232–51; Hamby, *Liberalism and Its Challengers*, 283–97; Greene, *Limits of Power*, 4–15; Wills, *Nixon Agonistes*, 81–82.

52.   Richard Nixon, *The Memoirs of Richard Nixon*, 259–68; Jules Witcover, *The Resurrection of Richard Nixon*, 98–108, 168–70; Ambrose, *Triumph of a Politician*, 60–61, 80–101; White, *Making of the President 1968*, 41–52.

53.   Ambrose, *Triumph of a Politician*, 133–61; Wills, *Nixon Agonistes*, 239–41; Witcover, *Resurrection of Nixon*, 339; White, *Making of the President 1968*, 129–37; Kathleen Hall Jamieson, *Packaging the Presidency: A History and Criticism of Presidential Campaign Advertising*, 241–42.

54.   Ambrose, *Triumph of a Politician*, 153–55, 164–70; White, *Making of the President 1968*, 137–38, 229–33, 238–41; Chester et al., *American Melodrama*, 439–75; Witcover, *Resurrection of Nixon*, 309–13, 342–49.

55.   David Maraniss, *First in His Class: A Biography of Bill Clinton.*

56.   Radosh, *Divided They Fell*, 209–14; Germond and Witcover, *Mad as Hell*, 79–80, 115–16; Bob Woodward, *The Agenda: Inside the Clinton White House*, 19.

57.   Radosh, *Divided They Fell*, 213–17; Woodward, *The Agenda*, 29–30; Milkis, *President and the Parties*, 310–12.

58.   Germond and Witcover, *Mad as Hell*, 281–88; Goldman, et al., *Quest for the Presidency*, 245–74.

59.   Germond and Witcover, *Mad as Hell*, 289–305; Radosh, *Divided They Fell*, 218–19; Goldman et al., *Quest for the Presidency*, 274–75.

Chapter 4: The Indirect Campaign

1.   See Crockett, *Opposition Presidency*, 62–68, for a description of Tyler's difficulties.

2.   Goebel, *William Henry Harrison*, 345; Van Deusen, *Jacksonian Era*, 144; Holt, *American Whig Party*, 104–105.

3.   Cleaves, *Old Tippecanoe*, 312–13.

4.   Robert J. Morgan, *A Whig Embattled: The Presidency under John Tyler*, 5–6, 149–53; Cleaves, *Old Tippecanoe*, 318; Goebel, *William Henry Harrison*, 345; Oliver Perry Chitwood, *John Tyler: Champion of the Old South*, 167–68, 172–73; Holt, *American Whig Party*, 104.

5.   Goebel, *William Henry Harrison*, 347; Cleaves, *Old Tippecanoe*, 320–21; Green, *William Henry Harrison*, 346.

6.   Goebel, *William Henry Harrison*, 352–54; Green, *William Henry Harrison*, 352, 357–60; Cleaves, *Old Tippecanoe*, 323–24; Holt, *American Whig Party*, 105–107, 111; Richard P. McCormick, *Presidential Game: The Origins of American Presidential Politics*, 198–99.

7. Goebel, *William Henry Harrison*, 363–64; Van Deusen, *Jacksonian Era*, 146–48.

8. Goebel, *William Henry Harrison*, 357–64.

9. Chitwood, *John Tyler*, 188–94.

10. Goebel, *William Henry Harrison*, 350–52; Cleaves, *Old Tippecanoe*, 321–26.

11. Chitwood, *John Tyler*, 177–83; Seager, *And Tyler Too*, 135.

12. Holt, *American Whig Party*, 109–10.

13. Dyer, *Zachary Taylor*, 282–83; Hamilton, *Zachary Taylor*, 94–95; Holt, *American Whig Party*, 320–27.

14. Hamilton, *Zachary Taylor*, 97, 109; Dyer, *Zachary Taylor*, 288–89; Van Deusen, *Jacksonian Era*, 256.

15. Robert J. Rayback, Millard *Fillmore: Biography of a President*, 180–86; Smith, *Presidencies of Taylor and Fillmore*, 43–46; Hamilton, *Zachary Taylor*, 95–97; Holt, *American Whig Party*, 327–29.

16. Dyer, *Zachary Taylor*, 293–95; Hamilton, *Zachary Taylor*, 44–45.

17. Hamilton, *Zachary Taylor*, 102–17; Bauer, *Zachary Taylor*, 239–42; Dyer, *Zachary Taylor*, 297–99.

18. Holt, *Political Crisis of the 1850s*, 62–64; Holt, *American Whig Party*, 344–45, 356–59; Hamilton, *Zachary Taylor*, 103–109.

19. Dyer, *Zachary Taylor*, 289–95.

20. Van Deusen, *Jacksonian Era*, 259–60; Holt, *American Whig Party*, 350–51.

21. Morgan, *From Hayes to McKinley*, 204–12; Nevins, *Grover Cleveland*, 150–71; Summers, *Rum, Romanism, & Rebellion*, 157–59.

22. Summers, *Rum, Romanism, & Rebellion*, 240–54; Williams, "Dry Bones and Dead Language," 133.

23. Morgan, *From Hayes to McKinley*, 213–25; Summers, *Rum, Romanism, & Rebellion*, xi, 173–75, 184–89, 191–93, 264.

24. Morgan, *From Hayes to McKinley*, 213–17; Nevins, *Grover Cleveland*, 162–69, 172; Summers, *Rum, Romanism, & Rebellion*, 179–84.

25. Morgan, *From Hayes to McKinley*, 226–30; Summers, *Rum, Romanism, & Rebellion*, 279–87; Nevins, *Grover Cleveland*, 181–83.

26. Morgan, *From Hayes to McKinley*, 404–12; Nevins, *Grover Cleveland*, 481–87; Knoles, *Presidential Election of 1892*, 13–15.

27. Nevins, *Grover Cleveland*, 491–93; Morgan, *From Hayes to McKinley*, 419; Knoles, *Presidential Election of 1892*, 64, 85–86.

28. Morgan, *From Hayes to McKinley*, 420–21; Nevins, *Grover Cleveland*, 481–98; Knoles, *Presidential Election of 1892*, 16–25, 86–89, 154–63.

29. Morgan, *From Hayes to McKinley*, 426–27, 434–35; Nevins, *Grover Cleveland*, 503–04; Knoles, *Presidential Election of 1892*, 167, 224–25.

30. Knoles, *Presidential Election of 1892*, 170–72, 216.

31. Nevins, *Grover Cleveland*, 499–501; Knoles, *Presidential Election of 1892*, 173–75; Welch, *Presidencies of Grover Cleveland*, 108.

32. Knoles, *Presidential Election of 1892*, 169–94; Morgan, *From Hayes to McKinley*, 429–32.

33. Broderick, *Progressivism at Risk*, 109–11; Robert M. Crunden, *Ministers of Reform: The Progressives' Achievement in American Civilization, 1889–1920*, 210–22; Cooper,

Warrior and the Priest, 188–91; Gould, *Reform and Regulation,* 142–43; Chace, *1912,* 116–23, 161–68.

34. Cooper, *Pivotal Decades,* 166–67; Broderick, *Progressivism at Risk,* 173–74.

35. Gould, *Reform and Regulation,* 144–45; Broderick, *Progressivism at Risk,* 134–41; Chace, *1912,* 192–97; Link, *Wilson and the Progressive Era,* 20–21.

36. Link, *Wilson and the Progressive Era,* 18–20; Cooper, *Warrior and the Priest,* 190; Broderick, *Progressivism at Risk,* 156–57; Gould, *Reform and Regulation,* 142–43.

37. Blum, *Politics of Morality,* 60–61; Cooper, *Warrior and the Priest,* 194–200; Broderick, *Progressivism at Risk,* 145–46.

38. Broderick, *Progressivism at Risk,* 35, 163–70; Chace, *1912,* 221.

39. Blum, *Politics of Morality,* 63; Cooper, *Warrior and the Priest,* 192–93; Broderick, *Progressivism at Risk,* 141; Chace, *1912,* 215–17; Wiebe, *Search for Order,* 217–18.

40. Cooper, *Warrior and the Priest,* 199–200; Broderick, *Progressivism at Risk,* 189–201; Chace, *1912,* 230–35.

41. Cooper, *Pivotal Decades,* 183–86; Wiebe, *Search for Order,* 217–18.

42. Link, *Wilson and the Progressive Era,* 233–34; Blum, *Progressive Presidents,* 77–78; Lovell, *Presidential Election of 1916,* 55–58; Gould, *Reform and Regulation,* 169.

43. Lovell, *Presidential Election of 1916,* 159–61; Link, *Wilson and the Progressive Era,* 225–29; Gould, *Reform and Regulation,* 170; Blum, *Politics of Morality,* 81.

44. Gould, *Reform and Regulation,* 168–71; Link, *Wilson and the Progressive Era,* 229; Blum, *Progressive Presidents,* 78–79.

45. Lovell, *Presidential Election of 1916,* 123; Gould, *Reform and Regulation,* 167.

46. Gould, *Reform and Regulation,* 171–75; Link, *Wilson and the Progressive Era,* 237–45; Lovell, *Presidential Election of 1916,* 105–106.

47. Lovell, *Presidential Election of 1916,* 64–70, 109–10; Gould, *Reform and Regulation,* 172–73; Link, *Wilson and the Progressive Era,* 244–45.

48. Lovell, *Presidential Election of 1916,* 108; Link, *Wilson and the Progressive Era,* 239–44; Blum, *Politics of Morality,* 124–25.

49. Ambrose, *Eisenhower: President-Elect,* 541–42, 546–53; Greene, *Crusade,* 115–17, 174–76, 187–88; Reinhard, *Republican Right,* 92–93; Gary W. Reichard, *The Reaffirmation of Republicanism: Eisenhower and the Eighty-third Congress,* 12–14; Stephen E. Ambrose, *Eisenhower: The President,* 14.

50. Pach and Richardson, *Presidency of Dwight D. Eisenhower,* 30–31; Ambrose, *Eisenhower: President-Elect,* 567–70; Reichard, *Reaffirmation of Republicanism,* 8–12; John W. Sloan, *Eisenhower and the Management of Prosperity,* 58.

51. Parmet, *Eisenhower,* 101; Greene, *Crusade,* 119; Ambrose, *Eisenhower: President-Elect,* 553–54.

52. Greene, *Crusade,* 210–15.

53. Jamieson, *Packaging the Presidency,* 44, 58–68, 82–86; Parmet, *Eisenhower,* 116–17; Greene, *Crusade,* 180–86.

54. Ambrose, *Eisenhower: President-Elect,* 569–70; Greene, *Crusade,* 215–20.

55. Sloan, *Management of Prosperity,* 58–59; Reinhard, *Republican Right,* 131–34; Ambrose, *Eisenhower: The President,* 294; Pach and Richardson, *Presidency of Dwight D. Eisenhower,* 115–22.

56. Pach and Richardson, *Presidency of Dwight D. Eisenhower,* 126–35; Reichard, *Politics as Usual,* 124–25; Ambrose, *Eisenhower: The President,* 350–73.

57. White, *Making of the President 1968,* 249–53; Witcover, *Resurrection of Nixon,* 349–57; Chester et al., *American Melodrama,* 482–95; Ambrose, *Triumph of a Politician,* 162–63, 172–75; Rowland Evans Jr. and Robert D. Novak, *Nixon in the White House: The Frustration of Power,* 305–10; Greene, *Limits of Power,* 21.

58. Chester et al., *American Melodrama,* 452–53; Ambrose, *Triumph of a Politician,* 166–72.

59. Ambrose, *Triumph of a Politician,* 175–79; White, *Making of the President 1968,* 254–56; Chester et al., *American Melodrama,* 495–99; Wills, *Nixon Agonistes,* 428.

60. Joe McGinniss, *The Selling of the President 1968,* 28–29.

61. McGinniss, *Selling of the President,* 34–37.

62. McGinniss, *Selling of the President,* 81.

63. McGinniss, *Selling of the President,* 62–72.

64. McGinniss, *Selling of the President,* 114–15.

65. Jamieson, *Packaging the Presidency,* 258; White, *Making of the President 1968,* 131–34.

66. Jamieson, *Packaging the Presidency,* 262–69.

67. Ambrose, *Triumph of a Politician,* 138–40; Greene, *Limits of Power,* 23–24; Chester et al., *American Melodrama,* 688–89; Jamieson, *Packaging the Presidency,* 233–34.

68. Unless Congress voted an exemption to the equal-time requirement, a debate would have to include Wallace.

69. White, *Making of the President 1968,* 400.

70. Ambrose, *Triumph of a Politician,* 180–93; Witcover, *Resurrection of Nixon,* 364–72, 392–93, 412–15; White, *Making of the President 1968,* 330–43, 367–68; Chester et al., *American Melodrama,* 694–702.

71. Ambrose, *Triumph of a Politician,* 196–206; White, *Making of the President 1968,* 353–61; Witcover, *Resurrection of Nixon,* 423–27; Chester et al., *American Melodrama,* 649–50, 719–26; William Safire, *Before the Fall: An Inside View of the Pre-Watergate White House,* 79–85.

72. Ambrose, *Triumph of a Politician,* 206–17; White, *Making of the President 1968,* 376–86; Safire, *Before the Fall,* 84–91; Witcover, *Resurrection of Nixon,* 428–47; Chester et al., *American Melodrama,* 726–35.

73. Ambrose, *Triumph of a Politician,* 500; Greene, *Limits of Power,* 142–43.

74. Ambrose, *Triumph of a Politician,* 580, 600–601, 646–49; Safire, *Before the Fall,* 645; Timothy Crouse, *The Boys on the Bus,* 305.

75. Germond and Witcover, *Mad as Hell,* 328–33, 342–46; Goldman et al., *Quest for the Presidency,* 276–83, 286–93; Theda Skocpol, *Boomerang: Health Care Reform and the Turn against Government,* 36–38.

76. Abramson, Aldrich, and Rohde, *Change and Continuity,* 43–44; Goldman et al., *Quest for the Presidency,* 402–404; Germond and Witcover, *Mad as Hell,* 403–16.

77. John H. Aldrich and Thomas Weko, "The Presidency and the Election Campaign: Framing the Choice in 1992," 262–63.

78. Germond and Witcover, *Mad as Hell,* 432, 441–43; Abramson, Aldrich, and Rohde, *Change and Continuity,* 54–55.

79. Germond and Witcover, *Mad as Hell*, 460–62, 488–92; Goldman et al., *Quest for the Presidency*, 543–48; Abramson, Aldrich, and Rohde, *Change and Continuity*, 55–63.

80. Goldman et al., *Quest for the Presidency*, 530–32; Germond and Witcover, *Mad as Hell*, 420–34, 468–70, 480–85; Abramson, Aldrich, and Rohde, *Change and Continuity*, 51–55, 61–63.

81. Germond and Witcover, *Mad as Hell*, 441–43; Elizabeth Drew, *On the Edge: The Clinton Presidency*, 19; Woodward, *The Agenda*, 55–56; Haynes Johnson and David S. Broder, *The System: The American Way of Politics at the Breaking Point*, 79–95; Skocpol, *Boomerang*, 41–47.

82. Abramson, Aldrich, and Rohde, *Change and Continuity*, 59–60, 66; Germond and Witcover, *Mad as Hell*, 3–19.

83. Woodward, *The Choice*, 354–55; Drew, *Whatever It Takes*, 70–71, 116–18.

84. Thomas et al., *Back from the Dead*, 15–16; Dick Morris, *Behind the Oval Office: Winning the Presidency in the Nineties*, 207–14, 221–31.

85. Bill Clinton, *Between Hope and History: Meeting America's Challenges for the 21st Century*, 6–7.

86. Elizabeth Drew, *Showdown: The Struggle between the Gingrich Congress and the Clinton White House*, 81–92, 140–49; Woodward, *The Choice*, 195–97, 352–53; Morris, *Behind the Oval Office*, 298–304.

87. Drew, *Whatever It Takes*, 130–37; Thomas et al., *Back from the Dead*, 135–36.

88. Skocpol, *Boomerang*, 191–97; Morris, *Behind the Oval Office*, 295–97, 319–25; Drew, *Whatever It Takes*, 56; Thomas et al., *Back from the Dead*, 203–04; David S. Broder, "Parceling Out Power to Both Parties," B3.

Chapter 5: From Campaigning to Governing: The Electoral Connection

1. On the question of candidate-centered politics, see Martin P. Wattenberg, *The Rise of Candidate-Centered Politics: Presidential Elections of the 1980s.*

2. To analyze this dynamic further, I constructed a logistic regression model using the ratings in tables 5-1 and 5-2. My dependent variable is a binary variable indicating whether the opposition party won or lost any of the forty-one elections in the data set. I coded the independent variables using an index in which I converted the star ratings to actual numbers. Each of the three explanatory variables by themselves is statistically significant. However, when I combine all three variables into one model, there appears to be a problem with collinearity. The variables seem to be too correlated with each other, making it impossible through this methodology to determine their relative influence. This problem should not be a surprise—as discussed both in the earlier chapters as well as the paragraphs above, when one factor of opposition victory is present in a successful campaign, all three are present, and when one factor is missing, often all three of them are missing or significantly weaker than in successful campaigns. To put it in words a campaign adviser would understand, all three factors are significant predictors of opposition party victory, but the statistical analysis cannot untangle which one is more important than the other. Until we come up with more precise and measurable concepts, it will be difficult to measure with precision the relative influence of these three variables on victory. We are left with the more rudimentary analysis above, which suggests an answer to this question—that is, that the

governing party in trouble is the foundation upon which all successful opposition party campaigns are built, with the other two factors building upon that opportunity.

3. For a fuller discussion of "third term understudies," see Walter Dean Burnham, "The Politics of Repudiation, 1992: Edging toward Upheaval."

4. See Patricia Heidotting Conley, *Presidential Mandates: How Elections Shape the National Agenda*.

5. Peterson, *Presidencies of Harrison and Tyler,* 29–30; Holt, *American Whig Party,* 111–12.

6. Brock, *Parties and Political Conscience,* 228–29; Holt, *Political Crisis of the 1850s,* 64–65; Van Deusen, *Jacksonian Era,* 261.

7. Morgan, *From Hayes to McKinley,* 232–35; Nevins, *Grover Cleveland,* 185–87; McFarland, *Mugwumps, Morals and Politics,* 52–53; Summers, *Rum, Romanism, & Rebellion,* 292–96, 302–303.

8. Williams, "Dry Bones and Dead Language," 140; Knoles, *Presidential Election of 1892,* 246–47; Morgan, *From Hayes to McKinley,* 436–37.

9. Gould, *Reform and Regulation,* 146; Cooper, *Warrior and the Priest,* 204–11; Chace, *1912,* 238–39; Broderick, *Progressivism at Risk,* 207–208; Link, *Wilson and the Progressive Era,* 22–24, 35; Kendrick A. Clements, *The Presidency of Woodrow Wilson,* 29.

10. Link, *Wilson and the Progressive Era,* 247–49; Gould, *Reform and Regulation,* 177; Lovell, *Presidential Election of 1916,* 170–80.

11. Ambrose, *Eisenhower: President-Elect,* 571; Pach and Richardson, *Presidency of Dwight D. Eisenhower,* 27.

12. Pach and Richardson, *Presidency of Dwight D. Eisenhower,* 124–25, 136.

13. Ambrose, *Triumph of a Politician,* 220–21; Greene, *Limits of Power,* 24–25.

14. Ambrose, *Triumph of a Politician,* 651–52.

15. Abramson, Aldrich, and Rohde, *Change and Continuity,* 67–72, 282; Burnham, "Realignment Lives," 364.

16. Drew, *Whatever It Takes,* 237; Thomas et al., *Back from the Dead,* 212.

17. Readers familiar with my source for tables 5-3 through 5-6 will notice some differences, most notably in the 1860 and 1912 elections. In 1860, Lincoln's popular vote and electoral vote advantages were over different candidates. Stephen Douglas came in second in the popular vote, but John Breckinridge came in second in electoral votes, making Lincoln's electoral vote advantage weaker than Rusk indicates. Similarly, Rusk computes the 1912 data based on the fact that Taft was Wilson's major party opponent. However, it was Theodore Roosevelt, not Taft, who came in second to Wilson in popular and electoral votes, making Wilson's advantage in both figures weaker than Rusk indicates. Finally, Van Buren's popular vote advantage in 1836 should be based on Harrison's vote, where Rusk apparently computes it by combining the three regional Whig candidates into one popular vote figure, thus minimizing Van Buren's performance.

18. On the question of presidential leadership as it relates to Congress, see Jon R. Bond and Richard Fleisher, *The President in the Legislative Arena;* James A. Thurber, ed., *Rivals for Power: Presidential-Congressional Relations,* 2d ed.; and Richard S. Conley, *The Presidency, Congress, and Divided Government: A Postwar Assessment.*

19. See Crockett, *Opposition Presidency,* 43–50, for a fuller description of this leadership choice.

20. This account is very brief and cursory. My full argument can be found in my earlier work, *The Opposition Presidency: Leadership and the Constraints of History.*

21. Robert B. Reich, *Locked in the Cabinet,* 202.

22. Nixon, *Memoirs,* 351–57, 764.

23. Ambrose, *Triumph of a Politician,* 580.

24. Admittedly, Nixon did pursue a more indirect attack against the New Deal system through his administrative powers, particularly through the "New Federalism" plan and his effort to reorganize the executive branch. Perhaps he would have enjoyed some success had he not simultaneously employed illegal means to attack the governing party. On Nixon's legitimate efforts, see Richard P. Nathan, *The Plot that Failed: Nixon and the Administrative Presidency.*

25. For those who doubt this grim assessment, *Economist* correspondents John Micklethwait and Adrian Wooldridge ably summarize the conservative perspective of Nixon's presidency in *The Right Nation: Conservative Power in America,* 68–71.

Afterword on the 2004 Election

1. See Campbell et al., "Symposium" on forecasting the 2004 presidential election in *PS: Political Science and Politics* 37 (October 2004): 733–67.

2. See Stephen Skowronek's post-2000 election analysis in "The Setting: Change and Continuity in the Politics of Leadership," 21–24.

3. See Joshua D. Clinton, Simon Jackman, and Doug Rivers, "'The Most Liberal Senator'? Analyzing and Interpreting Congressional Roll Calls," in *PS: Political Science and Politics* 37 (October 2004): 805–11.

4. "Kerry's 'Liberal Quotient,'" *Washington Times,* March 2, 2004, A18.

5. "The Presidential Candidates' 2d Debate: 'These Are the Differences,'" *New York Times,* October 9, 2004, A12.

6. Evan Thomas et al., *Election 2004: How Bush Won and What You Can Expect in the Future,* 79–81.

7. Gloria Borger, "A Republican for all Reasons," *US News and World Report,* May 31, 2004, 38.

8. Thomas, *Election 2004,* 28–39.

9. "The Presidential Candidates' 2d Debate: 'These Are the Differences,'" *New York Times,* October 9, 2004, A12.

10. David Brooks, "Kerry Off the Leash," *New York Times,* October 19, 2004, A27.

11. David S. Broder, "Need to Connect with Religious, Rural Voters Noted," *Washington Post,* November 4, 2004, A35.

BIBLIOGRAPHY

Abramson, Paul R., John H. Aldrich, and David W. Rohde. *Change and Continuity in the 1992 Elections.* Washington, D.C.: Congressional Quarterly Press, 1994.

Abramowitz, Alan. *Voice of the People: Elections and Voting in the United States.* Boston: McGraw-Hill, 2004.

Abramowitz, Alan I., and Kyle L. Saunders. "Ideological Realignment in the U.S. Electorate." *Journal of Politics* 60 (August 1998): 634–52.

Aldrich, John H. *Why Parties? The Origin and Transformation of Party Politics in America.* Chicago: University of Chicago Press, 1995.

Aldrich, John H., and Richard G. Niemi. "The Sixth American Party System: Electoral Change, 1952–1992." In *Broken Contract? Changing Relationships between Americans and Their Government,* ed. Stephen C. Craig. Boulder: Westview Press, 1996.

Aldrich, John H., and Thomas Weko. "The Presidency and the Election Campaign: Framing the Choice in 1992." In *The Presidency and the Political System,* 4th ed., ed. Michael Nelson. Washington, D.C.: Congressional Quarterly Press, 1995.

Ambrose, Stephen E. *Eisenhower: Soldier, General of the Army, President-Elect, 1890–1952.* New York: Simon and Schuster, 1983.

———. *Eisenhower: The President.* New York: Simon and Schuster, 1984.

———. *Nixon: The Education of a Politician, 1913–1962.* New York: Simon and Schuster, 1987.

———. *Nixon: The Triumph of a Politician, 1962–1972.* New York: Simon and Schuster, 1989.

Atkeson, Lonna Rae. "From the Primaries to the General Election: Does a Divisive Nomination Race Affect a Candidate's Fortunes in the Fall?" In *In Pursuit of the White House 2000: How We Choose Our Presidential Nominees,* ed. William G. Mayer. New York: Chatham House, 2000.

Bauer, K. Jack. *Zachary Taylor: Soldier, Planter, Statesman of the Old Southwest.* Baton Rouge: Louisiana State University Press, 1985.

Blum, John Morton. *Woodrow Wilson and the Politics of Morality.* Boston: Little, Brown, 1956.

———. *The Progressive Presidents: Roosevelt, Wilson, Roosevelt, Johnson.* New York: W. W. Norton, 1980.

Boller, Paul F. Jr. *Presidential Campaigns.* New York: Oxford University Press, 1985.

Bond, Jon R., and Richard Fleisher. *The President in the Legislative Arena.* Chicago: University of Chicago Press, 1990.

Brock, William R. *Parties and Political Conscience: American Dilemmas, 1840–1850.* Millwood: KTO Press, 1979.

Broder, David S. "Parceling Out Power to Both Parties." *Washington Post,* November 6, 1996.

Broderick, Francis L. *Progressivism at Risk: Electing a President in 1912.* New York: Greenwood Press, 1989.

Burnham, Walter Dean. *Critical Elections and the Mainsprings of American Politics.* New York: W. W. Norton, 1970.

———. "Critical Realignment: Dead or Alive?" In *The End of Realignment? Interpreting American Electoral Eras,* ed. Byron E. Shafer. Madison: University of Wisconsin Press, 1991.

———. "Realignment Lives: The 1994 Earthquake and Its Implications." In *The Clinton Presidency: First Appraisals,* eds. Colin Campbell and Bert A. Rockman. Chatham: Chatham House, 1996.

———. "The Politics of Repudiation, 1992: Edging toward Upheaval." In *The American Prospect* No. 12 (Winter 1993): 22–33.

Burns, James MacGregor. *The Deadlock of Democracy: Four-Party Politics in America.* Englewood Cliffs, N. J.: Prentice-Hall, 1963.

Busch, Andrew E., and William G. Mayer. "The Front-Loading Problem." In *The Making of the Presidential Candidates 2004,* ed. William G. Mayer. Lanham: Rowman and Littlefield, 2004.

Campbell, Angus, Philip E. Converse, Warren E. Miller, and Donald E. Stokes. *Elections and the Political Order.* New York: John Wiley, 1966.

Campbell, James E. *The American Campaign: U.S. Presidential Campaigns and the National Vote.* College Station: Texas A&M University Press, 2000.

Campbell, James E., et al. "Symposium: The 2004 Presidential Election Forecasts." In *PS: Political Science and Politics* 37 (October 2004): 733–67.

Canon, David T. *Actors, Athletes, and Astronauts: Political Amateurs in the United States Congress.* Chicago: University of Chicago Press, 1990.

Carmines, Edward G., and James A. Stimson. *Issue Evolution: Race and the Transformation of American Politics.* Princeton: Princeton University Press, 1989.

Ceaser, James W. *Presidential Selection: Theory and Development.* Princeton: Princeton University Press, 1979.

Chace, James. *1912: Wilson, Roosevelt, Taft & Debs—the Election that Changed the Country.* New York: Simon and Schuster, 2004.

Chester, Lewis, Godfrey Hodgson, and Bruce Page. *An American Melodrama: The Presidential Campaign of 1968.* New York: Viking, 1969.

Chitwood, Oliver Perry. *John Tyler: Champion of the Old South.* New York: Russell and Russell, 1964.

Chubb, John E., and Paul E. Peterson. "Realignment and Institutionalization." In *The New Direction in American Politics,* eds. John E. Chubb and Paul E. Peterson. Washington, D.C.: Brookings Institution, 1985.

Cleaves, Freeman. *Old Tippecanoe: William Henry Harrison and His Time.* Port Washington: Kennikat Press, 1939.

Clements, Kendrick A. *The Presidency of Woodrow Wilson.* Lawrence: University Press of Kansas, 1992.

Clinton, Bill. *Between Hope and History: Meeting America's Challenges for the 21st Century.* New York: Random House, 1996.

Clinton, Joshua D., Simon Jackman, and Doug Rivers. "'The Most Liberal Senator'? Analyzing and Interpreting Congressional Roll Calls." In *PS: Political Science and Politics* 37 (October 2004): 805–11.

Conley, Patricia Heidotting. *Presidential Mandates: How Elections Shape the National Agenda.* Chicago: University of Chicago Press, 2001.

Conley, Richard S. *The Presidency, Congress, and Divided Government: A Postwar Assessment.* College Station: Texas A&M University Press, 2003.

Cooper, John Milton, Jr. *The Warrior and the Priest: Woodrow Wilson and Theodore Roosevelt.* Cambridge: Belknap Press, 1983.

———. *Pivotal Decades: The United States, 1900–1920.* New York: W. W. Norton, 1990.

Crockett, David A. *The Opposition Presidency: Leadership and the Constraints of History.* College Station: Texas A&M University Press, 2002.

Crouse, Timothy. *The Boys on the Bus.* New York: Ballantine Books, 1972.

Crunden, Robert M. *Ministers of Reform: The Progressives' Achievement in American Civilization, 1889–1920.* New York: Basic Books, 1982.

Downs, Anthony. *An Economic Theory of Democracy.* New York: Harper Collins, 1957.

Drew, Elizabeth. *On the Edge: The Clinton Presidency.* New York: Simon and Schuster, 1994.

———. *Showdown: The Struggle between the Gingrich Congress and the Clinton White House.* New York: Simon and Schuster, 1996.

———. *Whatever It Takes: The Real Struggle for Political Power in America.* New York: Viking, 1997.

Dyer, Brainerd. *Zachary Taylor.* Baton Rouge: Louisiana State University, 1946.

Evans, Rowland Jr., and Robert D. Novak. *Nixon in the White House: The Frustration of Power.* New York: Random House, 1971.

Garraty, John A. *The New Commonwealth, 1877–1890.* New York: Harper and Row, 1968.

Germond, Jack W., and Jules Witcover. *Mad as Hell: Revolt at the Ballot Box, 1992.* New York: Warner Books, 1993.

Glad, Paul W. *McKinley, Bryan, and the People.* Philadelphia: J. B. Lippincott, 1964.

Goebel, Dorothy Burne. *William Henry Harrison: A Political Biography.* Indianapolis: Historical Bureau of the Indiana Library and Historical Department, 1926.

Goldman, Peter, Thomas M. DeFrank, Mark Miller, Andrew Murr, Tom Mathews, with Patrick Rogers and Melanie Cooper. *Quest for the Presidency 1992.* College Station: Texas A&M University Press, 1994.

Gordon, John Steele. *Hamilton's Blessing: The Extraordinary Life and Times of Our National Debt.* New York: Walker, 1997.

Gould, Lewis L. "The Republican Search for a National Majority." In *The Gilded Age,* rev. and enlarged ed., ed. H. Wayne Morgan. Syracuse: Syracuse University Press, 1970.

———. *Reform and Regulation: American Politics, 1900–1916.* New York: John Wiley, 1978.

Green, James A. *William Henry Harrison: His Life and Times.* Richmond: Garrett and Massie, 1941.

Greene, John Robert. *The Crusade: The Presidential Election of 1952.* Lanham: University Press of America, 1985.

————. *The Limits of Power: The Nixon and Ford Administrations.* Bloomington: Indiana University Press, 1992.

Greenstein, Fred I. "George W. Bush and the Ghosts of Presidents Past." *PS: Political Science and Politics* 34 (March 2001): 77–80.

Hamby, Alonzo L. *Liberalism and Its Challengers: From FDR to Bush,* 2d ed. New York: Oxford University Press, 1992.

Hamilton, Alexander, James Madison, and John Jay. *The Federalist Papers,* ed. Clinton Rossiter. New York: Mentor, 1961.

Hamilton, Holman. *Zachary Taylor: Soldier in the White House.* Indianapolis: Bobbs-Merrill, 1951.

Hetherington, Marc J. "Resurgent Mass Partisanship: The Role of Elite Polarization." *American Political Science Review* 95 (September 2001): 619–31.

Hofstadter, Richard. *The Idea of a Party System: The Rise of Legitimate Opposition in the United States, 1780–1840.* Berkeley: University of California Press, 1969.

Holt, Michael F. *The Political Crisis of the 1850s.* New York: John Wiley, 1978.

————. *The Rise and Fall of the American Whig Party: Jacksonian Politics and the Onset of the Civil War.* New York: Oxford University Press, 1999.

Jaffa, Harry V. "The Nature and Origin of the American Party System." In *Political Parties, U.S.A.,* ed. Robert A. Goldwin. Chicago: Rand McNally, 1961.

Jamieson, Kathleen Hall. *Packaging the Presidency: A History and Criticism of Presidential Campaign Advertising.* New York: Oxford University Press, 1984.

Johnson, Haynes, and David S. Broder. *The System: The American Way of Politics at the Breaking Point.* Boston: Little, Brown, 1996.

Jones, Charles O. *The Presidency in a Separated System.* Washington, D.C.: Brookings Institution, 1994.

Keith, Bruce E., David B. Magleby, Candice J. Nelson, Elizabeth Orr, Mark C. Westlye, and Raymond E. Wolfinger. *The Myth of the Independent Voter.* Berkeley: University of California Press, 1992.

Ketcham, Ralph. *Presidents above Parties: The First American Presidency, 1789–1829.* Chapel Hill: University of North Carolina Press, 1984.

Key, V. O., Jr. "A Theory of Critical Elections." *Journal of Politics* 17 (February 1955): 3–18.

King, Gary, and Lyn Ragsdale. *The Elusive Executive: Discovering Statistical Patterns in the Presidency.* Washington, D.C.: Congressional Quarterly Press, 1988.

Kleppner, Paul. *The Third Electoral System, 1853–1892: Parties, Voters, and Political Cultures.* Chapel Hill: University of North Carolina Press, 1979.

Knoles, George Harmon. *The Presidential Campaign and Election of 1892.* New York: AMS Press, 1942.

Landy, Marc, and Sidney M. Milkis. *Presidential Greatness.* Lawrence: University Press of Kansas, 2000.

Leuchtenburg, William E. *In the Shadow of FDR: From Harry Truman to Ronald Reagan.* Ithaca: Cornell University Press, 1983.

Link, Arthur S. *Woodrow Wilson and the Progressive Era, 1910–1917.* New York: Harper and Row, 1954.

Lovell, S. D. *The Presidential Election of 1916.* Carbondale: Southern Illinois University Press, 1980.

Lowi, Theodore J. *The Personal President: Power Invested, Power Unfulfilled.* Ithaca: Cornell University Press, 1985.

Lubell, Samuel. *The Future of American Politics,* rev. 3d ed. New York: Harper and Row, 1965.

Manchester, William. *The Glory and the Dream: A Narrative History of America, 1932–1972.* Boston: Little, Brown, 1973.

Maraniss, David. *First in His Class: A Biography of Bill Clinton.* New York: Simon and Schuster, 1995.

Mayhew, David R. *Electoral Realignments: A Critique of an American Genre.* New Haven: Yale University Press, 2002.

McCormick, Richard P. *The Presidential Game: The Origins of American Presidential Politics.* New York: Oxford University Press, 1982.

McFarland, Gerald W. *Mugwumps, Morals and Politics, 1884–1920.* Amherst: University of Massachusetts Press, 1975.

McGinniss, Joe. *The Selling of the President 1968.* New York: Trident Press, 1969.

Merrill, Horace Samuel. *Bourbon Leader: Grover Cleveland and the Democratic Party.* Boston: Little, Brown, 1957.

Micklethwait, John, and Adrian Wooldridge. *The Right Nation: Conservative Power in America.* New York: Penguin Press, 2004.

Milkis, Sidney M. *The President and the Parties: The Transformation of the American Party System since the New Deal.* New York: Oxford University Press, 1993.

Moore, Barrington Jr. *Social Origins of Dictatorship and Democracy: Lord and Peasant in the Making of the Modern World.* Boston: Beacon Press, 1966.

Morgan, H. Wayne. *From Hayes to McKinley: National Party Politics, 1877–1896.* Syracuse: Syracuse University Press, 1969.

Morgan, Robert J. *A Whig Embattled: The Presidency under John Tyler.* Lincoln: University of Nebraska Press, 1954.

Morris, Dick. *Behind the Oval Office: Winning the Presidency in the Nineties.* New York: Random House, 1997.

Nathan, Richard P. *The Plot That Failed: Nixon and the Administrative Presidency.* New York: John Wiley, 1975.

Neustadt, Richard E. *Presidential Power and the Modern Presidents: The Politics of Leadership from Roosevelt to Reagan.* New York: Free Press, 1990.

Nevins, Allan. *Grover Cleveland: A Study in Courage.* New York: Dodd, Mead, 1932.

Nichols, David K. *The Myth of the Modern Presidency.* University Park: Pennsylvania State University Press, 1994.

Nixon, Richard. *The Memoirs of Richard Nixon.* New York: Grosset and Dunlap, 1978.

Pach, Chester J., and Elmo Richardson. *The Presidency of Dwight D. Eisenhower,* rev. ed. Lawrence: University Press of Kansas, 1991.

Parmet, Herbert S. *Eisenhower and the American Crusades.* New York: Macmillan, 1972.

Peterson, Merrill D. *The Great Triumvirate: Webster, Clay and Calhoun.* New York: Oxford University Press, 1987.

Peterson, Norma Lois. *The Presidencies of William Henry Harrison and John Tyler.* Lawrence: University Press of Kansas, 1989.

Poage, George Rawlings. *Henry Clay and the Whig Party.* Chapel Hill: University of North Carolina Press, 1936.

Radosh, Ronald. *Divided They Fell: The Demise of the Democratic Party, 1964–1996.* New York: Free Press, 1996.

Rayback, Robert J. *Millard Fillmore: Biography of a President.* New York: Buffalo Historical Society, 1959.

Reich, Robert B. *Locked in the Cabinet.* New York: Alfred A. Knopf, 1997.

Reichard, Gary W. *The Reaffirmation of Republicanism: Eisenhower and the Eighty-third Congress.* Knoxville: University of Tennessee Press, 1975.

———. *Politics as Usual: The Age of Truman and Eisenhower.* Arlington Heights: Harlan Davidson, 1988.

Reinhard, David W. *The Republican Right since 1945.* Lexington: University Press of Kentucky, 1983.

Rockman, Bert A. *The Leadership Question: The Presidency and the American System.* New York: Praeger, 1984.

Rosenof, Theodore. *Realignment: The Theory that Changed the Way We Think about American Politics.* Lanham, Maryland: Rowman and Littlefield, 2003.

Rosenstone, Steven J., Roy L. Behr, and Edward H. Lazarus. *Third Parties in America: Citizen Response to Major Party Failure,* 2d ed. Princeton: Princeton University Press, 1996.

Rossiter, Clinton. *The American Presidency,* 2d ed. New York: Time, 1960.

Rusk, Jerrold G. *A Statistical History of the American Electorate.* Washington, D.C.: Congressional Quarterly Press, 2001.

Safire, William. *Before the Fall: An Inside View of the Pre-Watergate White House.* New York: Doubleday, 1975.

Schattschneider, E. E. *The Semisovereign People.* New York: Holt, Rinehart and Winston, 1960.

Seager, Robert II. *And Tyler Too: A Biography of John and Julia Gardiner Tyler.* New York: McGraw-Hill, 1963.

Simpson, Brooks. *Reconstruction Presidents.* Lawrence: University Press of Kansas, 1998.

Skocpol, Theda. *Boomerang: Health Care Reform and the Turn against Government.* New York: W. W. Norton, 1997.

Skowronek, Stephen. *The Politics Presidents Make: Leadership from John Adams to George Bush.* Cambridge: Belknap Press, 1993.

———. "The Setting: Change and Continuity in the Politics of Leadership." In *The Elections of 2000,* ed. Michael Nelson. Washington, D.C.: Congressional Quarterly Press, 2001.

Sloan, John W., *Eisenhower and the Management of Prosperity.* Lawrence: University Press of Kansas, 1991.

Smith, Elbert B. *The Presidencies of Zachary Taylor and Millard Fillmore.* Lawrence: University Press of Kansas, 1988.

Smith, Richard Norton. *Thomas Dewey and His Times.* New York: Simon and Schuster, 1982.

Stanley, Harold W. and Richard G. Niemi. *Vital Statistics on American Politics, 2003–2004.* Washington, D.C.: Congressional Quarterly Press, 2003.

Stone, Irving. *They Also Ran.* New York: Pyramid Books, 1964.

Storing, Herbert J. "The Creation of the Presidency." In *Toward a More Perfect Union:*

Writings of Herbert J. Storing, ed. Joseph M. Bessette. Washington, D.C.: American Enterprise Institute Press, 1995.

————. "A Plan for Studying the Presidency." In *Toward a More Perfect Union: Writings of Herbert J. Storing,* ed. Joseph M. Bessette. Washington, D.C.: American Enterprise Institute Press, 1995.

Summers, Mark Wahlgren. *Rum, Romanism, & Rebellion: The Making of a President 1884.* Chapel Hill: University of North Carolina Press, 2000.

Sundquist, James L. *Dynamics of the Party System: Alignment and Realignment of Political Parties in the United States,* rev. ed. Washington, D.C.: Brookings Institution, 1983.

Thomas, Evan, Karen Breslau, Debra Rosenberg, Leslie Kaufman, and Andrew Murr. *Back from the Dead: How Clinton Survived the Republican Revolution.* New York: Atlantic Monthly Press, 1997.

Thomas, Evan, et al. *Election 2004: How Bush Won and What You Can Expect in the Future.* New York: Public Affairs, 2004.

Thurber, James A., ed. *Rivals for Power: Presidential-Congressional Relations,* 2d ed. Lanham, MD: Rowman and Littlefield, 2002.

Tulis, Jeffrey K. *The Rhetorical Presidency.* Princeton: Princeton University Press, 1987.

Van Deusen, Glyndon G. *The Jacksonian Era, 1828–1848.* New York: Harper and Row, 1959.

Wattenberg, Martin P. *The Decline of American Political Parties, 1952–1988.* Cambridge: Harvard University Press, 1990.

————. *The Rise of Candidate-Centered Politics: Presidential Elections of the 1980s.* Cambridge: Harvard University Press, 1991.

Welch, Richard E., Jr. *The Presidencies of Grover Cleveland.* Lawrence: University Press of Kansas, 1988.

White, Theodore H. *The Making of the President 1960.* New York: Atheneum, 1961.

————. *The Making of the President 1968.* New York: Atheneum, 1969.

————. *The Making of the President 1972.* New York: Atheneum, 1973.

Wiebe, Robert H. *The Search for Order, 1877–1920.* New York: Hill and Wang, 1967.

Williams, R. Hal. "Dry Bones and Dead Language: The Democratic Party." In *The Gilded Age,* rev. and enlarged ed., ed. H. Wayne Morgan. Syracuse: Syracuse University Press, 1970.

————. *Years of Decision: American Politics in the 1890s.* New York: John Wiley, 1978.

Wills, Garry. *Nixon Agonistes: The Crisis of the Self-Made Man.* New York: Mentor, 1971.

————. *"Negro President": Jefferson and the Slave Power.* Boston: Houghton Mifflin, 2003.

Wilson, Woodrow. *Constitutional Government in the United States.* New York: Columbia University Press, 1908. In *Understanding the Presidency,* eds. James P. Pfiffner and Roger H. Davidson. New York: Longman, 1997.

Witcover, Jules. *The Resurrection of Richard Nixon.* New York: G. P. Putnam's Sons, 1970.

Woodward, Bob. *The Agenda: Inside the Clinton White House.* New York: Simon and Schuster, 1994.

————. *The Choice.* New York: Simon and Schuster, 1996.

INDEX

OTHER BOOKS IN THE JOSEPH V. HUGHES JR. AND
HOLLY O. HUGHES SERIES ON THE PRESIDENCY
AND LEADERSHIP

Printed in the United States
140064LV00003B/1/P